Jean J. Jusserand, Thomas Brown, John Savage, Paul Scarron, Jean
Baptiste Oudry

The Comical Romance and Other Tales

In Two Volumes. Vol. II

Jean J. Jusserand, Thomas Brown, John Savage, Paul Scarron, Jean Baptiste Oudry

The Comical Romance and Other Tales
In Two Volumes. Vol. II

ISBN/EAN: 9783744694872

Printed in Europe, USA, Canada, Australia, Japan

Cover: Foto ©Thomas Meinert / pixelio.de

More available books at **www.hansebooks.com**

THE COMICAL ROMANCE, AND OTHER
TALES. BY PAUL SCARRON. DONE
INTO ENGLISH BY TOM BROWN OF
SHIFNAL, JOHN SAVAGE, AND OTHERS
WITH AN INTRODUCTION BY J. J.
JUSSERAND.

ILLUSTRATED FROM THE DESIGNS OF OUDRY.

IN TWO VOLS.—VOL. II.

.

LONDON: LAWRENCE AND BULLEN. 169
NEW BOND STREET, W. MDCCCXCII.

CONTENTS.

PART III.

CONTENTS.

SCARRON'S NOVELS.

PART III.

SCARRON'S COMICAL ROMANCE.

CHAPTER I.

WHICH MAY SERVE FOR AN INTRODUCTION TO THIS THIRD PART.

IN the last chapter of the second part of this romance, you have had little Ragotin all bloody with the several repeated buttings he received from the ram, whilst he slept in a low chair in the comedian's chamber, and which, occasioned him to go out thence in a great fury. But he had received so deep a wound from Madam Star's eyes, and was withal so desirous of knowing the issue of the operator's scheme, that he could only afford himself time to wash his face and hands before he returned. As he was just entering the inn again, his brain was so disturbed, what with the blows, and what with the darts, that he mistook an advocate then walking by to the hall for Ferdinando the operator. He therefore accosted him very civilly, and began with him after this manner:

"Sir, I am happy in meeting you so luckily; I have long desired this opportunity, and I was just going to your lodgings, in great haste, to have a farther account from you of what concerns either my life or death. I don't doubt but you have employed the utmost of your art, in schemes, to serve me all the time you slept; and I desire you to believe I would by no means be ungrateful in my acknowledgments. Tell me then, I beseech you, dear doctor," continued he, "will this little charming shining star suffer me to share any of her influence?" The advocate, who understood not a tittle of all the fine words had been spoken to him, and taking them for raillery, was not long before he interrupted him.

"Monsieur Ragotin," quoth he, "if it had been a little later I should verily have thought you had been drunk, notwithstanding, I cannot help believing that you are either a madman or a fool. To whom, for God's sake, do you think you are talking?" added he, "and what a devil makes you to talk to me of schemes, and the influences of stars? Do you take me either for an astrologer or a magician? Prithee consider a little, Monsieur Ragotin," proceeded he, "don't you know me?"

"Ah! sir," replied Ragotin, "how unkind you are; I thought I had too well informed you of my malady to have been refused a remedy. Alas! I could not . . . ."

He was just proceeding with another tedious harangue, when the advocate left him in a great passion, telling him at parting, "That he was a great sot for a little man." Ragotin would have followed him, but that he at length perceived his mistake, and therefore was glad to retire with shame. He had so great regard to his reputation, as to keep this a secret; and I'll assure you, I had never come to know it had not the advocate one day told it me, among others of his friends, to divert us. The little fool afterwards turned into the inn, and went directly to the comedian's apartment, which he had no sooner entered, but he heard a proposition made by Mrs. Cave and Destiny to quit Mans, and retire to some other post. This vexed him so heartily, that he was like to have dropped down from his height on the floor, and which he might have safely done, since he had no great way to fall. But what concerned him most was, that the time of their departure was to be the next morning, when they were to bid adieu to the good town of Mans, and particularly to its inhabitants, who had been their constant auditors for some time. They purposed to take their way to Alençon after the old rate, having been assured that the pestilence was not there, as they had been before informed. I say they took their way after the old rate, for these sort of people have a constant rule of travelling, in like manner as the sun has in the Zodiac. The journeys they had made and were to make in this country, were first from Tours to Angers, from Angers to La Flèche, from La Flèche to Mans, from Mans to Alençon, from Alençon to Argentin or Laval, no matter which, according to the road they have a mind to take, either to Paris or Brittany, both being alike to them, and indifferent to us in the composition of this romance. This resolution being made by all the men and women players unanimously, they proposed to play one of their best plays before they left Mans, to the end they might leave their audience there in good humour. What this play was never came to my knowledge. That which obliged them to go away so suddenly, was by reason that the Marquis of Orse, on whose account they had stayed so long, was commanded instantly to court; insomuch that being like to have no benefactor left after he was gone, and the Mansean audience diminishing every day, they purposed to go where they might be better used: Ragotin would needs be endeavouring to oppose this resolution, for which purpose he gave a great many reasons, whereof he had always store at command, which nevertheless were little or nothing regarded. This vexed the little man extremely, insomuch that he begged of the company not to go presently out of the province of Mayne, but to take first the tennis-court which was in the suburbs of Montfort, and afterwards they might go to Laval in Mayne likewise, whence they might easily come into Brittany, according to their promise made to Monsieur la Garouffière. This opinion of Ragotin's Destiny would by no means agree to, affirming that if they took his advice, they should make no work on it, the pitiful tennis-court mentioned by him being a great way out of the town, and more than that, on the other side of the river, which would hinder the better sort of people from coming near them ; when the great tennis-court, in the sheep-market of Alençon, was just in the middle of the town ; and, more-over, surrounded with all the best houses, and that therefore it were better to give something more for such a place, than anything for the despicable tennis-court at Montfort, whose good market was the only reason that Ragotin had to speak for it.   This last proposition was agreed to by the whole company, therefore they immediately ordered a waggon to be got ready for their baggage, and horses for their women.   The care of procuring these was left to Leander, who having a great many intrigues in Mans, was the likeliest man to have the best acquaintance there. Next day, before they set out, they presented a comedy tragedy ; tragi-comedy, or pastoral, I know not whether, but which had the success that you may imagine.   The players were admired by everybody, and Destiny performed wonders, especially in his manner of taking leave of the audience, for he expressed his acknowledgments and unwillingness to leave them with that tenderness and force, that he charmed them to that degree that, as I am informed, some among them wept.   Ragotin was so concerned that his proposal had not been followed, that he remained for some time like a dolt, sitting in his chair, even after the rest of the company were gone, and where I believe he had sat till now, had not the marker of the tennis-court let him know that nobody was left, which he had nevertheless no small trouble to make him com-prehend.   Being at last prevailed upon to be gone, he rose from his chair and went home, where he resolved to go find out his company the next morning, and discover to them what shall be related in the following chapter.

CHAPTER II.

THE criers of *aqua vitæ* had not yet waked those that were in a profound sleep, when Ragotin being already dressed, was going to propose to the strolling company his inclinations to be admitted amongst them. He went then to the players' lodgings, whom he found neither up nor awake, and happened to have the discretion to leave them as he found them ; nevertheless could not help entering one chamber, where he found Olive abed with Rancour. This last he desired to get up, and walk with him to La Cousture, a fine abbey in the suburbs of that name, and thence to go to breakfast at the Great Golden Star, where he had ordered a collation to be prepared for them. Rancour, who was one of those who love to eat at other men's cost, was almost as soon got ready as the proposition was made him, and which you may easily be inclined to believe, if you consider that these sort of people are accustomed to dress and undress behind the scenes, to act different parts, which will admit of but little delay. Ragotin and Rancour then marched on towards the abbey of La Cousture ; but we must suppose they called in at some church or other by the way to say a short prayer, for Ragotin's thoughts he had in his head would not admit of a long one. He nevertheless acquainted Rancour with nothing of the matter, for fear it might have kept him from his breakfast, which he knew he had a greater in-

clination for than to give ear to anything he could tell
him. They came to the inn, where being entered the little
man began to fly in a great passion, because the *petits
pâtéz* he had ordered were not ready. To which the
hostess answered without rising off the seat where she sat,

"Truly, Monsieur Ragotin, I know not how you could
expect I should divine when you would come ; but since
you are now here the *pâtéz* shall not be long after you.
Pray walk into the hall, where you'll find a cloth laid, and
a Westphalia ham to stay your stomach."

This she spoke after a grave, hostess-like manner, and
which inclined Rancour to be on her side ; who turning to
Ragotin, cried, "Sir, pray let us comply with my hostess's
proposal, and take a glass or two while our breakfast is
getting ready."

They sat down to table, which in a very short time after
was covered, and they breakfasted after the manner of
Mans, that is to say, very heartily. They drank the same,
and put about several healths, among which the reader may
imagine Madam Star's was not forgot. Little Ragotin
tossed up above a dozen glasses successively, sometimes
sitting, and sometimes standing with his hat in his hand.
But at last he would needs drink his mistress's health on
his knees and bare-headed, which made him to look just
for all the world as if he had been doing penance at the
door of some church. It was then that he earnestly re-
minded Rancour of his promise to assist him in the
conquest of Madam Star's heart. Whereupon Rancour,
half angry, or at least feigning to be so, answered him a
little roughly.

"I thought, Monsieur Ragotin, you had known me to be
a man that never embarked without ammunition—I mean,
engaged in anything that I were not able to bring about.
Be satisfied then I will omit no opportunity to serve you.
I tell you so again, and have ways in my head whereby to
compass it. But I see one great obstacle in our way, and

that is our sudden departure from hence ; the only method therefore that I can advise you to bring about your ends, is to resolve to be admitted amongst us. You have all the qualifications for it that can be desired. You have a good mein, a strong voice, a good tone, and a better memory, and, in a word, seem to have nothing about you that looks country. You look as if you had lived all your lifetime at court, having so much the air of it, that you might be known for a courtier above a mile off. You need not," proceeded he, "to act above a dozen times before you'll be able to outdo all our young pretenders, who must resign their parts to you, and then leave the rest to me. As for your mistress," quoth he, "you'll have but a tough bit of her at first, you must manage her with policy, whereof I know you to have sufficient ; however a little instruction cannot be amiss. I would advise you therefore not to let her know your design at your first admittance of our company, that being certainly the way to lose her, but rather to keep her in suspense till you have a convenient opportunity to make your addresses, and after you have sufficiently won upon her by your conversation, which I dare promise you'll soon do."

The little man had been so attentive to Rancour's discourse, that he was almost ravished into an ecstasy, imagining he had already, as we say, the wolf by the ears ; when coming to himself all of a sudden, as it were out of an apoplexy, he started from the place where he sat, and went to the other side of the table to embrace Rancour, whom he thanked heartily for his counsel, and begged of him to continue his friend in this affair ; protesting at the same time that his only design in inviting him to breakfast was to have declared his mind to him concerning his being admitted of his society, and which he resolved forthwith to be. After this they reckoned with their landlady, and Ragotin paid all. When they were out of doors they took their course directly towards the strollers' lodgings, which was not far off. They found the women up and dressed ;

but Rancour had no sooner opened Ragotin's design to them than he was interrupted by a messenger from Leander's father, who sent his son word by him that he was sick to death, and desired to see him before he paid that debt to nature which all men sooner or later must. This obliged all the company to lay their heads together to consult how they should bear up against an accident so unexpected. Leander took Angelica aside, and told her his time was now come to live happy if she would but contribute towards it, otherwise he must be unfortunate though rich, and poor though he had a good income. She promised him all the favours that lay in her power, and particularly those you will meet with in the following chapter.

CHAPTER III.

THE Jesuits of La Flèche not having been able to make
Leander continue his studies, and perceiving his inclinations ran high to be a player, presently concluded he must
be in love with some actress or other, which they were
altogether confirmed in when, after the departure of the
company, they found he had followed them to Anvers.
They therefore thought themselves obliged to acquaint
his father therewith by a messenger on purpose, which they
soon after did, and who arrived just as a letter was delivered
the old gentleman from Leander, whereby he gave his
father to understand that he designed for the wars, and
therefore desired a sum of money to accoutre himself
This stratagem had been laid between Destiny and he,
when he first discovered his quality to him at the inn
where he was wounded. His father soon finding the cheat,
flew into an excessive passion, which together with his
great age, threw him into a distemper that quickly ended
his days. Perceiving his end to approach, he called one of
his tenants to him, and commanded him immediately to go
find out his son, which he told him he was most likely to
do among the strollers. This the farmer knew as well as
he, having been the person that had furnished Leander
with money from the time he left the college, so that understanding there was a company of strollers at Mans, he made
all the haste he could thither, and found his young landlord

as you have heard in the foregoing chapter. Ragotin was desired by the company to leave them for some time to confer with the tenant newly arrived, which you may imagine he was very unwilling to do, yet at last he retired into an adjoining chamber, where he waited with great impatience till their business was over. They had no sooner got him out of the room but Leander brought in his father's tenant, who immediately related the bad condition the old gentleman was in, as likewise his earnest desire to see his son before he died. Thereupon Leander immediately craved leave to comply with his father's dying request, which was judged by the whole company reasonable to be granted. It was then Destiny revealed the secret of Leander's quality, which he had all along kept private, and which he did not come to the knowledge of till after the ravishing of Madam Angelica, as you may have read in the second part of this true history. He thought it now high time to let it be known, as well to disabuse Mrs. Cave, who could not get it out of her head but that Leander was either the principal, or accessory in the carrying off her daughter, as to oblige him who had done him the honour to be his serving-man, and would have continued such had he not found himself obliged to tell who he was, while he was in quest of Madam Angelica. He was moreover so far from consenting to the carrying away of Angelica, that having met her ravishers he had hazarded his life in her assistance ; but not having been able to resist so many people, he had been dangerously wounded, and left for dead upon the *place*. All the company then immediately asked his pardon for not having treated him suitable to his quality, which they nevertheless thought themselves the more excusable for, in not having had any knowledge of the matter before. Madam Star added, she had always suspected something from the great store of wit and merit she had observed in him, and which she was afterwards confirmed in, especially when she saw her mother Mrs.

Cave's letters from him ; nevertheless did not know what to think when she saw him so employed in her brother's service. Then began Mrs. Cave to speak, addressing herself to Leander, after the following manner :—

"Truly, sir, after I had in some measure discovered your quality, by the letters you writ to my daughter, I had no small reason to distrust your sincerity, being not inclinable to believe that a person who was to have so good an estate after his father's death, would ever condescend to marry a poor stroller. But," continued she, "I thank heaven the time is at length come that you are to be made happy in plentiful possessions, and I am to be delivered from a future possibility of being any more imposed upon by your false pretensions."

Leander being extremely surprised at these words, quickly replied : "All you say, madam, I am likely to possess, would not render me a jot happy, if I were not assured at the same time of the possession of your daughter Angelica. Without her I renounce all the fortune which nature and my father's death shall cast upon me ; and declare to you, before all this good company, that I go with so much willingness to enter upon my succession, upon no greater account than to return speedily to perform my promise to marry your daughter, which I here once more confirm, and will speedily accomplish, provided both she and you will do me the honour to afford your consents. And if so," added he, " I would not have you to think that I design to carry her to my own home ; that is not at all in my intentions, for I have found so much pleasure in a strolling life, that I could never be persuaded to quit so many worthy companions that have so largely contributed towards it."

After this obliging declaration, both the actors and actresses speaking all together, returned him their most humble acknowledgments, averring at the same time, that Mrs. Cave and her daughter would not be a little to blame if they refused so advantageous a proffer. Angelica, for

her part, said no more than became one that was at her
mother's disposal, only she bid Leander at parting to
hope, if he continued in the same mind at his return.
After all the mutual endearments and tears that commonly pass between parting friends, it was agreed that
Leander should go the next morning upon one of the
horses that had been hired ; but which he refused, choosing
rather that of his tenant, which he thought would carry
him better, and would leave the hackney for his companion. "But we forget all this while," quoth Destiny, "that
Monsieur Ragotin is waiting without to speak with us.   Is
there anybody among us," added he, " that knows what he
would have ? " Hereupon Rancour, who had been silent
for some time, opened his mouth, to let them understand
that he knew, and that that very morning he had treated
him with a breakfast to procure himself an opportunity to
acquaint him that he had a mind to be admitted of the
company, without pretending to any share in the profits,
having sufficient of his own, and which he would rather
choose to spend in seeing the world, than to live altogether
at Mans, as he had been advised to do.   Hereat Roquebrune presently advanced to give his opinion, that he
ought not to be admitted, and that for these reasons :

"Because," said he, "two poets under one roof never
agree, it being with them as with women, where there are
more than one there are too many.   Besides," quoth he,
"Ragotin's shape would never suffer him to be an ornament to the stage, but would rather disgrace it.   For,"
added he, "what parts could he propose to act ?   As for
the principal ones Monsieur Destiny would not permit him
to undertake them, and for the second best they belong to
Olive.   And then for a nurse or a confidant," continued
he, "he must not pretend to either of them, his person
being altogether as deformed in a disguise as out of one.
Therefore," concluded he, "'tis my opinion in few words,
that he ought by no means to be received."

"And 'tis mine," replied Rancour, "that he ought by all means to be received, for where there is occasion to represent a dwarf none can be so proper; and then for a monster, as that in *Andromeda*, it were better to have a natural one at hand, than to be at the trouble to contrive one that would be only artificial." He added farther, that as for speaking a part, he could assure them he would be like another Orpheus, that drew everything after him. "For," proceeded he, "whilst Olive and I were seeking after Madam Angelica, we overtook him riding upon an ass no bigger than himself, and repeating the adventures of Pyramus and Thysbe, with so good an emphasis, that several rustics that were then going the same way, came up with him, and gave so constant attention with their hats off, that they would not leave him till they came to the inn where we all baited. If then," continued he, "he could gain so far upon these rustics, what will he be able to do when he comes to speak before men of sense?"

This relation made everybody to laugh, and the company was thereupon resolved to hear Ragotin speak for himself. He was sent for in, and after about a dozen low *congées* he began his harangue in the following manner:—

"Illustrious personages, and august senate of Parnassus," quoth he, fancying himself, no doubt, speaking at the bar of the President's Court in Mans, where he had been admitted advocate but a little before, "it is a common saying, that evil company corrupts good manners, and on the contrary, good must needs improve them."

This exordium, so well begun, made the company believe he was about to preach a sermon, therefore they turned their hands one way and t'other, and could hardly forbear laughing. Some critics perhaps may think much of the word sermon; but why might not Ragotin be thought capable of performing such a task, when he had several times sung ballads to the organs? But however, he proceeded:

'   " I find myself so destitute of virtues, that I desire to be admitted of your illustrious society for improvement. You are the Muses' interpreters, the living echoes of their dear darlings, and your merits are so well known throughout all France, that you are admired even beyond the poles. As for you, ladies," quoth he to the women, "you charm all that do but look upon you ; and it is impossible to be within the hearing of your harmonious voices, but one must needs be ravished into ecstasy. In fine," said he, "you are mere angels of flesh and blood ; and all the poets have thought themselves happy in celebrating your praises. And for you, gentlemen," continued he, "no Alexander nor Cæsar ever equalled the valour of Monsieur Destiny nor of the other heroes his companions, and therefore you must not wonder if I am ambitious of increasing your number by one, which will be easy for you to suffer me to do, if you can but consent to it. I promise you moreover," proceeded he, " that I will be no manner of charge to ye, neither will I pretend to any share in the profits of our performances, but all along continue your most humble and most obedient servant." Ragotin having thus ended his harangue, he was desired to withdraw for a minute, that what he had said might be considered. He withdrew, and the company were just going to proceed according to form, when the poet Roquebrune threw himself in again to make a second opposition to Ragotin's preferment, but he was presently thrust out by Rancour, who had pushed him more violently but that he had regard to his new suit which was bought with the money he had lent him. At length it was agreed that Ragotin should be admitted amongst them for the diversion of the company. He was thereupon called in, the accustomed ceremonies passed, was enrolled in the register, took an oath of fidelity, had the word given by which the strollers knew one another ; and after all, supped with the whole caravan.

CHAPTER IV.

OF LEANDER'S DEPARTURE; THE STROLLER'S GOING FOR ALENÇON, AND RAGOTIN'S MISFORTUNE.

AFTER supper everybody would be congratulating Ragotin upon the honour he had received, and which made him to swell so enormously, that he burst the waist-band of his breeches in two places. In the meantime Leander took occasion to entertain his dear Angelica with love-stories, and to whom he reiterated his design to marry her, which he pronounced with so much softness and tenderness that she could answer him only with tears, whereof she shed abundance. I know not whether these proceeded from her joy at the fair promises he made her, or through her concern for his so sudden departure; however it was, it is certain they exchanged several mutual endearments, which were not in the least interrupted by Mrs. Cave. But at length night drawing on apace, it was convenient they should both retreat. Leander took leave of the company and went to bed. Next morning he got up betimes, and set out with his father's tenant, with that expedition that he quickly arrived at his journey's end, where he found the old gentleman very ill, who nevertheless told him he was glad to see him. He likewise expressed to him as far as he was able, the great grief his absence had caused him, as also that he was now come seasonably to receive his last blessing, together with his estate, although he had been advised to disinherit him for

the ill courses he had taken.   The rest of Leander's affairs
we shall learn at his return.

The actors and actresses being got ready dressed, took
care to pack up their baggage as fast as they could, that
they might be ready to depart in good time.   At length all
was prepared, and nothing was wanting except a horse for
one of the women, which they had before provided, but
were disappointed in.   They therefore had desired Olive to
get another just as Ragotin entered the room, who hearing
their proposition, told them there was no occasion, by
reason he had one that would carry double, and if they
pleased, either Madam Star or Angelica should ride
behind him.   This he urged the rather because he told
them it was impossible they should reach Alençon in one
day, being above ten leagues off ; but being obliged to
make two of it, his horse would serve well enough for the
purpose he proposed.   Whilst he was thus recommending
his contrivance, Madam Star interrupted him, affirming
she could not ride double ; this vexed the little man extremely, but which he was a little after the better
satisfied with, when Angelica told him she would.   They
breakfasted all together that morning, and the operator
and his wife were invited ; but whilst the collation was
getting ready, Ragotin took an occasion to talk farther
with Signor Ferdinando, to whom he made the same
speech he had done before to the advocate, whom he had
taken for him ; to which the magician answered, that he
had tried all that lay within the compass of his heart to
serve him, but without effect, which made him inclinable to
believe that Madam Star knew more of magic than he ;
that her charms were more powerful, and, in a word, that
she must needs be a dangerous person, not fit to be conversed with.   Ragotin would have replied to these reflections on his mistress, but that he was just then called
upon to wash his hands, and sit down to table, which they
all did at the same time.   Inezilla protested to all the

company, and chiefly the women, that both she and her husband were extremely concerned at their so speedy leaving them, and would willingly have waited on them to Alençon, to have had their conversation longer, had they not been obliged to mount their stage and act their farces, which her husband chose rather to do at Mans when they were gone, than to incommode them by doing it in the same town whither they were going ; it being certain the people would sooner run after them where they paid nothing, than go to see a play where they must pay.

The company thanked both the husband and wife for their civilities, and returned them a thousand acknowledgments for their good will. The women wept, and a great many compliments passed between both parties ; only the poet, who upon other occasions would have talked as much as four, upon this spoke not one word, the parting with Inezilla being so cruel a thunder-stroke to him, that though he fancied himself all over covered with laurel, the common preservative against thunder, yet could he not secure his carcass. The waggon being loaded, and ready to set out, Mistress Cave took her place as she had done formerly, in the beginning of this romance, Madam Star mounted upon a horse which Destiny led, and Angelica got up behind Ragotin, who took care to avoid the like accident in mounting as had before befallen him. All the rest went on foot in the same order as they came to Mans.

When they were got to a little wood about a league from the town, a stag that was then hunting by the Marquis of Lavardin's servants happened to cross the road, which Ragotin's horse that went before perceiving, was extremely affrighted at, which obliged Ragotin to quit his stirrups ; he at the same time clapped his hand on the carbine he had by his side, and thinking to kill the stag, happened to touch the trigger before he had well mounted the piece ; whereby, being greatly charged, the carbine recoiled, and threw him off, and striking at the same instant against

Angelica's side, forced her off likewise, but who received little or no harm.   As for Ragotin, it was his misfortune to fall against the stump of a tree, which was about a foot out of the ground, whereby he got a bump on his left temple, which however by a bandage with a piece of silver instead of lead was soon cured.

This accident caused a great deal of laughter in the company, after they saw there was no more harm done, which they would otherwise have forborne.   The little man nevertheless was extremely enraged at their making a jest of his misfortune.   Being remounted, together with Angelica, he would needs charge his carbine again, but which she would by no mean suffer him to do.   They then proceeded on their journey, and at last came to a little inn where they were to bait.   The actors for their parts must take an afternoon luncheon, and the actresses proposed to lie on the bed, as well to repose themselves as to observe how lustily their companions ate and drank.   The briskest drinkers were Rancour and Ragotin, who were so hotly engaged to Angelica's health, which they thought nobody had observed, that she was forced to call out to the latter to bid him drink less, and take more care of his charge for the future.   This caused a cessation of arms, or rather of glasses between the two combatants.   After some time the reckoning being paid, and the horses brought out, they all set forwards on their journey.   The weather was fair and the road good, which permitted them to arrive betimes at a town called Vivain.   They there went to the Sign of the Cock, being the best inn in the town.   The hostess, who was none of the best-natured women in the province of Maine, made a great deal of difficulty to receive them, telling them she had no bedroom for them.   Her company it seems was a general receiver, an exciseman, and four or five pedlers.   Rancour thinking to give a cast of his office, told his landlady they desired only a chamber for the women, and as for the men, they would pig in anywhere.

This calm dealing somewhat abated the pride of our lady hostess. She admitted them therefore, and they did not unload their waggon, but locked it up in a stable which they found at the bottom of the yard. The women had a chamber assigned them, where the company all supped together. After supper the men retired, leaving the women to go to bed in two beds, viz., Madam Star in one, and Mrs. Cave and her daughter Angelica in the other. You may imagine they did not forget to take the key in the inside of the door, as did not likewise the two receivers, who had ordered their portmanteaus top full of money to be brought into their chambers. But the unwary pedlers were not so cautious, for they took not that care, but admitted Rancour and Olive to lie in the same room where they had their packs.

There were three beds in that room, whereof the pedlers had two, and Rancour and Olive the third. Rancour slept not a wink all night, watching for an opportunity to put his design in execution when the pedlers were asleep. At last he got up, thinking they were fast, and going softly towards the packs, was interrupted by one of the pedlers, who being overtaken with a looseness, was forced to rise to ease his belly. This made Rancour to return in some haste to his bed. In the meantime the pedler who had been used to lodge in this inn, and knew all the ways out and in, went to a door that opened into a little gallery, at the end whereof was the house of office. This he did not to incommode the venerable comedians with a bad smell. When he had done he went to return from whence he came ; but instead of going the right way, descended on the other side, and went by a private door into the receivers' chamber, where approaching the first bed he met, and believing it his own, he heard an unknown voice demand of him who was there ? This caused him to turn, without saying a word, to the other bed, where he heard the same thing, but spoke with a more angry accent.

This last person called out at the same time for a candle,
affirming there was somebody in his room. Hereupon the
host made the servant to rise immediately, and see what
was the matter; but before she could possibly strike a
light, the pedler had got out of the room, and was coming
into his own chamber; but before he came, Rancour that
had heard all the difference between him and his neighbours, for there was only a thin partition between them,
resolved to lose no time, and therefore having dexterously
untied the cords of one of the packs, took out thence two
pieces of linen, which having done he fastened the cords
again as artificially as if they had never been opened; for
he knew perfectly well that secret, known only to those of
his fraternity, as well as he did their marks and ciphers.
He was just going to attack another of the packs when
the pedler entered the chamber, who hearing him walk
about demanded who was there? Rancour, who never
wanted an excuse at a pinch, after having thrust the two
pieces of linen into his own bed, told him the maid had
forgot to set him a chamber-pot, and that therefore he was
looking for the window to piss out at; whereupon the
pedler, who was not yet got into bed, replied, " Stay, sir, if
you please, I'll go open it for you, for I know better where
it is than you do." This having not only said but done,
he immediately leapt into bed, and left Rancour to piss
out at the window, which he did as copiously as when he
bedewed the merchant of lower Maine, while he lay with
him in an inn at Mans, as you may find he did in the sixth
chapter of the first part of this romance. He afterwards
went directly to his bed, without shutting the window.
The pedler cried out to him that he ought not to have left
it open, and he cried out to the pedler that he might shut
it if he pleased, for as for his part he should not trouble his
head about it any more, having scarce been able to find the
way to his bed when it was shut.

The pedler fearing Rancour had a mind to make a

squabble of it, rose without any more ado and shut the
window, and afterwards groped his way out to bed again.
All this while the host and hostess were brawling like mad
at their maid to light the candle, which she was endeavouring to do, but as the proverb has it, " The more haste the
less speed," this sorry wench had been above an hour
blowing the small coal before she could raise a spark of fire.
This caused her master and mistress to curse her at no
common rate, and the receivers began to be more and more
enraged to find they could not get a candle, when they had
called for one so often.   At length it was lighted, and the
host, hostess, and servant went together into the receivers'
room, where finding nobody, they told them they had done
ill to alarm all the family for no reason.   But they on the
contrary maintained they had both seen and heard a man
in their chamber, and more than that, had talked with him.
The host hearing this, went immediately into the strollers'
chamber, and demanded of them and the pedlers whether
any of them had been in their neighbours' room ?   They all
answered, " No, none of us has been out of bed except that
monsieur yonder," meaning Rancour, "who was forced to rise
to piss out at the window, your maid not having set him a
chamber-pot."   Hereat the host presently fell upon the
servant for her neglect, and afterwards went to the receivers
again, telling them they must needs have dreamt that
somebody was in their room, since not a soul had been
stirring that way as he could hear of.   After this he left
them, wishing them to go to sleep again, it not being yet
day.   As soon as it was well light Rancour got up, and
demanding the key of the stable, went to hide the purchase
he had got in the waggon.

CHAPTER V.

WHAT HAPPENED TO THE STROLLERS BETWEEN VIVAIN
AND ALENÇON, TOGETHER WITH ANOTHER OF
RAGOTIN'S MISFORTUNES.

ALL the heroes and heroines of our strolling company got
out betimes. They took the high road to Alençon, and in
a little while arrived safe at Bourg le Roy, The King's Town,
called by the vulgar Boulercy. Here they dined, and
stayed some time, during which, they debated whether they
should go by Arsonnay, a village about a league from Alençon, or whether they should take to the other side to avoid
Barrèe, a road where in the hottest summer there is dirt,
and wherein the horses often plunge up to their bellies.
Being not able to conclude the matter amongst themselves,
they consulted the waggoner, who told them his horses would
carry them through the worst of quagmires, they being the
very best for draft of any in Mans. Also that they had not
above half a mile of bad way, whereas if they went by the
common of St. Pater, they would find the roads dirtier and
to longer continue so. He remembered them likewise, that
the horses and waggon only would go in the dirt, and that the
foot people might step over into the fields and walk there
secure. At length they pitched upon the former road, and
Madam Star desired the waggoner to let her know when
they came to the dirt, because she chose rather to go on
foot in good way, than to ride on horseback through bog.
Of the same mind were Angelica and Mrs. Cave, who had

some apprehensions that the waggon might overturn. When they were just about entering this bad way, Angelica slipped off from Ragotin's horse's crupper, Destiny set down Madam Star, and some others of the company handed Mrs. Cave out of the waggon. Hereupon Roquebrune whipped up upon Star's horse, and followed Ragotin, who went just after the waggon.

When they were got into the very worst of all the road, and where there was only room for the waggon to pass safe, they met about twenty carriers' horses, driven by five or six country fellows, who bawled out like mad to the waggoner to stop ; but which he little regarding, requiring the same thing of them in a much higher tone, and alleging that he could turn on neither side without inevitable plunging in the bog. The carriers, thinking to get the better by their expedition, trotted briskly up to him, and gaped out so loud that the waggoner's horses took fright and broke their traces, throwing themselves at the same time into the bog, whilst the waggoner, endeavouring to keep his waggon from following them, weighed one of the wheels too much on the other side, which finding no firm ground to support it, overthrew the whole machine in the mud. Ragotin being extremely incensed against the carriers, for having been the occasion of this accident, thundered out anathemas against them like one possessed, and thinking to come at them on the right side, where he saw the way open, rid furiously against them with his carbine cocked ; but he had no sooner entered the mud than he stuck so fast, that he was fain not only to disengage his legs from out of his stirrups, but likewise to quit his saddle, and leap off into the bog, where he presently sunk so deep that he was up to his armpits, and had been quickly to his chin if he had not extended his arms.

This unexpected accident caused all the passengers that travelled in the fields to stop and lend their assistance.

Poet Roquebrune likewise, who had hitherto out-braved all
the assaults of fortune, was now glad to retire to a dry
place. The carriers perceiving so many men for their
enemies, all armed with fusees, thought it but prudence to
retire as fast as they could, and take to another road. In
the meantime it was judged highly necessary to remedy
the disorder that had happened as soon as possible, and
therefore they proposed to begin with Monsieur Ragotin
and his horse, who were both in no small danger of being
suffocated. Olive and Rancour were the two first
that ventured to assist them; but the nearer they approached the deeper they sunk into the mud, insomuch
that having tried several places, and found them all alike
Rancour, who had always an expedient at hand in cases
of necessity, proposed without laughing to draw Ragotin
out of the danger wherein he was, by one of the cart-ropes,
one end to be fastened on his neck and the other to the
horses, who were then got out into the dry road.

This proposition made all the company to laugh, except
Ragotin, who was not a little afraid of its being executed
upon him. Nevertheless, at last the waggoner, who had run
a great hazard in getting out the horses, did the like for
him; for seizing him fast by the collar, he at several pulls
drew him out of his hole, and dragged him into the fields
where his company were waiting for him, who could not
forbear laughing to see him in that pickle. This done, the
waggoner returned to bring out the horse, who beginning
to exert himself, by the help of a little whipping, flounced
about in the mud, and at length got quite out. Last of all
Olive, Rancour and the waggoner, being all over bemired
with dirt, joined to get out the waggon, which they soon
performed by their united endeavours, and loaded it once
more with the baggage. The horses were put again into
the traces, and Ragotin remounted his courser, though
that with some difficulty, his girths being all broken
Angelica would by no means get up behind him again,

for fear of spoiling her clothes Mrs. Cave and Madam Star chose to walk on foot likewise, all whom Destiny accompanied to the sign of the Green Oaks, which was the only inn to be met with between Mans and the suburbs of Montfort. Here they stayed, not caring to enter the town in the condition they were in. After those that had took the most pains had drunk to refresh themselves, they spent the rest of the day in drying their clothes, having taken fresh to put on out of their trunks, which variety had been presented them by the gentry of Mans. The actresses supped but lightly, having lost their stomachs through the great fatigue they had undergone in walking, and which inclined them to go early to bed.

The actors not only ate but drank heartily before they would go to bed. They were in about their first sleep, being near eleven at night, when a company of men came and knocked at the gate of the inn, inquiring for beds. The host answered his lodgings were full, and besides, that it was an unseasonable time of night for them to require any. Notwithstanding this answer they knocked the more, and threatened to break down the gate in case it were not speedily opened to them. Destiny, who had always carried Saldagne in his mind, thought that this must needs be he, who was come to carry Star away by force; but having looked out of the window, perceived by the help of the moon, which then shone very bright, a man among them with his hands tied behind him; which having whispered to his companions who were already prepared to receive Saldagne, Ragotin cried out it was Monsieur la Rappinière, who had got some highwayman in his custody, for that he was in quest of one. They afterwards were confirmed in this opinion, when they heard them from without command the host in the king's name to open the gates. "But why the devil," quoth Rancour, "could they not have carried their prisoner to Mans, or to the Viscounty of Beaumont, or at worst, why could they not go to

Fresnay ? At all which places there are prisons, whereas there is none here. There must," proceeded he, " be some mystery in this." The host thought himself however obliged to open to La Rappinière, who entered with ten archers and a prisoner bound after the manner I have told you. This prisoner was in a merry humour, and could not forbear laughing, especially as often as he looked upon La Rappinière, which he often did steadfastly, and which was the reason he was not carried to Mans.

Now you must know La Rappinière having had notice there were several robberies committed, and houses broken open and pillaged thereabouts, had set himself diligently about looking after the rogues. As it happened, whilst he and his archers were hunting for them near the forest of Persaine, they saw a man come out of the wood who, per-ceiving a company of horsemen, returned with haste in again, which caused La Rappinière to believe he must needs be one of those he looked after. Having caught him, they were extremely surprised that he answered only confusedly, and yet at the same time laughed in La Rappinière's face, who the more he looked upon him the more he fancied he had seen him somewhere, but could not remember where. The reason of his not being able to recollect himself was, that at the time of their acquaintance short hair and long beards were worn, but this man had long hair and no beard, and moreover wore different clothes from what he did when they were acquainted. All this entirely disguised him from La Rappinière's knowledge. La Rappinière, when he went to bed, which he did after he had well supped, committed him to the custody of two of the archers, who tied him to an old-fashioned bench in the kitchen, and so went to sleep in their chairs, leaving him to do the like if he pleased on the pavement. Next morning Destiny was up first in the house, who going into the kitchen, saw the archers asleep in their chairs, and a man with his hands tied behind him, fastened to a bench, and lying along awake upon the stones ;

who making a sign to him, to come near him, he was not a
little surprised, when the prisoner asked him if he did not
remember he was once robbed on the Pont-neuf, at Paris, and
that he had lost among other things a small picture in a box ?
" I was then," continued he, " with the Sieur la Rappinière
who being at that time our captain, forced me to attack
you. You know all that passed besides. I have learned,"
proceeded he, " that you have been informed of all by
Doguin, on his death-bed, and I have likewise understood
that La Rappinière has restored you your box, nevertheless,
you have now a fair opportunity to revenge yourself on
him. As for my part," added he, " should they carry me
to Mans, as I do not know but they may, I should be
surely hanged there ; but then," concluded he, " it is also
in yours and my power to make him dance the same dance.
It is but joining your evidence with mine, and you may
guess how a jury of Mans would deal with him."

Destiny having heard this left the prisoner, and waited
for La Rappinière's rising. Being come down he met him
in an entry, when taking him aside, he acquainted him
with all that the highway-man had told him, adding withal
that he might well see he was not revengeful, since he
declined taking advantage of what he had heard, and
instead thereof, advised him to be gone, and leave the
criminal to shift for himself. La Rappinière would have
stayed till the actresses were stirring, had not Destiny
frankly told him that Madam Star could not behold him
without the most just indignation imaginable. He
insinuated to him moreover, that if the under-baily of
Alençon should come any ways to hear of his crime, he
would certainly send quickly to seize him. This he
himself was likewise inclinable to believe, and therefore
having first unloosed the prisoner, and set him at liberty,
he mounted on horseback, together with his archers,
pretending to them he had been mistaken in the man, and
went his way without paying his reckoning, according to

custom, and likewise without returning Destiny thanks ; but which last omission was wholly to be attributed to the disorder and confusion he was in. After he was gone, Destiny called up Roquebrune, Olive and the decorator, and they went together into the town, to the great tennis-court, where they found six gentlemen playing a *partie*. They presently went to inquire for the master of the court, when those that were in the gallery, knowing they were players, acquainted the six gentlemen therewith, and that there was amongst them one of a better mien than ordinary. The gentlemen after a little while finished their *partie*, and went up stairs to be rubbed and dried, whilst Destiny came into the court, and discoursed the master.

At length the gentlemen came down again half dressed and saluted Destiny, asking him several questions concerning his company, particularly how many they were ? Whether there was any good actors among them ?   If they had good clothes ?   And whether their women were handsome ?   All which questions Destiny answered to their satisfaction, in return for which civility, they offered him all the service they were capable of doing him ; and having desired the master to help them on with the rest of their clothes, told Destiny they would gladly drink with him, if he would but have patience till they were quite dressed.

Destiny accepted their proffer, being glad to get as many friends as he could to assist him, in case Saldagne should pursue him, which he was yet under an apprehension of. In the meantime the hire of the tennis-court was agreed on, and the decorator was dispatched to the joiner, to give him orders to fit up a playhouse according to his model. The gentlemen being at length dressed, Destiny addressed himself to them with so graceful a mien, and so much good sense, that they soon conceived a more than ordinary kindness for him. They demanded of him where his company lay, and having understood that it was at the

Green Oaks in the suburbs, they proposed to go and drink a glass, and eat a bit with him and his friends where he pleased. A place was named, and they met all except the women, where they breakfasted heartily. You may imagine their discourse was chiefly about acting and plays. They afterwards went together to the women's lodgings, whom they found just sitting down to dinner, which was the reason the gentlemen stayed but little with them; but nevertheless long enough to offer them all the service and protection imaginable, which was much in their power to perform being the very top gentry of that town.

After dinner their strolling baggage was carried to the Golden Cup, being the lodging Destiny had taken for them, and after a little while their theatre being ready, they began to act, in which exercise we will leave them to show they were no novices, and return to see what became of Saldagne after his fall.

CHAPTER VI.

SALDAGNE'S DEATH.

You have seen in the twelfth chapter of the second part of this true history how Saldagne kept his bed in the Baron d'Arques' house in Vervelle's apartment, on account of a fall he had had, as likewise, how his servants had got so unmercifully drunk in a country inn, not above two leagues off from the said house, that Vervelle's man had no small trouble to make them comprehend that the lady they had in charge was escaped, and that the man his master had sent along with them had followed her on another horse. After they had a little rubbed their eyes, yawned three or four times apiece, and stretched out their arms as often to adjust their shin-bones, they put themselves into a posture of pursuit. Vervelle's man nevertheless led them a quite contrary way to what the lovers had taken, and that by his master's orders, so that having wandered about for two or three days in a fruitless search they at last returned to their master Saldagne, who was not yet either out of his bed or cured of his fall; they related to him how the lady had got from them, but that the person whom Monsieur Vervelle had procured them was gone in quest of her.

Saldagne was like to run mad at the first hearing this news, and soon gave his servants to understand, that it was well for them he was confined to his bed, for had he been able to stand, or to lift but one leg from off the sheets, he would have made them sensible by innumerable kicks and bastinadoes that their intolerable negligence was not to be excused by bare words. He flew into that violent passion, and thundered out so many curses against them, that he quite baffled the surgeon's art, and brought the fever again so upon him, that when he came at night to dress him, he apprehended a gangrene in his thigh, from the great inflammation his disorder had occasioned there. He also observed a kind of livid colour on the part, which being a farther bad symptom, caused him to go immediately and find out Vervelle, to whom he related the whole unfortunate accident. Vervelle seemed much astonished at the relation, and wondered how the occasion of such an accident could happen, which he nevertheless knew well enough, having been informed of all before by his servant. He notwithstanding pretended a great deal of ignorance, and went immediately to visit Saldagne; till having inquired the cause of his alteration, and hearing it from his own mouth, he at length redoubled his grief by confessing to him that he had been the contriver of what had befallen him, and that rather to have done him a service than diskindness, which had never been in his thoughts. "For," said he to him, "you may remember nobody would entertain this woman when you ran away with her; and I declare to you, that though I did suffer your wife, my sister, to lodge her within my father's house, yet was it only with design to procure an opportunity to restore her to her brother and friends. Tell me, I beseech you," proceeded he, "what do ye think would have become of you, if information had been given in against you, and you had been taken up for a rape? Could you have procured your pardon, think you? and don't you yet know that the king never passes by crimes of that nature? You fancied perhaps," added he, "that the meanness of her known birth, and the baseness of her profession, would in a great measure have got you excused; but do not flatter yourself in that, for I would have you to know, that she is the daughter both of a gentleman and gentlewoman,

and therefore your hopes would have failed you there.
Besides," continued he, "though all the efforts of justice
should not have been able to hurt you, yet remember she
has a brother who would surely have been revenged on
you for debauching his sister. He is a man of courage,
you know, and you have experienced it in divers rencounters ; therefore one would think that single consideration should incline you rather to value than persecute
him as you have long done. It is high time now to cease
that vain pursuit, or you may quickly come to repent of
not having done it."

This discourse that one would have thought might have
both inclined Saldagne to have reflected and repented,
served rather to increase his resentments, and made him
entertain strange resolutions ; which though he dissembled
for the present to Vervelle, yet he endeavoured afterwards
to put in practice. He made what haste he could to get
cured, and as soon as he found himself in a condition to
mount a horse, took leave of Vervelle, and at the same
time posted away towards Mans, thinking to have found
the company of strollers there ; but being informed they
were gone thence to Alençon, he forthwith resolved to
follow them thither. Passing by Vivain he baited his men,
and three cut-throats he carried along with him, at the
Cock, where the strollers had lodged. He was no sooner
come into the yard but he heard a great noise. Upon
inquiry into the matter it appeared to be the pedlers, who
being going to a fair at Beaumont had on the road
discovered the theft committed on them by Rancour, and
were therefore returned to complain of their hostess, requiring satisfaction ; but who told them she thought herself
not obliged to make it them, by reason they did not
intrust her with their packs, but had had them carried into
their chamber. "That's true," quoth the pedlers, "but why
the devil did you put us to lodge in the same room with
those jugglers, those mountebanks, for no doubt it was
some of them that robbed us ?"

" Well," replied the hostess, " but did you find any of
your packs slit or torn, or the cords unloosed ? "

" Neither of all three," answered the pedlers, " and that
is it which most surprises us, for we found the cords tied
after the same manner we had left them."

" How then would you have me to repair your loss ? "
quoth the hostess. " Get you about your business for a
company of impudent rogues."

The pedlers were just going to reply, when Saldagne
swore that if they did not cease their bawling he would
beat them most unmercifully. The poor pedlers seeing so
many lusty fellows all disguised, thought it but prudence
to hold their peace, however waited for an opportunity when
they were gone to renew their dispute with the hostess.
After Saldagne and his men and horses had refreshed
themselves a little, they set forward for Alençon, where
they arrived very late.

Saldagne for his part could not sleep a wink all night,
and that for thinking on the manner of revenging himself
on Destiny for taking his booty from him ; and as his inclinations had been always brutal, so were the resolutions
he came to. Next day he resolved to go to the play,
which was *Pompey the Great* of Corneille, and sent one of
his companions before to take places for four. As for
himself he came muffled up in his cloak to avoid discovery,
but the rest were in *querpo*, being not known. All the
time the play was acting he was as much tormented as the
audience was pleased, for all admired at the admirable
action of Madame Star, who represented Cleopatra.
When the play was ended, Saldagne and his friends stayed
behind all the company, being resolved to attack Destiny
before they went away. But how luckily were they prevented, for this company of strollers had gained so far
both upon the nobles and all the best citizens of Alençon
of either sex, that they never came to the theatre, or
returned thence, without a great number to attend them,
The same night a young widow lady, by name Ville-Fleur,

invited the actresses to supper in Saldagne's hearing, which
they out of modesty declined accepting; but being
pressed thereto with a great deal of obliging compulsion,
they at length consented; and promised to come. After
this they retired, but accompanied, as were the men, with
a great number of persons of the best note. Among the
rest were those gentlemen that Destiny found at the
tennis court when he first came to hire it.

This second defeat almost made Saldagne despair, till at
length he resolved on one of the most villainous actions
that could be thought on by man; and that was to carry
off Star as she came out of Madam Ville-Fleur's house,
and to stab all those that opposed him, under covert of the
night. The three actresses went to wait on the lady
pursuant to their promise, and great numbers of gallants
came likewise to wait on them. Now Saldagne imagined
it as easy to carry off Star at this juncture as he had
found it before, when she was conducting on horseback by
Destiny's man. He took therefore one of the strongest
horses he had, and putting him into the hands of one of
his men, placed him at one of the doors of Madam Ville-
Fleur's house, which opened into a narrow street near the
palace, believing that upon some slight pretence or other
he might get her out of the house, and then he would
mount her on horseback, and carry her whither he pleased.

Whilst he was thus feeding his fancy with vain chimeras
and imagining his booty already in his possession, an
ecclesiastic who loved good company, and had scraped
some small acquaintance with our strollers, happened to be
going that night to officiate his vespers at Madam Ville-
Fleur's, and who perceiving a lackey, whose livery he did
not know, to stand at her door, began to inquire of him
who he was, what he did there, and whether his master
was in the house? To all these questions the fellow
answered so confusedly that the priest had just reason to
believe him a rogue. He went therefore up into the room,
where all the company was, and gave them an account of

what he had observed, telling them moreover, that he feared there was an ambuscade laid for somebody or other, for that he had heard several people walking about in the darker part of the narrow street.

Destiny had taken notice that one of the audience had hid his face in his cloak, and having his enemy Saldagne always in his thoughts, did not doubt but it was he ; nevertheless he concealed his imaginations and thought it sufficient for the present only to guard the women to Madam Ville-Fleur's house, where they were to sit up all night, with as much company as they could get ; but when he came to understand from the ecclesiastic, what I have before told you, he immediately concluded that Saldagne was once more contriving to carry off his dear Star. This caused him and his company to enter into an immediate consultation what they had best to do.

At last they agreed they would wait the event, and if nobody appeared among them before they broke up, they would go away with as much caution as they could. When they had just determined what to do, an unknown person entered the room, and inquired for Madam Star. Upon her coming, he informed her that a lady of her acquaintance desired to speak with her in the street, and begged she would only come down for a moment. Everybody then presently knew that this was the method Saldagne had proposed to himself to procure the possession of his mistress by, and therefore immediately got themselves into a posture to receive him. It was not thought fit that any of the actresses should be suffered to go down, and therefore they borrowed one of Madam Ville-Fleur's chamber-maids for that purpose. She was no sooner got into the street but Saldagne seized her, and offered to mount her up on his horse ; but he was not a little surprised when he perceived himself surrounded on all sides with armed men, whereof some had come by the great door round the market-place, and others by the lesser door.

Hereupon Saldagne, who had always had no more consideration than his horse, and scarce so much, let fly a pistol among them, and slightly wounded one of the actors before he well knew whether they were come as friends or enemies. This rash attempt had half a dozen shot immediately returned, whereof one entered his head, and two others his body. His companions who were out upon the scout hearing a noise of several discharges, instead of coming up to assist their friend, fled incontinently, as such rascally bullies commonly do where they find any resistance. A light was forthwith called for, to view the wounded man who was fallen on the ground ; but nobody knew him except the strollers, who assured the company it was Saldagne. He was thought to be dead, though he really was not, and which occasioned the bystanders to lend his lackey their assistance to throw him athwart his horse. Being carried after this manner to his lodging, when he came there his host presently discovered some signs of life in him, and consequently did all that lay in his power to recover him, which notwithstanding proved ineffectual, for he died the next day. Being dead his corpse was carried into his own country, where he was received with feigned sorrow by his sisters and their husbands, both lamenting outwardly their loss, though inwardly they were not a little glad of his death ; and I dare be bold to say, that Madam Saint Far his wife, wished him no better fate. In the meantime Justice was fain to bestir her stumps a little in the quest of the murderers, but nobody being found, nor anybody making a complaint ; (besides, the persons that could be most suspected being of the best gentry of the town,) the prosecution was let fall. The actresses were conducted to their lodgings, where they learnt the next day that Saldagne was dead, which caused them to rejoice exceedingly, being thereby out of danger of any future disturbance, meeting everywhere with friends, except in him and his adherents.

CHAPTER VII.

THE SEQUEL OF MRS. CAVE'S HISTORY.

THE day after Saldagne's death Destiny and Olive went to return their hearty thanks to the ecclesiastic, at that time Prior of St. Lewis, for having delivered them from a plague they could never otherwise have hoped to have got rid of. This priory was a title rather honorary than beneficial, belonging to a little church situate in an island made by the river Sartha, and between the two bridges of Alençon. You must not wonder if both the actors and actresses of this company received benefit from a priest, since you might have perceived throughout the whole comical adventures of this famous history, how many services and good offices have been done them by curates. This prior, who before had had but a slender acquaintance with our strollers, by this signal token of kindness had contracted so great a friendship with them, that they interchangably visited and ate together almost every day.

Now one day, while monsieur the prior was in the strollers' chamber, which, by the by, you must take notice was on a Friday, when they did not act, Destiny and Madam Star entreated Mrs. Cave to proceed with the account of her life. She for her part was at first a little loth to comply with their request, till at length being prevailed upon, and having coughed three or four times, spit as often, and as some will have it, gravely wiped her mouth with her handkerchief, she just began to get herself

into a readiness to speak, when the prior was offering to be
gone, believing, it seems, that she might have something
to deliver which she would not have everybody know. He
was notwithstanding stopped by all the company, and unanimously desired to stay, they assuring him they would
be exceeding glad to have him take part of their adventures.

"And I dare say," quoth Star to him, being a woman of
a ready wit, "you yourself have had a share of some in
your time, for you don't by any means seem to me to be a
person that has always worn a cassock."

These words confounded the prior a little at first, but
who afterwards coming to himself, frankly owned he had
had adventures in his time, which possibly might not prove
unacceptable in a romance, in the room of many fabulous
stories it is commonly stuffed with. To which Star briskly
replied, that she was very well satisfied they would be entertaining, and therefore immediately engaged him in the
relating of some of them the first opportunity they should
have. Her request he promised to gratify, and then Mrs.
Cave proceeded with her account after the following
manner :—

"The dog that frightened us prevented what I was then
going to say, and what ye shall now hear. The proposal
the Baron of Sigognac caused to be made to my mother, by
the good curate, afflicted her no less than it pleased me,
as I have already told you ; but what yet increased her
affliction was, that she could not propose a way to herself
how she might get out of his house. To do it alone she
thought would be to little purpose, since she could not
think to get far before he would certainly send and overtake her, and perhaps abuse her to boot. Moreover we
thereby ran a risk of losing our baggage, which was the
only thing we had left to subsist on. At length fortune
offered us an opportunity to escape the most plausible that
could be, which was this. This baron, who had always

hitherto been of a morose inflexible temper, was now all of
a sudden changed from his insensible brutality to the
softest of passions, love, and that to so great an excess, that
he became even sick with the violence of it; nay more,
sick to death. At the beginning of his illness my mother
would needs be frequently offering her service, but she no
sooner came near his bed than he always began to rave.
This my mother perceiving, and being a woman of no
common contrivance, she immediately applied herself to his
servants, telling them that she observed her daughter and
she were rather an hindrance to their lord's recovery than
a help, and therefore desired of them to procure us horses
for ourselves, and a waggon for our baggage, and she
would be gone. This the servants would by no means
hearken to, till at length the curate coming, and having
understood the baron was raving, resolved forthwith to
deliver him from the occasion thereof, and immediately
setting about it soon provided us with all those necessaries
we required.

"Next morning we loaded the cart with our equipage,
and after having taken leave of the servants, but especially
of the obliging curate, we set forth and arrived at night at
a little town of Perigord, whose name I have forgot, but
which I nevertheless remember to be the same place from
whence a surgeon had been fetched to my mother, when
she was wounded by the Baron of Sigognac's servants, who
took us for gipsies. We alighted and went to an inn,
where we were immediately discovered for what we were;
for the chamber-maid no sooner saw us but she cried out
aloud to her companions, ' Courage, my heart! we shall
quickly have play acted here, since the rest of the company are
arrived.' This gave us to understand there were some strollers
already in the town, which we were heartily glad of, being
in hopes that we might have the good fortune to join with
them, and so get our livelihoods. Wherein, as it happened,
we were not deceived, for the morning following, after we

had just discharged our waggon and horses, two actors who had heard of our arrival came to see us, who acquainted us that one of their companions with his wife having quitted their company, we if we pleased might have their places; which if we would but condescend to accept he promised himself to perform wonders. My mother who was always very obliging accepted their proffer, and it was agreed she should have the chief parts, another woman that was among them the second, and I such as they should allot me, or think me capable of, for I was but then thirteen or fourteen years of age at farthest. We continued acting here about fifteen days, this town being not sufficient to maintain us any longer.

My mother pressed heartily to be gone, having a dread upon her that as soon as the baron was recovered he might make search after us, and give us some affront. We consequently set out and rid near forty leagues before we pitched upon any place where to act. The master of the company, whose name was Belle-fleur, talked of marriage to my mother, but which she absolutely refused, conjuring him at the same time not to trouble himself with making love to her, since she began to be somewhat old, and moreover had entered into a vow never to marry again. Belle-fleur hearing my mother's resolution, troubled her no more with his addresses. We rubbed on three or four years with success. At length I began to grow up, and my mother became so crazy that she could not well act her parts wherefore the company having a tolerable opinion of my performance, I was substituted in her place. Belle-fleur, who found he could not have my mother, demanded me of her for his wife; but which favour she again denied him, having a mind to take the first opportunity to retire to Marseilles. But falling afterwards sick at Troyes in Champagne, and fearing to leave me behind her unmarried in case she should die, she communicated to me Belle-fleur's request. Present necessity obliged me to accept the proffer, though he was old enough to be my father, yet considering he was a very honest man, I was the easier induced to consent to marry him. My mother then had the satisfaction to see me married before she died, which happened in a few days after. I was concerned as much as a good daughter ought to be, which nevertheless wore away in a little time. I began then to apply myself altogether to my business again, and in a short time became with child. The day of my lying down being come, I brought into the world this daughter Angelica you see here, who has cost me so many tears, and is like to cost a great many more if I continue much longer in this world."

As she was going to proceed, Destiny interrupted her, telling her she might promise herself a great deal of satisfaction for the future instead of disquiet, since so rich a gentleman as Leander had desired her daughter for his wife. Whilst Mrs. Cave was about to finish her relation, Leander entered the room and saluted all the company. He was all dressed in black, and attended by three footmen in black likewise, which presently gave everybody reason to conceive that his father was dead in earnest. The prior left the company and went his way ; and 'tis here I conclude this chapter.

CHAPTER VIII.

THE END OF MRS. CAVE'S HISTORY.

AFTER Leander had finished his compliments upon his arrival, Destiny told him he must desire leave both to condole him for the loss of his father, and to congratulate him on account of the great estate he had left him. Leander thanked him for both, but as for his father's death, told him, he had long expected it with impatience.

"Nevertheless," added he, "I do not intend to forsake my profession, which has always been so pleasant to me, however, must desire that my appearing on the stage may be dispensed with, till such time as we are got farther off the place of my nativity."

This request was forthwith granted by all. After which, Madam Star desired to know of Leander what title she must salute him by for the future. His answer was, that his father's title was Baron of Roche-pierre, which he had a right to use if he pleased, but that having resolved to continue among them, he determined to be called by no other name than that of Leander, being the same under which he had been so happy as to be thought acceptable to his dear Angelica. "This name therefore," quoth he, "I am resolved to carry along with me to my grave, as well for the reason just mentioned, as to convince ye all, that I am indispensably disposed to perform punctually what I promised to the company at my departure hence."

At these words embraces were renewed, many sighs

breathed forth, some tears shed, and all in general approved
the generous resolution of Leander, who approaching
Angelica, bestowed a thousand endearing protestations on
her ; all which she returned with so much wit and good
nature, that he was more and more confirmed in his
resolution.   I would willingly give you the particulars of
their entertaining each other, but that I am not in love as
they were.   Leander told the company farther, he had
regulated all his affairs, and put new tenants into most of
his farms, who having paid fines amounting in all to near
6,000 livres, he had brought the same along with him, to
the end that in case the company wanted money, he might
supply them.   He received abundance of thanks for this
noble offer.

Then Ragotin, who had hardly appeared in the two
foregoing chapters, came forward, and desired that since
Monsieur Leander had been pleased to declare he would
not act whilst the players continued in this country, that
he might have his parts, which he promised he would
perform to all the advantage imaginable.   Whereupon,
Roquebrune, who had always been his opposite, rose up,
and said, "That he humbly conceived Leander's parts
belonged rather to him, than to such a whipper-snapper as
he."   This word made all the company to laugh ; after
which Destiny acquainted the two candidates that their
several merits should be considered, and justice be speedily
done them.   Then Mrs. Cave was desired to go on with
her history ; but first the Prior of St. Lewis was to be sent
for, to the end that having heard hers, he might be the
better able to relate his own.   Great attention was given,
and she began again thus :

"As I remember I left off at my lying-in of Angelica, I
have already told you the two strollers came to desire us
to join with them, but did not tell you, that those two were
Olive and another who left us afterwards, in whose room came
our poet Roquebrune.   But to come to the greatest of my

misfortunes, I must tell you, that one day as we were acting the *Menteur* (*Liar*) of Monsieur Corneille, in a certain town of Flanders, a footman that had been keeping a place for his lady that was not yet come, left it, and went a drunkening, whereby another lady got the place. Soon after, the lady to whom the place belonged came, and finding it taken up, very civilly told the other lady that that place belonged to her, and therefore desired her to let her have it. The other answered that if she had a place there, she might take it if she pleased, but that for her part she would not move an inch from where she sat. Words thus arose, and from thence they came to blows. The ladies cuffed each other heartily, which would have signified little, had not the men interposed; who instead of parting the fray, increased it, taking to either party, and raising factions against one another. This was principally caused by the ladies' relations, who both got what friends they could on their side. Then was there nothing to be heard but squeaking and clashing of swords, all which we only looked upon from the stage, till at length my husband, who at that time played the part of Dorante, seeing so many swords drawn, and not caring to look on, leapt in among them with his sword drawn likewise, and endeavoured to appease the tumult; when a certain person from one of the parties, taking him no doubt for his enemy, gave him such a home thrust, as paid him notably for his meddling.

"This was given unperceived by my husband; for had he seen it, he would no doubt have parried it, being not a little skilled in fencing. This thrust nevertheless pierced his heart, whereof he immediately fell dead to the ground, which occasioned all the audience quickly to shift for themselves. I then threw myself off from the stage into the pit, and went to assist my wounded husband, but to my great grief found him stark dead. Angelica, who then might have been about thirteen or fourteen years of

age, came down immediately to me, together with the rest
of the company, who all joined with me in my just complaints, for the loss of so good a husband. I buried him
the best I could, after that the coroner had sat upon him,
who demanded of me if I would have his warrant to take
up the murderer. I answered, I should be willing to have
justice done upon him, but feared I had not wherewithal
sufficient to prosecute him, and so declined it. We quickly
forsook this town, and went a strolling on farther, being
obliged to act for our maintenance ; but our company was
now by no means good, having lost its principal actor. I
was for a long time so grieved at my husband's death,
that I could not give my mind to get up my parts, but
herein Angelica always supplied me from her memory,
when we were on any scene together. At length we
came to a town in Holland, where you know that you,
Mr. Destiny, your sister Star, and Rancour, came to us,
and offered to join us if we so pleased, whereof we were
not a little glad, being almost quite broke before. The
rest of my adventures have been common to us all, whereof
you know as much already as I can pretend to tell you,
and that from Tours, where our porter killed one of the
intendant's officers, even to this city of Alençon, where we
now are."

Here Mrs. Cave ended her history, shedding a great
many tears, which Madam Star did likewise, comforting
her all she was able, for the great misfortunes she had
undergone, but withal remembered her, she had the less
reason to be concerned now, since she was so near to an
alliance with so worthy a gentleman as Leander. Mrs.
Cave sobbed so violently that she could not find time to
answer her, neither can I to continue this chapter any
farther, and therefore conclude it.

CHAPTER IX.

HOW RANCOUR UNDECEIVED RAGOTIN CONCERNING
MADAM STAR ; TOGETHER WITH THE ARRIVAL OF
A COACH FULL OF GENTRY, AND SOME OTHER
COMICAL ADVENTURES OF RAGOTIN'S.

THE play went· on prosperously, and one or other was
acted every day, with great satisfaction to the audience,
which consisted of the better sort, and was generally very
numerous, amongst whom nevertheless happened no disorders, by reason Ragotin was kept behind the scenes,
having no parts yet given him ; but which he grumbled at,
though he had been promised some when occasion served.
He made his complaints almost every day to Rancour,
whom he put a great confidence in, though, by the way, he
was one of the very worst of men. As he plagued him one
day above the rest, Rancour said to him, " Monsieur
Ragotin, disturb yourself no more about this matter, for I
must tell you, there is a great deal of difference between
the bar and the stage. If a man have not a more than
ordinary assurance he will be easily put out on the stage ;
besides, the speaking of verse requires no common capacity,
and is more difficult to do than you may fancy. You must
observe nicely the pointing of verse, and when you speak
it on the stage, run one verse into another, that it may
seem prose, and consequently be natural and easy. You
must not sing it out, and stop at the cesures, or at the end
of a verse, as the vulgar do, but pronounce it always with a

good grace, and a becoming action. I would have you therefore," continued he, " to wait a little longer before you come on the stage, and in the meantime, you may act in some private masquerade or farce, to bring your hand in. You may there play the part of a second Zany, or Merry-Andrew, and I think we have a habit within that will be very fit for you, having formerly belonged to a little boy called Godenot, who had sometimes represented that person. But," added he, " we must first speak to Monsieur Destiny and Madam Star about it."

This they did the same day, and it was ordered that next morning Ragotin should represent the said person. He was instructed by Rancour in what he was to say, who as you may have observed in the first part of this romance, was altogether inclinable to farce. The plot of what they played was an intrigue which Rancour unravelled in favour of Destiny. As Rancour was preparing to begin, Ragotin appeared upon the stage, to whom the former spoke thus : " Little boy, my pretty Godenot," quoth he, " whither art thou going in such haste ? " Then addressing himself to the company, after having chucked him under the chin and felt for his beard, " Gentlemen," said he, " I have always hitherto thought that Ovid's metamorphosis of pismires into pigmies who had at that time war with the cranes, was only a fable, but now I find it to be true ; for certainly this is one of that race, or else the little man revived, concerning whom, about seven or eight years since, there was a song made to this effect :

THE SONG.

" ' My mother would needs have me wed,
  But a pigmy, alas ! is the man,
  For call him husband who can,
That scarce takes up a foot of the bed ?
Yet still this of him may be said,
  That if he be not, he be not a man,
  He is, he is, he is, he is, he is as much as he can.'

At the end of every verse Rancour turned and winded
Ragotin about as if he had been a puppet, making him to
appear in so many ridiculous postures, as made the
company to laugh heartily. The rest of the song I have
left out as superfluous to our romance.

After Rancour had ended his song, he showed Ragotin
to the company, telling them he was risen again from the
dead ; and to make what he said appear, took off his mask,
and exposed him barefaced, which caused him not only to
blush for shame, but likewise to redden with anger. He
nevertheless was fain to bear it ; however to revenge himself, told Rancour that he was a downright blockhead for
making his song with such old-fashioned rhymes. " But,"
quoth Rancour, " I think you are a greater blockhead for a
little man, since you could not distinguish betwixt an old
song and a new one, this having been made above a
hundred years ago. Also," continued he, " it is with
rhyming as with language, custom must regulate all ; for
since, as Monsieur Rogula has it, who reformed the French
tongue, we cannot give a reason why we pronounce so
and so, no more ought our ancestors to do why they wrote
after this manner ; and whereas whatever is most ancient
is always most valued, so ought my song to be for the
same reason."

While Ragotin was going to answer, Destiny entered,
complaining of the long stay his man Rancour had made,
and whom having found in a hot dispute with Ragotin, he
immediately demanded the cause of their dispute, but
which he could nevertheless never come to know, since
they answered him both at a time, and so loud that they
made him stark mad. His passion being thus raised, he
thrust Ragotin against Rancour with great indignation,
and whom Rancour returned again against him with like
fury, till at last they had tossed him about from one to
the other so long, that he fell down on his face, and afterwards marched away on all fours under the curtains.

This the audience all rise up to see, protesting this mute action was worth all the rest of their farce, which they could not proceed any farther with, by reason the actors had quite laughed themselves into confusion.

Notwithstanding this affront, Ragotin still solicited Rancour to bring him in favour with Madam Star, and the better to incline him to it, often treated him ; which was very welcome to Rancour, who did not scruple to feed heartily at the little man's cost. But as he was wounded with the same dart, he had not the heart to speak either for Ragotin or himself. One day above the rest Ragotin pressed him so close that he found himself obliged to tell him, " Monsieur Ragotin, this Star, no doubt, is of the nature of those in the firmament, which the astrologers name wandering, for I have no sooner at any time begun to open your passion to her, but she twinkles and leaves me without an answer. Yet how should she answer me," quoth he, " if she will not hear me ? But I believe I have discovered the occasion of her indifference," proceeded he, " and which no question may surprise you ; but a man that has a mind to be satisfied in anything must be prepared against all events. This Monsieur Destiny, whom she calls her brother, I fancy not to be so, for I surprised them the other day caressing after that manner as such near relations are not wont to do, and therefore am rather inclinable to believe he is her gallant, and am more deceived than ordinary, if on the same day that Leander and Angelica marry, they do not marry likewise. Otherwise, I should think her the most indiscreet woman in the world," added he, " to slight your generous proffer. You that are a man of quality and merit, without taking notice of your graceful mien. I tell you this," continued he, " that you may have the more reason to remove her from your heart, since you will not otherwise fail to torment yourself like one of the damned."

The little man, both poet and advocate, was so confounded at this discourse, that he had nothing left to say, but immediately quitted Rancour, shaking his head, and crying after his wonted manner, " Serviteur ! Serviteur," &c·

Afterwards Ragotin resolved with himself to go to Beaumont le Vicomte, a little town about five leagues distant from Alençon, where there was a market kept every Monday. The reason of his going he told the company was to receive a certain sum of money that was owing him in that town by a merchant. " But how will you do to go," quoth Rancour to him, " since your horse has been lately pricked in shoeing, and is lame ? he will never be able to carry you so far."

" It may be not," answered Ragotin, " and therefore I'll hire one that shall, and if I cannot meet with one to my purpose, I can at last walk on foot, it is not so far. I don't question," added he, " but I shall meet with some company that will go from hence." He sought after but could not find a hackney to be let, which induced him to enquire of a pedler that lived next door to his lodgings, if he were not disposed to go, and finding he was, he desired the favour of him for a companion ; which the pedler agreed to, in case he would be going by one o'clock in the morning, when the moon would be just up, which he with little difficulty consented to.

Now a little before they set out, a poor nail-smith was gone towards the said market to dispose of his nails, which he was accustomed to make every week ready for Mondays on purpose. This nail-smith being upon the road on foot, with his wallet upon his back, and hearing no noise of travellers, either before or behind him, thought he had been got out too early ; besides, he was a little afraid, when he considered he was to pass under several gibbets where men's quarters hung, which obliged him to step aside out of the road, and to go lie down upon a bank, where he fell asleep, Some little time after Ragotin, and the pedler came by, but who said not a word to each other,

thc little man's thoughts being wholly taken up with
reflections on what Rancour had told him. When thcy
came near to the gibbets, Ragotin asked the pedler if hc
would not count the persons that were hanged. The
pedler answered, " with all his heart." Then they went
forwards into the middle of them, and began to count ; but
at length having met with one that was dropped down, and
was very stiff and dry, Ragotin, who had always thoughts
worthy himself, asked of his companion to assist to hclp
him up, and set him against one of the posts, the which
they easily performed by help of their staves.   This donc,
they counted fourteen hanged, besides this last and so went,
on their journey.

They had not gonc far, before Ragotin had a maggot
come into his head, to turn about and call to the dead
person to come after him, which he did in these words :
So ho ! you, will you come along with us ? "   The nail-
smith, who it seems did not sleep very sound, hearing this,
rose presently from his post, thinking some fellow travellers
had desired his company, and cried, " With all my heart,
I come, I come," and immediately began to follow them.
The pedler and Ragotin, thinking verily it had been the
dead corpse that came towards them, ran away as hard as
they could drive ; whereat the nail-smith began to run
likewise, crying all the way, " Stay, stay, I come, I comc."
As the nail-smith ran, his nails he had on his back made a
great noise, which inclined Ragotin and thc pedler the
more to believe that it was the corpse they had set up
against the gibbet, or else the ghost of some other person
that dragged chains after him ; for the vulgar are of
opinion there's never a ghost that appears, but he has a
chain fastened to him.   This belief made them to tremble
so much that they could not run any farther, so that their
legs not being able to support them longer, they dropped
down.

This gave thc nail-smith opportunity to come up with

them, whom they at first were miserably affrighted at ;
but he having bid them good morrow, and telling them
they had given him a great deal of trouble to overtake
them, they began to come to themselves, and saw he was
no ghost. They then joined companies, and continued
their journey prosperously to Beaumont where Ragotin did
what he had to do, and returned next morning to Alençon ;
where he found his friends just risen from dinner, to whom
having related the story of his adventure ; they laughed so
heartily, that they were almost ready to burst. The
women for their parts were so extremely tickled, that they
haw-hawed out so loud, that they were heard across the
way, and which it is probable they would have continued
much longer, had they not been interrupted by the arrival
of a coach full of country gentry. This coach belonged to
one Monsieur de la Fresnay, who was about to marry his
daughter, and was come to Alençon to entreat the strollers
to come and act a play at her wedding. This lady, who
was none of the wisest, desired they would act the *Sylvius*
of Mairet. This the actresses were hardly able to forbear
laughing at, telling her that if her ladyship would have
that, she must procure them a book, for they had not one
by them ; the lady answered, she would lend them one ;
adding withal, that she had all the pastorals bound up
together in one volume, viz those of Ragan, being *The Fair
Fisher-woman*, *The Love-hater*, *Plocidon*, *The Mercer*, &c.,
together with several others whose titles she had forgot.

"Such plays as these," quoth she to them, "are proper
for you strollers that act always in the country, and cannot perhaps go to the expense of such sumptuous habits,
as the *Death of Cinna*, *Heraclius*, *Rodogune*, and the like,
would require. Moreover, the verse in pastorals savours
not so much of bombast, as that of heroic poems. Besides,
pastorals are of a nature more conformable to the simplicity
of our first parents, who wore nothing but fig-leaves even
after they had sinned."

Her father and mother were all the while hearkening to their daughter's discourse with great attention and wonder, imagining that the greatest orators of the kingdom could not be able to utter anything beyond it. After this, the strollers desired time to prepare themselves, and had eight days given them. The company parted after dinner, just as the Prior of St. Lewis happened to come in. Madam Star told him he had done well to come, having saved Olive the trouble of looking after him. The actresses seated themselves upon the bed, and the actors in chairs. The door was shut, and the porter had orders to send away everybody that came to speak with them. After silence proclaimed, the prior began his history, as you may find in the following chapter, if you'll but take the pains to read it.

CHAPTER X.

" THE beginning of this history," quoth the prior, "cannot
but be a little tedious, since it consists chiefly of genealogy.
Nevertheless, this sort of beginning is necessary to introduce
a perfect understanding of the matter in dispute. I shall
not endeavour to disguise my condition, since I am in my
own country. In another it may be I might have passed
for what I really was not, which nevertheless I have never
yet done. I have always been very sincere in this point.

" I am then a native of this city, the wives of my two
great grandfathers were gentlewomen, and had a *de* tacked
to their surnames. But as you know, the eldest sons going
away with the greatest part of the estate, leaves but little
for the younger children ; who according to custom, are
either obliged to go into orders, or else to marry some
inferior person or other, suitable to their conditions,
provided she be but rich and honest, pursuant to the
proverb which has been a long time current in this country,
'More money and less honour.' So that my two grand-
mothers were married to two rich tradesmen, the one a
woollendraper, and the other a linendraper. My father's
father had four sons, whereof my father was not the eldest.
My mother's father had two sons and two daughters,
whereof she was one, and married to the second son of the
woollendraper, who had left off his trade to follow petty-

fogging, whereby he fooled away most of his estate, which was the reason he left me but little. My father had formerly thrived very much by his trade, and married a very rich woman for his first wife, who died without children. He was pretty well advanced in years when he married my mother, which she consented to rather out of duty than inclination, insomuch that there was more of aversion on her side than love, which no doubt was the reason they were thirteen years married before they had the least hopes of having any children. At last my mother was big, and when the time of her lying in was come, she brought me into the world with a great deal of pain, having been four full days in labour.

"My father, who was at that time employed in prosecuting a man that had killed his brother, was overjoyed, when at his return the women gave him joy of a son. He treated them all as well as he could, and made some of them drunk, having given them strong white wine on the lees, instead of perry ; which he has many a time after told me, and whereat we have laughed heartily. Two days after my birth I was baptized. My name signifies little to be mentioned. I had for godfather the lord of the place, a very rich man, and my father's neighbour ; who having understood by the lady, his wife, that my mother was with child, after so many years' marriage, desired he might hold what God sent her to the font. What he desired was readily granted. My mother having no more children than me, bred me with all the care imaginable, and perhaps a little too nicely for one of her quality.

"As I came to grow up it was observed I would be no fool, which occasioned me to be mightily beloved by everybody, especially my godfather, who had but one only daughter, that had been married to a gentleman a relation of my mother's. She had two sons, one elder by a year than I, and one younger by a year, but both who were as backward in parts as I was forward ; which occasioned my

godfather to send for me always when he had any of the
better sort of company (which you must know he often
had, being accustomed to treat all the princes and great
lords that passed by our town), to divert them, which by
dancing, singing and prattling I did. For this purpose I
was always kept in a better garb than ordinary, and had
surely made my fortune, had not death taken him away
suddenly as he was on a journey to Paris. I nevertheless
was not so sensible then of his death as I have been since.
My mother sent me to study, and I profited extremely ;
but when she understood my inclinations ran towards the
church, she took me from the college and brought me into
the world, notwithstanding her vow to devote her first-fruits
to God, if He should please to give her any.

"She proved quite contrary to other mothers, who do all
they can to prevent their children falling into ill courses,
for she was continually feeding me with money, Sundays
and holidays especially, to go a gaming, or to the tavern.
Nevertheless having some discretion of my own, all my
liberties and abilities amounted only to making merry
sometimes with my neighbours. I had contracted a more
than ordinary friendship with a young lad, son to a certain
officer belonging to 'Lewis XIII.'s Queen Dowager, who
had likewise two daughters. He lived in that fine park
which as you may have heard was one of the greatest,
delights of the ancient Dukes of Alençon. His house
there had been given him by the aforesaid Queen Dowager,
his royal mistress, who had an appendage upon that
duchy. We led a pleasant life in this park, but that still
like children, never thinking of what was to come."

"This officer of the Queen's was called Monsieur du
Fresne, who had a brother an officer likewise, who belonged
to the king. This brother required du Fresne to send his
son to him, which he could by no means refuse to do.
Before the lad went for the court he came to take leave of
me, and I must own the parting with him raised the first

grief I ever felt. We lamented our separation reciprocally ; but I had much greater reason two months after, when I heard from his mother the news of his death. I showed as much concern at the loss of him as I was capable of showing, and went immediately to join with his sisters in their grief for him, which was exceeding great. But as time lessens all things, when this sad remembrance was a little over, Madame du Fresne came and desired my mother that I might teach her younger daughter to write, whose name was Mademoiselle du Lys, to distinguish her from her elder sister, who bore the name of the family. The reason of her troubling me, she said, was because her writing-master had been newly gone, and though there were several others in the town, yet none would teach abroad, and truly she thought her daughter's quality too great to go to school. She excused herself very much for this liberty she had taken, but withal intimated, that this familiarity might end in something more important, meaning a marriage, which was soon after agreed on privately between my mother and her. My mother had no sooner proposed this employment but I readily accepted it, and went immediately after dinner to wait on my scholar, finding a secret spring within, that pushed me on more than ordinary, though I knew not at that time what it was.

" I had not been above eight days in this exercise, before the young lady, my scholar, who was much handsomer than her sister, began to be very familiar with me, calling me in raillery her little master. It was then I began to find something in my heart I had been but little acquainted with before, and the young lady, for aught I could perceive, began likewise to feel the same. We were from that time inseparable, and were never so well pleased as when we were left alone together, which happened not seldom. This sort of conversation lasted about six months, before we presumed to discover the sentiments of our hearts, which nevertheless our eyes had spoke sufficiently all the while. One day I had a mind to try to make a copy of verses in her praise, to see how she would receive them ; but having never made an attempt of that kind, I was afraid I should not succeed in it. Notwithstanding I immediately set myself about reading the best romance-writers and poets I could find, having rejected those of the *Melesines, Robert the Devil, Amon's Four Sons, The Fair Maguelonne, John of Paris*, &c. which are trifling compositions, and only fit for children. At last looking by chance into Marot's Works, I met with a roundelay very proper for my purpose. This I immediately transcribed word for word, and which is as follows :

A ROUNDELAY.

" ' Your face and tongue so pleasing prove,
　　That I both gaze and hear ;
　And whilst your charms invite to love,
　　Your chains am glad to wear :
　But since you make of me a slave,
　　And use me at your pleasure,
　Why may not I my mistress have
　　To occupy my leisure ? '

" I gave her these verses, which she read with a great deal of pleasure, as I could perceive by her countenance. After having read them she thrust them into her bosom, whence they not long after fell upon the ground, and were taken up by her eldest sister, contrary to her knowledge, which however she afterwards came to know, by means of a lackey. She thereupon asked her sister for them, and perceiving she made some difficulty to let her have them, she flew into a great passion, and went and complained to her mother, who forthwith ordered her sister to give them her, which she presently did. This sort of proceeding gave me a great deal of hopes, while a serious reflection on my condition made me as much to despair.

" Now whilst we thus pleased each other with our

fancies, my father and mother being pretty well advanced
in years, determined to marry me, and one day made me
acquainted with their intentions. My mother discovered
to my father the project she had laid with Madame du
Fresne, but he being a man of more sense than ordinary,
absolutely rejected it ; saying, that that young lady's quality
was too great for mine, and besides, she had too little
money to support it, well knowing she would expect to be
maintained according to her condition. But as I was the
only son of my father, who was tolerably rich, as likewise
heir to an uncle, who had no children, by the custom of
Normandy, many families looked upon me as worthy their
alliance, and consequently made me to stand godfather to
divers children, with several young ladies of the best
quality in our neighbourhood, those being the common
means to promote marriage, which nevertheless had no
effect upon me, having been before entirely devoted to my
dear Du Lys. I was notwithstanding so continually persecuted by my parents to marry some other, that to avoid
their importunities, I resolved to go to the wars, although I
was not then above sixteen or seventeen years of age. New
levies being made in this city to go to Denmark, under
command of the Count of Montgomery, I enlisted myself
privately with three younger brothers, my neighbours. We
set out in pretty good equipage, and my father and mother
were so extremely concerned at my departure, that the
latter was almost like to die with grief. How Du Lys
bore my so sudden leaving her, I could not tell then, but
which I understood afterwards from herself.

"We embarked at Havre-de-Grace, and sailed very
successfully till we came within sight of the Sound ; but
then arose so furious a tempest that the like was scarce
ever known before. Our ships were soon separated, and
that which I was in, commanded by the count himself, was
driven very luckily to the mouth of the Thames, where by
the help of a reflux we quickly got up to London, the

capital city of England. There we stayed about six weeks, during which time I had opportunity to survey the rarities of that superb city, and above all, the shining court of its king, who was then Charles I. of that name. The Count of Montgomery returned afterwards to his seat, Port Orson in Normandy, whither I did not care to go, and therefore desired of him to permit me to go for Paris, which he did. I embarked then on board a vessel bound for Rouen, where I not long after arrived safe, and from thence went partly by boat, and partly by land to Paris. There I met with a near kinsman of mine, who was the king's wax-chandler. I begged of him to make use of his interest to get me into the Guards. He promised he would, and did it, but was fain to be my surety, for at that time nobody was to be admitted without one. I was received into Monsieur de la Rauderie's company. My cousin lent me money to equip myself, for in my sea-voyage I had spoiled all my clothes. I thus became equal to many cadets of good families who carried muskets as well as I. About that time the princes and great lords of France rose against their king, and among them Monsieur the Duke of Orleans; but his majesty, through the policy of the great Cardinal Richelieu, broke all their measures, but that not without taking a journey first to Brittany with a gallant army. We arrived at Nantes, where the first person made an example of was the Count of Calais, who had his head struck off there. This raised a terror in all the others, insomuch that they sued to his majesty for peace, which being granted, the king returned to Paris. In our way we stop at Mans, where my father came to see me, old as he was, having been before acquainted by my cousin, that I was in the king's Guards. He begged of my captain to discharge me, which he obtained with some difficulty, or rather, for some consideration. We then returned to this city, where it was agreed, the only way to keep me at home was to marry me.

"A surgeon's wife that was neighbour to a cousin-german of mine, hearing this, brought along with her the under-baily's daughter of a town about three leagues off, under pretence of devotion, being Lent-time, but her true reason was to entrap me if possible. Having seen her but once, I was desired to do it again at my cousin's house, which I did, and after about an hour's conversation with her, she went her way, when all the company told me she was a mistress for me ; to which I bluntly replied, I did not like her. My reason was not because she was not rich and handsome, being both in perfection, but because all the beauty in the world could have no power upon me, as long as my dear Du Lys was in my thoughts.

"I had an uncle, my mother's brother, of a severe temper, who coming one night to our house, after having rallied me extremely for the slights I had put upon the under-baily's daughter, told me I must resolve to go and visit her at her own house, in the Easter holidays, there being those of a much greater quality than I who would be proud of such a match. I answered neither one way nor other, but when the holidays came, I was forced to go thither with my said cousin, the surgeon's wife, and a son of hers. When we came, we were very courteously received and treated for three days together. We were also carried to all the said under-baily's farms, at every one of which we were handsomely entertained. We went likewise to a large village, about a league off this gentle-man's house, to pay a visit to the curate of the place, who was a brother to this lady's mother, and who gave us a very civil reception. At last we returned home as we came, that is, as to what concerned me, as little in love as before. It was nevertheless resolved, that in a fortnight's time our marriage should be concluded ; which term being expired, I was compelled to return to the baily's house, together with three cousin-germans, two advocates, and an attorney of this jurisdiction ; but as good luck would have it, they could agree upon nothing, wherefore the business was put off till May next. But that saying is certainly true, that 'man proposes, and God disposes,' for a little before the said time, my mother fell sick, and my father four days afterwards, both whose maladies ended in death, the former dying on Tuesday, and the latter on Thursday following. Although I was very sick myself, yet I made shift to go visit my aforesaid severe uncle, who was extremely ill likewise, and who died in less than a fortnight's time. Some time after all this, the baily's daughter was proposed to me anew, but which I would hear nothing of, having now no parents to force me. My heart was altogether in the aforesaid park, where I frequently walked, but never half so often as I had done in imagination. One morning, when I thought nobody had been stirring in the Sieur du Fresne's house, I walked leisurely before it, and was not a little surprised, when I saw Du Lys singing at the window an old song, which had for its upholding

"'Ah! why is he from me, the man that I love?'"

"This obliged me to draw nearer, and to make her a very low bow, which I accompanied with this or the like expression—'I could wish with all my heart, Madame, you had the satisfaction you so much desire; and were it in my power to contribute towards it, I would do it, with as fervent a passion as ever I have showed to approve myself your most humble servant?' She returned my salutation, answering me not a word, but continuing to sing on, she changed the burthen of her song to

"'Ha! see him before me, the man that I love.'"

"You may imagine this was not heard by one that was deaf, and having been a little in the wars, I had courage enough to reply, though not in verse—'I should have just reason to believe you sincere, madam, if you would but oblige me so far as to open the door.' At the same time she called to the lackey, spoken of before, and bid him to open the door to me. I went in, and was received not only by her, but likewise by her father, mother, and elder sister, with all the civility and good will imaginable. Her mother asked me why I was so great a stranger, and why they had not seen me as frequently as they were wont? My mourning, she told me, was no just excuse, since I must be allowed to divert myself now as well as before; and in a word, she gave me to understand that I should always be extremely welcome to her house. My answer was only to show the little merit I had to pretend to, and which I expressed in some few ill-ordered phrases as I had done before. But at length all concluded with a breakfast of milk, which you know in this country passes for a good treat."

" And which is notwithstanding none of the worst, sir," quoth Madam Star. " But pray go on."

" When I was taking leave to be gone, the mother asked me if I would not give myself the trouble to accompany her and her daughter to see an old relation of theirs that lived about two leagues off; I answered, she did me wrong to ask me the question, when an absolute command would have been much more obliging to me. The journey was pitched upon for next day. The time came, and the mother got up upon a little mule they had in the house, the elder sister rid her father's horse, and I carried behind me my dear Du Lys. What discourse we had upon the road I'll give you leave to guess, for as for my part I have forgot it. All I am able to tell you is, that Du Lys and I often stole from the company, and went to recreate ourselves in an adjoining grove, which had a little river that ran through the midst of it, upon whose banks we had the pleasure both to hear the warbling of the birds, and the purling of the stream, to which we added our mutual endearments, and

many innocent caresses which passed between us. It was
there we entered into a resolution to divert ourselves con-
siderably at the approaching Carnival.

"Some time after this journey, while I was making cider
in the suburb called La Barre, and which joins to Du
Lys's father's park, she came running to me, whereby I
presently guessed she had something more than ordinary
to say to me. After having chid me a little for finding me
in that condition, she took me aside, and told me that the
gentleman whose daughter was at Monsieur de Planche-
Planete's brother-in-law's, had brought another gentleman
his friend to make love to her, and whereof she thought fit
to get an opportunity to come and tell me. 'It is not,'
added she, 'that I distrust my power of refusing him, but
because I had rather you should find out some means to
send him packing.' To this I replied, 'Go you and make
much of him, that he may not be gone before I come, and
I'll assure you he shall not be there by to-morrow this time.'
She left me extremely well pleased, and I immediately put off
my cider to my servants' management, and went directly
home ; where taking a clean shirt, and another suit of clothes,
I hasted to find out my companions ; for you must know
there were fifteen of us young fellows, who had each a
mistress, and were all jointly engaged to cut any man's
throat that should offer but to interfere with either. I
acquainted them with what I have already told you, and
all concluded that this gallant, who was a gentleman of
Lower-Maine, must be found out, and be forced to return
from whence he came. We went then forthwith to his
lodging, where he was at supper with the other gentleman his
introducer. We did not stick to tell him downright that he
must speedily be gone, and that there was nothing to be got
for him in that country. The introducer replied, that we
did not know what they were come about, and that when
we did, we would not be so much concerned at it. Then I
stepped up, and clapping my hand to my sword, said, 'If I

have her heart, I have it, and if you do not quit her this
minute, I'll quickly send your souls a wool-gathering.' One
of them replied, that the contest was not equal, and that if
I were alone I durst not have said so much. To which I
answered 'You are two, and here is a gentleman and I,
taking one of my comrades, that will presently go and
dispute the matter with you farther.'

" The gentlemen accepted the challenge and we were all
going out when the master of the house and a son of his
prevented us, persuading the gentlemen that their best way
was to be gone, and not to stand disputing with us, whom
they were positive they would get nothing by. They took
their advice, and we never heard a word of them after.
Next morning I went to wait on my dear Du Lys, telling
her all that had passed, wherewith she seemed very well satisfied, and gave me abundance of thanks for delivering her
from her lover. The winter now approaching, the nights
began to be long, and which we passed away at ' Questions
and Commands,' and such like sorts of plays, but which
being every night repeated, at length grew tedious, and
therefore I determined to give a ball. I conferred with Du
Lys about it ; and she consented to it. I asked her father's
leave, and he granted it me. The following Sunday we
danced all day, and which we continued to do often, till at
length there came so many people that Du Lys desired me
to give it over, and think on some other diversion. We then
resolved to get up a comedy and act it, which we not long
after did accordingly."

Here Madam Star interrupted the prior, saying, " Sir,
since you are upon comedy, pray give me leave to ask you,
if this history of yours be much longer, for it begins to grow
late, and supper-time approaches."

" Ah Madam ! " quoth the prior " there is twice as much
to come yet."

Then it was thought necessary to put it off to another
opportunity, that the actors might have time to dress for the

play ; and had it not been for that reason, Monsieur Vervelle's arrival would have interrupted it, who got easily into the chamber, by reason the porter was asleep. His coming surprised the company extremely. He very court-eously embraced them all, and chiefly Monsieur Destiny, whom he hugged closely more than once. Afterwards he began to tell them the occasion of his journey, which you shall have in the ensuing chapter, although it be very short.

CHAPTER XI.

THE prior of St. Lewis would have been gone, but Destiny stopped him telling him that supper would be ready very speedily, and he should keep Monsieur Vervelle company, whom they had entreated to sup with them. The hostess was called up, and ordered to get something extraordinary. Clean linen was laid, good cheer made, many healths drunk, and a great deal talked. After the cloth was taken away, Destiny desired to know of Vervelle the occasion of his coming into those parts. He answered, It was not on account of his brother-in-law Saldagne's death, which his sisters lamented no more than he, but by reason of a business of importance he had to negotiate at Rennes in Brittany ; so that being that way bound, he could do no less than turn a little out of the road to visit so good a friend as, him. Destiny thanked him heartily for the honour he had done him, and afterwards informed him of all the ill designs Saldagne had had against him ; which you may have seen in the Sixth Chapter of this Third Part, as likewise with the manner of his death. Vervelle shrugged up his shoulders at this relation, saying he had deservedly met with what he had so industriously sought after. After supper Vervelle made himself acquainted with the prior, whom Destiny recommended to him for a very worthy gentleman. Having sat up a little with them, the prior retired, when Vervelle took Destiny aside, and demanded of him what made Leander in mourning, and how he came to have so many lackeys after him all in black likewise. He satisfied him quickly in his demands, and moreover acquainted him that he was returned with design to marry Madame Angelica. "And you," quoth Vervelle, "when do you design to marry? Methinks it is high time to let the world know who you are, which cannot be done without a marriage;" adding withal, that if his business had not called him suddenly away, he would have stayed to see both his and Leander's marriage solemnized. Destiny answered, it was necessary for him to know Madam Star's mind before he declared himself. Hereupon Star was presently called, and the marriage proposed to her; whereto she readily answered that she ever would be ruled by the advice of her friends. At last it was agreed that when Vervelle had finished his affairs at Rennes, he should return by Alençon, and then all matters should be concluded. The same was agreed upon between the company and Mrs. Cave concerning her daughter's match with Leander. Then Vervelle took his leave of the good company, and went to bed. Next morning he set forth for Brittany betimes, and arrived not long after at Rennes, where he immediately went to wait on Monsieur la Garrouffière, who, after the accustomed compliments, told him there was a company of strollers in that town, one of which had a great resemblance of Mrs. Cave.

This caused him to go next day to the play, where having seen the person mentioned to him, he was forthwith inclined to believe that he must needs be a relation of Cave's, he was so like her. After the play was ended he went upon the stage, and inquired of him what country he was of, whence he came, how long he had been a player, and by what means he got into the company. To all which questions he answered so directly that it was no hard matter for Vervelle to guess that he was Mrs. Cave's brother, who had been lost ever since his father was killed at Perigord by the Baron of Sigognac's page. This he frankly owned, adding withal, that he had never been able to meet his sister since. Then Vervelle let him know she was at that time in a company of strollers at Alençon ; that she had met with many misfortunes, but that now she was like to have large amends made her by a gentleman of 12,000 livres a year, who was suddenly to be married to an only daughter of hers ; and farther, that this gentleman was now along with them, and acted among them. He also acquainted him that the marriage was to be consummated at his return to Alençon, and that it was very necessary he should go along with him, both to see his sister and to wish his niece joy. The stroller was extremely pleased at this news, and promised to be going as soon as he pleased ; but we must leave him a while packing up his Awls, and return before him to Alençon, The prior of St. Lewis came the same day that Vervelle went away, to acquaint the strollers that the bishop of Sées had sent to speak with him to communicate some matter of importance to him, that he was very sorry that he had not then leisure to perform his promise, but that however there would be no time lost, for while he was at Sées they might go to Fresnaye, to act *Sylvia* at the wedding of the lord's daughter, and at his return he would certainly finish what he had begun. He went forthwith, and the strollers immediately set themselves about preparing for their departure likewise.

CHAPTER XII.

WHAT HAPPENED AT THE JOURNEY TO FRESNAYE, AS
LIKEWISE ANOTHER MISFORTUNE OF RAGOTIN'S.

THE night before the wedding a coach and several saddle-
horses were sent for the strollers. The actresses went in
the coach, together with Destiny, Leander, and Olive.
The others rid·on the horses, and Ragotin mounted his
own nag, which he still kept, because he could not sell him,
and who was now cured of his lameness. He would have
fain persuaded either Star or Angelica to have got up
behind him, giving for reason that they might ride much
easier than in the coach, which jolted people together ; but
however neither of them would accept his proffer. To go
from Alençon to Fresnaye, it was necessary to pass through
the Forest of Persaine, which was in the province of Maine.
They had not gone above a mile into this forest before
Ragotin called out to the coachman to stop, alleging he
saw a troop of horsemen coming towards them. It was
not however thought necessary so to do, yet every one
would be upon his guard. When he came near the horsemen, Ragotin gave notice it was La Rappinière with his
archers. Hereat Madam Star began immediately to look
pale, which Destiny perceiving, told her she had no reason
to fear any insult being offered her there, by reason La
Rappinière would never pretend to any such thing in the
presence both of archers and Monsieur de la Fresnaye's
servants, whose house they were also near.

La Rappinière knew well that it was the strolling company which were coming towards him, and therefore advancing to the coach side, with his accustomed impudence saluted the actresses, to whom he made very coarse compliments ; which they returned cold enough to have put any one out of countenance that had not so much brass in his forehead as La Rappinière had. He told them he was looking after robbers that had robbed some tradesmen near Balon, and that he was informed they were coming that way. Whilst he was thus talking to the strollers, one of the archer's horses, that was a little wanton, leapt upon Ragotin's horse's neck, which he going backward to avoid, happened among a parcel of dead trees, whereof one pointing directly towards him, took him under his waistcoat, and hung him from his saddle ; which being willing to disengage himself from, he spurred his horse lustily, and thereby remained like a scarecrow trussed up in the air ; for his horse no sooner felt his favours than he left him crying he was killed, run through, and I know not what. The standers-by laughed so heartily to see him hanging in this posture, that they had no manner of regard to assisting of him. Indeed they called once or twice to the footmen to unloose him, but they ran away on the other side laughing. In the meantime his horse was run quite away, and would not suffer himself to be stopped.

At length, after everybody had laughed their bellyfull, the coachman, who was a strong lusty fellow, stepped down from his seat, and approaching Ragotin, lifted him off from his tenter-hook, and took him down. The company gathered about him, and made him believe he was wounded, but that they could not get him cured till they came to the next village, where there was a good surgeon, and therefore that in the meantime they must apply some green leaves to him, to keep the wound from festering, which they immediately did. They afterwards put him into the coach in Olive's room who came out. Whilst this passed, the footmen and Olive went after his horse that would not be stopped, and notwithstanding his being got a great way, brought him back again to his master. This done La Rappinière left the company, and they continued onwards of their journey towards the gentleman's house, where they soon after arrived, and sent thence for a surgeon, whom they had privately instructed what he was to do. He seemed to probe the imaginary wound that Ragotin had, whom they had put to bed. He likewise pretended to tent it, and afterwards bound it up, telling his patient that if it had been never so little on the other side, he had been no longer a man of this world. He then ordered him a strict diet, and so left him to his repose.

The little man was so imaginarily afflicted at this accident, that he could not but believe he was desperately wounded. He therefore did not think fit to rise to assist at the ball which was given after supper. This ball was furnished with music from Mans, the musicians of Alençon being gone to a wedding at Argenton. Several country-dances went about, and the strollers danced divers French ones. Destiny and Star performed a saraband together, which was admired by all the company, consisting as well of country gentry as peasants. Next day the strollers played the pastoral which the bride had desired. Ragotin caused himself to be carried to the sight of it in a chair, with his night-cap on. Afterwards they made good cheer, and the next morning after breakfast, having been well paid, set out for Alençon again. As soon as the coach was brought out, they did what they could to disillusion Ragotin concerning his imaginary wound, but all to no purpose, for he still persisted he felt the pain of it. They nevertheless put him into the coach, and arrived safe at Alençon. Next day they would not act, the actresses being desirous of a little respite. The same day the prior of St. Lewis returned from Sées, who going to visit our company, Madam Star told him he could never meet a better opportunity than now to finish his history. He required no further entreaty, but proceeded as you may find in the following chapter.

CHAPTER XIII.

THE CONTINUATION AND CONCLUSION OF THE PRIOR OF ST. LEWIS'S HISTORY.

"IF the beginning of this history," quoth the prior, "where you have met with nothing but joy and contentment, has been tiresome to you, the rest you are about to hear, I fear, will be much more. This consists of nothing but the reverse of fortune, despair, and grief, for past pleasures. To begin then where I left off:

"You must know that after our comrades and I had got up our parts, and rehearsed several times, we played perfect one Sunday night, in Monsieur du Fresne's house; the rumour of which being got abroad in the neighbourhood, so many people crowded thither, although we took what care we could to keep the park gates shut, that we found no small difficulty to get to the stage, which we had had raised for us in a middling sort of a hall. This place being not near large enough for our audience, two thirds of the company were forced to stand without; whom to get rid of, we promised, that on Sunday following we would play again in the town, and in a more spacious room. We performed our parts indifferent for young beginners, only one among us, who was to act the secretary of King Darius, the death of that monarch being the subject of our play, acquitted himself so ill, that although he had not above two lengths to speak, which he performed well enough at our rehearsal, yet when he came to act, he was

so fainthearted that we were forced to thrust him on upon
the stage ; where he spoke so extremely ill, that made all
the audience to laugh.   The tragedy being ended, I began
the ball with Du Lys, which lasted till midnight.   We
took a great deal of pleasure in this exercise, and without
saying aught to anybody, quickly got up another play ; I
nevertheless did not omit to make my ordinary visits in
the meantime.   One day as we were sitting together by
the fireside, a young gentleman happened to come in, to
whom we gave place.   After we had discoursed a while, he
put his hand in his pocket, and pulled out a picture in wax
in relievo very well done, and which he said was the picture
of his mistress.   After all the ladies had seen it round, it
came to my turn to look on it.   When I had considered it
a little, I found it was made for Du Lys, to whom I fancied
this gallant pretended.   I therefore without any more ado
threw the box, picture and all, into the fire, where the little
bustum melted immediately ; and when the owner thereof
would have snatched it out, I threatened to throw him out
at the window.   Monsieur du Fresne, who loved me as
much at that time as he hated me afterwards, swore he
would force that intruder to make more haste out than he
had done in ; and going to perform his oath, the young
spark skipped over everybody's head, and ran out in
confusion.   I followed him without anybody in the company being able to hinder me ; and having overtaken him,
told him that if he took anything amiss, we had each of us
a sword by our sides, and were in a convenient place to
decide the difference.   But his answer was he had nothing
to say to me ; and so went his way.

" The Sunday following we acted the same play we had
done before, according to our promise, in a great hall
belonging to a neighbour, by which means we had fifteen
days to study the other play.   I designed to adorn it with
some interludes of dancing ; and for that purpose chose
out six of my companions that danced the best, and made

the seventh myself. This interlude consisted of shepherds
and shepherdesses that were desperately in love with each
other. In the first entry Cupid appeared, and in the others
the shepherds and shepherdesses, all dressed in white, and
their habits all beset with narrow blue-ribbon knots, which
was the colour Du Lys delighted in, and which I have worn
ever since, although for some reasons I will tell you hereafter
I afterwards added some bows of fillemot. These shepherds
and shepherdesses made their entries two by two, and when
they were altogether, formed the letters of Du Lys's name.
Love let fly a dart at each shepherd, and threw flames at
the shepherdesses, all which bowed the knee in token of
submission. I had composed some verses to be sung in
this interlude, which were performed, but the great length
of time has made me to forget them ; and if I had
remembered them, I should never have dared to repeat
them before you, that are such able judges.

" Having kept the acting of our second play secret, we
were not so embarrassed with company as we had been
before. The play was, *The Amours of Sacripantus, King
of Circassia, with Angelica ;* the story taken from *Ariosto.*
We performed the interlude likewise, and I would have
begun as we were wont to do after the play, but Monsieur
du Fresne opposed it, alleging, We must needs be too
much tired ; and therefore dismissed us. We resolved,
however private we had done it now, to make the represen-
tation of this play more public ; which we afterwards
performed before everybody, in my godfather's hall on
Shrove-Sunday. In the daytime Du Lys desired, if I
intended to have the ball that night, that I would begin it
with a young lady a neighbour of hers, who was then
dressed in blue taffeta as well as she ; which I did. Whilst
we were dancing there arose a whispering among the company, some whereof cried out aloud, ' He's mistaken, he's
deceived ;' which made both Du Lys and I laugh, and
which the other lady perceiving, cried, ' The people are in

the right, for you have taken one for the other.'   To which
I answered abruptly, 'Pardon me, madam, I know what
I do.'   ·

"At night I masked myself with three of my comrades,
and carried a flambeau, to prevent my being known.   In
this equipage we went into the park, and afterwards to the
house.   My three companions entered only, and I stood
at the door.   Du Lys observing the three masquers,
presently found I was not among them; when coming to
the door, she immediately discovered me, and spoke to me
these obliging words: 'Disguise yourself after what
manner you please, I shall always know you.'   After having put out the flambeau, I came up to the table, where
there was a box and dice set.   I took up the box, and
began to rattle it; whereupon Du Lys asked me who I
would be at: I made a sign I would be at her.   She
replied, 'How much will you throw at?'   I pointed to a
knot of ribbons and coral bracelet which she wore on her
left arm.   Her mother would by no means have her
venture that, but she burst out a-laughing, saying, 'She
was not afraid of venturing it?   I threw and won, and
afterwards made my fair adversary a present of my
winnings.   The same did my companions to the elder
sister, and the other ladies that were come to pass their
evening there.   After this we took our leaves, but as we
were going out Du Lys came behind me, and untying the
ribbons that held my mask on, it immediately fell off;
whereat I turning about, she said to me, 'Thus people are
to be used that go away before their time.'   I was a little
ashamed, but nevertheless very glad to have any opportunity to talk farther with her.   The others unmasked
likewise, and we went in again, and spent that night very
agreeably.

"The last night of the carnival I gave the ball again,
when we were fain to take up with the lesser company of
musicians, the greater being pre-engaged by other gentry.

During Lent we were forced to lay aside diversions a little, to give way for devotion, and I can assure you for our parts, Du Lys and I never wanted a sermon. The feast of Easter approaching, young Madame du Fresne asked me, laughing, if I would carry her and her sister to St. Pater, a village about a quarter of a league off the suburbs of Montfort, whither people are wont to go out of devotion on Easter-Mondays, and where one meets all the beau-monde. I answered, I would willingly wait on them both thither, or any whither else. The day we were to go being come, as I was going out of our house to fetch the ladies, I met a young fellow, a neighbour of mine, who asking me whither I was going in such haste, I told him to the park, to wait on the young ladies there to St. Pater. To which he replied, I might save myself the labour, for to his certain knowledge their mother would not permit them to go along with me. This news stunned me so much that I had not a word to say, but going into my house set myself about thinking what might be the occasion of so sudden an alteration. After having reflected a good while, I could guess at nothing but my little merit and mean condition. This considered, I could not but exclaim extremely against their carriage to me, since they had seemed well enough pleased as long as I diverted them with balls, interludes, plays, and serenades, which I frequently did to my no small charge, but now that those ceased they slighted me. The anger I conceived, made me resolve to go to the assembly at St. Pater without them, whilst they it seems were waiting for me in the park.

"The time being passed that I had promised to come, Du Lys and her sister, with some other ladies their neighbours, went without me. After having paid their devotion in the church, they came out into the churchyard, and seated themselves on the wall under a great shady elm. Some time after I passed by, but that at a distance. Du Fresne made a sign to me to come near, which I took no notice of, making as if I did not see them. Some neighbours that were with me told me a lady beckoned to me, but I seemed not to hear them neither, and going on, cried at the same time, 'Come, let's go and drink a bottle at the Four Winds,' which we did. I were no sooner got home to my house but a widow who had been formerly our confidant, came to speak with me, telling me briskly that she wondered how I could neglect doing myself the honour of waiting on the young ladies Du Fresne to St. Pater; acquainting me moreover, that Du Lys was very much concerned at the disappointment, and that I must endeavour speedily, by some means or other, to make a compensation for my fault. I was extremely both surprised and pleased to hear this, and having let her know all the reason I had to do so, which I have acquainted you with before, I went along with her to the park gate, where the ladies were. I left her to make my excuse, for I could not pretend to do it myself, being so extremely troubled that I should not have remembered what I said. Then the mother addressing herself to me, told me I ought not to have been so credulous as to mind all people said, and that she believed what had been told me was done by somebody that envied me; and lastly, she assured me I should always be unfeignedly welcome to her house; and thither we immediately went. I had then the honour to give my hand once more to Du Lys, who also told me she had been extremely concerned at my carriage, especially when I seemed not to take notice of the sign her sister made me at St. Pater. I asked her pardon humbly, yet made her but confused excuses, being not entirely come to myself.

"I would have been revenged on the young man that had so imposed upon me, had not Du Lys entreated me not so much as to think of it; adding, that I ought to be satisfied with finding the contrary of what he had told me. I obeyed her in this, as I did in everything always after.

We passed our time the most agreeably that could be, and experienced what is commonly said of lovers—that 'their language is chiefly that of the eyes.' One Sunday after vespers we gave each other to understand by this mute language that we should after supper go up the river, and have only such persons with us as we could best fancy. For this purpose I sent presently to hire a boat, and immediately after went myself with the company I had pitched upon, to the park-gate, where the ladies waited for us ; but as ill luck would have it, three young men that were not of our company, were at that juncture talking with them. They did what they could to shake them off, but they observing it, seemed the more desirous to stay. This was the reason that when we came up to the gate we thought fit to pass by, contenting ourselves with only tipping them the wink to follow us, which they soon after did, but the young fellows along with them ; which we perceiving, immediately entered our boat, and landed near one of the gates of the city, where we met the Sieur du Fresne. He forthwith demanded of me where I had left his daughters? I not knowing presently what answer to make, told him frankly I had not had the honour to see them all that night. Having heard this, he took his leave, bidding us good-night, and went towards his park, at the gate whereof he overtook his daughters ; whom asking where and with whom they had been, Du Lys pertly answered, with such a one, naming me. At that the father reached her a sound box of the ear, together with, 'You lie,' at the end on't ; 'for' continued he, 'had he been with you though it were much later, I should never have asked you the question.'

"Next day the widow I mentioned before came again to let me know what had happened the night foregoing, and acquainted me that Du Lys was extremely angry with me, not only at the box of the ear she had received on my account, but also at my disappointing her, she intending to

have got quickly rid of those impertinent young fellows.
I excused myself as well as I could, and declined going
near her for four days together. But one day, as she and
her sister sat with some other young ladies on a bench
before a shop in the street next the city-gate which I was
going out at towards the suburbs, I passed by them,
moving my hat a little, but without so much as looking
upon or saying anything to them.   The other ladies immediately asked what was the meaning of my so cold de-
portment, which they scarce took to be civil. Du Lys
gave them no answer, but her elder sister told them she
did not know the reason, and that if they had a mind to be
satisfied farther, they must know it from myself; adding
withal, ' Come let us go place ourselves a little nearer the
gate, that he may not be able to get by us as he comes
back without taking more notice ? '   I quickly returned,
when this good sister catching me hold by the cloak, and
pulling me to her, said, ' How comes it, haughty sir, that
you can pass by your mistress without taking notice ? '
and at the same time forced me to sit down by her ; but
when I turned to embrace her, and tell her the reason, she
flung away like a mad thing.   I stayed a little longer with
them and after went my ways.   I resolved then not to go
near my mistress for some days longer, the which I performed, but it seemed as so many ages to me ; till at length
one morning meeting Madame du Fresne, she stopped
me, asking what had made me so great a stranger to her
house.   I answered, It was on account of the ill humour of
her younger daughter. Whereupon she immediately
promised to make up the difference, and for that end bid me
meet her within an hour at her house.   I was not a little
impatient till I had obeyed her, and therefore went
punctually at the time appointed.

    " As I was going up to her chamber according to her
direction, I met Du Lys coming down ; who perceiving me,
made so much haste by me, that I could not stop her.   I

afterwards went into the chamber, where I found her sister, who began immediately to simper ; whereupon I told her how briskly her sister had gone by me, but she assured me that was all feigned, and that to her knowledge, she had gone a hundred times to the window, to look whether she could see me, and farther, that she was now gone but into the garden, whither I might follow her if I pleased. I took the hint, and went to the garden-door, but found it locked, whereupon I begged of her to open it, but she would not, which her sister hearing from the top of the stairs came down and opened it for me, by a trick she had got. I went in, but Du Lys ran from me as if she had been mad. I followed and overtook her, and catching her by one of her sleeves, pulled her down upon a camomile bank, clapping myself at the same time down by her, I made her all the excuses I was capable of making, but she continued inexorable ; at length I acquainted her that my passion was not to be fooled with, and therefore if she did not quickly think fit to let me know her mind, despair might drive me to the doing of something which she might repent having been the cause of. This nevertheless wrought nothing upon her, the which perceiving, I drew my sword out of the scabbard, and presenting it to her naked, desired she would be pleased to thrust it through my heart ; telling her at the same time, that it was altogether impossible for me to survive a deprivation of her favours. She thereupon rose to be gone, informing me she had never yet killed anybody, and that when she was so disposed I should not be the first person. Then I stopped her, and begged she would stay and see me do it myself, to which she answered coldly, I might do as I pleased, for she should not go about to hinder me. At that, I clapped the point to my breast, and put myself into a posture to fall upon it, which she observing, immediately grew pale, and kicked away the hilt from the ground, so that the sword falling down, she assured me, that that action had

extremely frighted her, and begged I would let her see
no more such sights. I answered, I were willing to obey
her, provided she would be less unkind to me for the future,
which she promised to be. We afterwards embraced so
lovingly that I could have wished to have had a quarrel
with her every day of my love, to occasion so charming a
reconciliation. Whilst we remained in these transports, her
mother entered the garden, and told us she would have
come sooner, but that she imagined we had no need of her
interposing to reconcile us.

"One day, as the Sieur du Fresne, his wife, Du Lys and
I, were walking together in the park, this good mother told
me aside that she had been a faithful advocate in my behalf.
She might easily speak this without her husband's hearing
it, since he was very deaf. We both thanked her, but that
rather by gesture than words. A little after, Monsieur du
Fresne took me aside, and told me his wife and he had
agreed to give me their younger daughter in marriage
before he went to court to wait his quarter in his turn, and
therefore desired I would put myself to no more charges
in serenades or the like.

"I returned him my acknowledgments, but after a confused manner, being more than ordinarily transported at so
unexpected a happiness. But I well remember, I told
him I should never have dared to have asked his daughter
in marriage, as well considering my small merit, as the in-
equality of our conditions. To which he replied, that as
for merit, he was well satisfied I had sufficient, and for
quality, everybody knew I had that would very well supply
it ; meaning, I suppose, my estate.

"I don't remember what reply I made, but this I know
well, that he invited me that night to supper and there it
was concluded that the Sunday following we should have a
meeting of our friends to finish the nuptials. He acquainted
me likewise what portion he designed to give his daughter,
but as for that, I told him I had sufficient for us both,

and therefore required her person only. Then I thought myself the most happy man in the world. But, alas! that happiness did not last long, for one night before we were to be married, as Du Lys and I were sitting upon a grass-plat, we perceived at a distance a councillor of the Præsidial-Court coming to pay a visit to the Sieur du Fresne, his kinsman, whereat both she and I conceived the same thought at a time, and began to be both concerned, though we knew not well at what, which nevertheless the event of what we feared made but too perspicuous. For next day, when I went to meet the company at Du Fresne's house, according to agreement, I found Du Lys at the court gate crying. Upon asking her what she ailed, I could obtain no answer; whereupon I entered the house, and found her sister in the same condition. I asked her likewise what was the meaning of so many tears. She answered sobbing, I should know but too soon. Then I went up into the chamber and found her mother, but she no sooner saw me than she went out, without scarce speaking a word to me, for tears, sobs, and sighs had so disturbed her that all she could do was to look pitifully upon me, and cry, 'Ah, poor young man!' I resolved to know the cause of this sudden change, and therefore immediately went to Monsieur du Fresne's chamber, where I found him sitting in an elbow-chair. At my coming in, he told me bluntly he had altered his mind, and would not now marry his younger daughter before the elder, and though he did, it should be sure not to be before his return from court.

"I answered upon these two heads: First, that his elder daughter would not be at all displeased to have her younger sister married before her, provided it were to me, since she had always loved me as her brother, and more than once professed as much. And secondly, I acquainted him I would willingly stay for her ten years, instead of three months that he should be from home. At last, he

told me in plain terms that I must think no more of his
daughter, and so turned from me. Having heard this, I
immediately determined to go home and kill myself. But
as I was drawing my sword for that purpose, the aforesaid
widow, that had formerly been our confidant, came in upon
me where I was, and prevented me in that design, by
telling me she came from Du Lys, and that she desired by
her, not to afflict myself, but have patience, and matters
might perhaps change to my advantage. She farther informed me from her that I had her mother and sister sure
to my interest, and above all, herself, whose kindness and
constancy to me was unalterable. She likewise told me
the sisters had resolved as soon as their father was gone to
give me an opportunity to continue my visits as before.

"Though this discourse was extremely pleasing to me,
yet could it not altogether comfort me, for I afterwards
fell into so deep a melancholy that despair suggested to me
to consult the Devil about my fate. Hereupon, a little
before Monsieur du Fresne's departure, I went to a large
copse, about half a league from the town, where it was the
vulgar report that evil spirits inhabited, and where 'tis
certain the fairies who are no doubt the Devil's imps, had
formerly been. I went a great way into this copse, and
when I thought I was far enough, began to call upon and
invoke the spirits to assist me in this worst of misfortunes ;
but after I had prayed and bawled for some time to no
purpose, and only heard the birds warble, which I interpreted to be their concern for my misfortune, I returned
home to my house not at all satisfied ; then, throwing
myself upon the bed, I was immediately seized with so wild
a frenzy that I even lost my speech, insomuch that 'twas
thought I could never have escaped death. Du Lys was
ill at the same time, and much after the same manner, and
that has inclined me to believe ever since there is something
more in sympathy than ordinary ; for as the cause of
our sickness was the same so was its effect ; and this we

understood by our doctor and apothecary having both the
same ; but as for our surgeons, they were several. I
recovered a little before Du Lys, which made me to go (or
I might rather say, be carried) to see her. When I came
to her house, I found her in bed, and her father gone to
court. She no sooner saw me than she seemed to recover,
which made me desire her to rise but she no sooner got out
of bed than she fainted away in my arms. This made me extremely sorry that I had requested so unreasonable a thing
of her, and therefore I had her immediately put to bed again,
where, after some time, I left her to recover by sleep, which
perhaps she could not have done had I stayed with her.

" Not long after we were both entirely recovered, and
passed our time very pleasantly all the while her father
continued absent, till at last returning again, he was
informed by some secret enemies of ours that I had kept
his daughter company ever since he had been from home.
This made him to rave extremely, and to forbid his wife
and daughters seeing me any more ; which I learnt afterwards by our confidant ; as likewise, that they had notwithstanding engaged in a resolution to see me often, and
informed me of the means by this widow. The first was,
that I should observe when this unkind father came into
the city, when I might go to his house, and continue there
till his return, and that was understood by his knock. Then
were I to step behind the tapestry, and afterwards, whilst
either a man, maid, or one of his daughters took off his
cloak, I might very easily slip out behind him, and he
should never hear, by reason (as I have told you before) he
was deaf. This contrivance I frequently made use of ; but
being at length discovered, I was forced to have recourse to
another ; and that was, to meet my mistress and friends in
our confidant's garden, which I did several times, but at last
that plot was likewise detected. We then made use of the
churches for our meeting, but which also came to be known.
So that at last we had nothing to rely upon but common

chance, that now and then afforded us an interview in one
or other of the walks of the park, but then we were fain to
use a great deal of caution to prevent being seen.   One day
after I had been with Du Lys a considerable time, for we
dived to the very bottom of our misfortunes, and took all
the measures imaginable to surmount them, I must needs
accompany her to the lower court gate, where being just
come, we perceived at a distance her father coming directly
towards us from the town.   To fly was to no purpose, for
he had already seen us.   She then immediately entreated
me to think of some invention to excuse us : I put off that
task to her, alleging, she had the more subtle capacity.
In the meantime the old gentleman came up to us, and
whilst he was going to scold, she told him, that I having
understood he had some rings and other jewels by him (for
he had jewellers always at work for him, being as covetous
as he was deaf), I was come to know if he would please to
furnish me with some, to present to a young lady at Mans
whom I was going to marry.

"He was easily inclined to credit my pretence, and
carrying me upstairs, showed me several, whereof I chose
two, one a small diamond, and the other a rose of emeralds.
We presently agreed on the price, which I paid him down
on the spot.   This expedient gained me a continuance of
my visits for some time, till at length, beginning to
grow jealous of the cheat, he demanded of his daughter
why I did not make more haste to Mans.   She thereupon
advised me to go thither for a little time, the which
I did.

"This city is one of the pleasantest in the whole kingdom,
as ye know well, and where there is the most quality, which
induced me to make plenty of acquaintance.   I lodged at
the Green Oaks, where also lay at the same time an
operator, who kept a stage to sell his physic on, but that
only till such time as he could get a company of strollers
together to act, that being his principal design.   He had

already got several persons of quality, and among others a count's son, whose name I shall beg leave to conceal; a young lawyer of Mans, who had formerly belonged to a company, together with a brother of his, and an old comedian, who was a great proficient in farce. He besides expected a young lady from Laval, that had promised him to run away from her father for that purpose. With this man I got acquainted; and one day, for want of better discourse made him acquainted with all my misfortunes, whereupon he persuaded me to engage with him in his design, and that might prove a means to make me forget my hard usage. I readily accepted his offer, and would have certainly engaged in it, had but the lady that was expected come. But it seems her parents had been acquainted of her intentions, and therefore took care to frustrate them, which obliged me to quit the undertaking. Love notwithstanding furnished me with a stratagem to renew my conversation with Du Lys without suspicion, and that was to carry the lawyer before mentioned, and another young man of my acquaintance, to both whom I had discovered my design, along with me to Alençon. They soon after appeared in this city, one under the title of a brother, and the other a cousin-german of an imaginary mistress of mine. I carried them to the Sieur du Fresne's house, whom I had before desired to pass for my relation, which he condescended to do. He did not fail likewise to say a great many fine things in my favour, assuring them they had pitched upon a very deserving person to make an alliance with, after which he invited us to supper. My mistress's health was drank, and Du Lys pledged it. After my friends had continued about four or five days in this city they returned to Mans, but I stayed behind, and had a freer access than ever to my mistress. At last Monsieur du Fresne asked me why I delayed so long to conclude my marriage, which made me to apprehend that my stratagem might be at length discovered, and then I should shamefully be driven out of the house as before. This made me to enter into the most barbarous resolution that ever man in despair conceived, and which was, to kill Du Lys to prevent another's ever having the possession of her. For this purpose I got a poignard, and going to her, desired her to take a walk out with me, which she granted. I thereupon led her before she was aware into a brambly part of the park quite out of any pathway. There I discovered to her the cruel design despair had suggested to me to preserve her to myself, and at the same time drew the naked poignard out of my pocket. She looked so charmingly upon me, and spoke so many soft things to divert my intentions, that she at length found it no difficult matter to disarm me. She seized the poignard then, and throwing it into the bushes, told me she must be gone, and that she should not care to trust herself any more with me alone. She was going to tell me farther, that she never had deserved this usage at my hands, when I interrupted her, desiring she would but afford me a meeting next day at her confidant's. She promised, and accordingly came. I saluted her, and we lamented our common misfortune together, and after a great deal of discourse, she advised me to go to Paris, and promised that though I stayed away ten years, yet would she not entertain anybody else in the meantime, which nevertheless she did not keep to. When I was about to take leave of her, which you may imagine I could not do without a great many tears, she said she thought it necessary that her mother and sister should be of the secret, and therefore the widow was immediately sent to call them, whilst I continued alone with her. It was then we opened our minds to each other more than we had hitherto done; whereupon at length she told me, that if I had thoughts of carrying her away, she would willingly consent to it, and follow me wheresoever I pleased; and that if any were sent out after us, and should overtake us, she would pretend to be with child by me. However my love was so honourable towards her, that I would by no means consent to any hazard of her reputation on my account, but leave the event of all things to fortune. In the interim her mother and sister came, and we broke our resolutions to them, which caused fresh tears and embraces on all sides. In short, I took my leave of them in order to my journey to Paris. Before I set out I writ a letter to Du Lys, the contents whereof I have forgot, but you may imagine I omitted nothing therein that might serve to raise her compassion, and my confidant that carried it assured me she could not read it for weeping, and much less return an answer.

"I have forborne telling the several other adventures that happened during our amour, to the end I might not trespass too far on your patience ; such as the jealousy Du Lys conceived at a cousin-german of hers that came to see her, and lived at her father's for three months together, as also on account of the gentleman's daughter that brought the gallant whom I sent away packing ; together with several rencounters I had by night for her sake, in two whereof I was wounded, once in the arm, and another time in the thigh. But to end all digressions, I must even let you know that I departed at last for Paris, where I arrived safe, and continued about a year. Not being able to maintain myself there equal to what I had done in this city, as well by reason of the excessive dearness of provisions, as by having diminished my fortune by the expenses I were at on account of Du Lys, as you have heard before, I was fain to put myself to one of the king's secretaries, who had been married to his predecessor's widow. Though this lady conferred many favours upon me, yet was I always so blind as not to perceive them, though some of them were so open that most of the family took notice of them.

"One day having bought some holland for neckbands and wristbands to my shirts, and given them to some of the maid-servants to make, my mistress came by and observed them ; when asking who they were for and understanding they were mine, she bid them to finish them as soon as they could, but leave the lace for her to put on. Afterwards whilst she was working on them, I by chance entered the chamber, when she called to me, and told me she was at work for me ; which surprised me so much, that I could only return her thanks, and so went out. But one morning, to my great wonder, whilst I was writing in my bed-chamber, which was not very far off hers, she sent for me by one of her lackeys. Whilst I was going to wait on her, I heard her rave like mad against one of her chamber-maids and her waiting-gentlewoman, in these words, ' Get ye out of my chamber, ye blunderers, ye buffleheads ! You know not how to do anything as ye should.' As they went out I came in ; whereupon, having rallied them yet a little longer, she bid me shut the door, and come and dress her, and particularly to take the clean smock from the toilet, and put it on for her. At the same time she stripped off her foul one, and exposed herself naked to my sight. I was so greatly ashamed of this action of hers, that I told her I should be less serviceable to her that way than her maids, therefore desired her to send for them again ; which she was nevertheless obliged to do by the sudden arrival of her husband. I had no reason to doubt of her intentions, but as I was young and timorous, was likewise apprehensive of some unlucky accident, and therefore resolved to ask leave speedily to be gone, which I did soon after, whereto the husband answered nothing, and the wife sullenly turned her chair toward the fire, and bid the butler clear the table.

"After this, I went down to supper with the steward ; and being at table, a niece of my lady's, of about twelve years old, came to me from her aunt, to know whether I had the courage to eat before I went. I forget what answer I sent her, but I well remember she immediately

fell sick, and was forced to keep her bed. Next morning
betimes she sent for me to go for a physician. When I
came near her bedside, she catched me by the hand, and
told me, I had been the occasion of her illness. This
augmented my former apprehensions, and therefore the
same day I 'listed myself in the troops that were then
raising at Paris for the Duke of Mantua, and departed
without saying aught to anybody.

" Our captain came not along with us, leaving the
command of his company to his lieutenant, who was a
common robber. The same were the two serjeants, for
they plundered wherever they came ; the lieutenant and
one of the serjeants were at last hanged by the provost of
Troyes in Champagne, but he spared one of the serjeants
on account of his being brother to a *valet de chambre* of
the Duke of Orleans. We hereby remained without a
leader ; whereupon the soldiers with common consent
pitched upon me to command the company, which consisted
of four-score men. I took this post upon me, with that
authority as if I had really been their captain. I drew out
my company, mustered them, and distributed arms amongst
them, which I received at St. Reine in Burgundy. At
length we filed off to Ambrun in Dauphine, where our
captain came to us, expecting scarce to find a man in his
company ; but when he perceived all I had done, and that
I had preserved sixty-eight of the men, having lost only
twelve in our march, he hugged me heartily, and gave me
the colours and his table.

" The army was one of the finest that ever went out of
France, but which had the ill success you may have heard
of, merely through the bad intelligence between the
generals. After its defeat, I stayed at Grenoble, to avoid
the barbarity of the peasants of Burgundy and Champagne,
who murdered all that fled in such great numbers that it
introduced the plague into those two provinces, the which
afterwards likewise spread throughout the whole kingdom.

Having stayed some time at Grenoble, where I had got a
great deal of acquaintance, I at length resolved to go for
this city, where I was born ; but travelling out of the high
road, for the reason above mentioned, came at length to a
small town, called St. Patrice, where the lady of the
manor's son was raising a company of foot, to go to the
siege of Montauban. I 'listed under him, and he having discovered something more than ordinary in my countenance,
after having demanded of me who I was, and being told
the truth by me, he desired me to accept the tutelage of a
young brother of his, to whom he had given the colours,
which I readily did. We departed then for Nocus in
Provence, being the place of rendezvous for the regiment ;
but before we had been there three days, our captain's
steward robbed his master and fled. He gave orders to
have him pursued, but it proved to no purpose. He then
desired me to take the keys of his coffers, which I did not
keep long, by reason he was commanded from the regiment to wait on the Cardinal Richelieu, who then headed
the army for the siege of Montauban and other rebellious
towns of Guyenne and Languedoc.

"He nevertheless carried me along with him, and we
found his eminence in the town of Albi ; thence we waited
on him to the aforesaid rebellious city, but it continued not.
long so after this great statesman's setting down before it.
During this march we had a great number of adventures,
which I don't think fit to bring you acquainted with, for
fear of proving tiresome, having but too just reason to
believe I have been so too much already."

To this Star replied, he "would deprive them of a great
deal of pleasure if he did not continue his adventures to the
end." He went on then, after the following manner : —

"I got a great acquaintance in this illustrious cardinal's
house, and that chiefly with the pages, whereof there were
eighteen of Normandy, who all made extreme much of me,
as did likewise the rest of his eminence's servants. As

soon as the town was surrendered our regiment was disbanded, and we returned to St. Patrice.

"The lady of the manor had a suit at law with her eldest son, and was going to Grenoble to prosecute it. As soon as we were got home, we were desired to accompany her thither, the which I had no manner of mind to do, having determined to go as I told you before. We were however prevailed upon to comply with her request, which I had not since repented of ; for whilst we stayed at Grenoble soliciting this suit, the late king of France, Louis XIII., happened to pass by that way into Italy, and I had the honour to meet in his retinue all the great lords of this country, and amongst the rest the governor of this city who being well acquainted with Monsieur St. Patrice, after having offered me what money I wanted, recommended me heartily to him, so that I had then no reason to complain. I met likewise five young men of this city, three whereof were gentlemen, who had been my intimate acquaintance. I treated them the best I could, both at our house and at the tavern. One day, as we were coming from breakfast at an inn in the suburbs of St. Laurence which is on the other side of the water, we happened to stop upon the bridge to see the boats pass, when one of the five told me seriously he very much wondered I had not inquired of them after Du Lys. I told him I durst not, for fear of hearing that which would not please me. They replied, I had done wisely to slight her that had broke her word to me. I thought I should have died at this news, but however must know more to the same purpose ; for they immediately acquainted me farther, that my departure for Italy was no sooner heard of there, than Du Lys was married by her parents to a young man whom they named to me, and to whom I had the most aversion of any of her pretenders.

"Then I began to break out and rail at her, in all the ill language that jealousy could suggest. I called her tigress, traitoress, and the like, for that she could suffer herself to be married, when she knew I was so near, and would certainly require an account both from him and her. I then took a purse out of my pocket which she had given me, wherein I kept a bracelet of hers, and a blue ribbon, and putting a stone into it, to make it sink, threw it in a great passion into the river, uttering these words at the same time; ' So may I blot her out of my memory, as I abandon this purse to the pleasure of the waves.'

"These gentlemen were not a little surprised at my proceeding, and therefore told me they were extremely sorry they had let me know so much; which nevertheless I should have come to the knowledge of some way or other. They added moreover, to comfort me, that what Du Lys had done was wholly by compulsion; for they perfectly perceived an aversion in her to the person; and which was demonstrable enough, in that she languished all the time she was married to him, and died not long after. This news increased my grief and comforted me at the same time. I took leave of these gentlemen, and went home, but so altered, that young Madame St. Patrice, the good lady's daughter, observed it, and asked me what I ailed. I gave her no answer; yet at length, upon pressing me farther, I told her the story of my whole adventures, together with the news I had just then heard. This good-natured young thing (being extremely concerned at the relation, which might be perceived by her crying) went immediately and told it to her mother and brothers, who all assured me they commiserated my misfortune, and would do all that lay in their power to redress them, but that in the meantime I must be comforted and have patience. The suit betwixt the mother and the son ended by an arbitration, and so we returned. I then began to think of settling in the world. The house where I was would have been sufficient to have afforded me a character, had I been disposed to marry, but though several good

matches were offered me, yet would I accept of none.
Then I returned to my former resolution of being a
Capuchin, and required the habit, but I met with so many
obstacles in this intention, which would be but tedious for
you to hear, that I soon quitted that design likewise.
About this time the king commanded the Arrierban of the
gentry of Dauphiné to go to Casal. Monsieur de St
Patrice desired me to go along with him, which I could
not well refuse. We departed and arrived there, and you
know what was the success of it. The siege was raised,
the town given up, and peace concluded through the
mediation of Mazarin. This was the first step he made
to the cardinalship, and to that prodigious grandeur which
he arrived to afterwards in the government of France. We
returned to St. Patrice, where I still persisted in becoming
a recluse, but Divine Providence ordered it otherwise.

"One day Monsieur de St. Patrice, perceiving my resolution, told me he would advise me to take orders as a
secular priest. I replied I had not capacity : He answered,
there were those that had less. I resolved then upon it,
and took orders upon an allowance of a hundred livres a
year that Madame St. Patrice gave me. I said my first mass
in our parish church, and upon which occasion my patroness
treated about thirty priests and several gentry of the neighbourhood. I lived with too rich people to want preferment,
for in six months time I got a considerable priory, and two
other small benefices. Some years after, I had a very large
priory and a very good curateship given me, for I had taken
a great deal of pains in my study, and was arrived to that
perfection in preaching, that I could mount the pulpit
before the best auditory, and even in presence of any bishop·
I managed my revenues with discretion, and in a short time
got together a considerable sum of money, wherewith I
retired into this city, where I think myself extremely happy
in meeting with so good company, as likewise in having
done them some small service."

" Rather," quoth Star, " the greatest that could be done for anybody."

She was going to say more, when Ragotin started up and said he would write a comedy upon this story, which would afford a more than ordinary decoration for the stage: For example, a fine park with a great wood and river, with lovers walking and fighting, and a priest saying his first mass in it. What could be finer? This made all the company laugh, when Roquebrune, who had all along contradicted Ragotin, told him " You will never be able to do anything in the matter. You know nothing of the rules of the stage ; besides you must change the scene, and continue three or four years upon it."

Then the prior said, " Gentlemen, pray don't dispute upon this point, for I have taken care of it myself already. You may remember that Monsieur du Hardy never observed rules so strictly, no more than some others of our late poets have done, such as the author of *St. Eustace*, &c. Monsieur Corneille likewise would not have been so nice in this particular had not Monsieur Scudery been so severe on his *Cid*. But for the most part these are such faults as the better sort of judges term beautiful ones. I must tell you," quoth the prior, " I have composed a play on the subject of my adventures myself, and have called it *Fidelity Preserved after Hope Lost*. I have also taken for my device a withered tree with only a few blasted leaves on it, and a spaniel-dog lying at the root of it with this motto out of his mouth, ' Deprived of hope yet always faithful.' My play hath been acted several times."

" The title you have chose for it," quoth Star, " is as much *à propos* as your device and motto, for though your mistress has proved false to you, yet you continue constant to her, resolving never to marry any other." The conversation ended by the arrival of Monsieur Vervelle and Monsieur la Garrouffière, and here ends this chapter, which no doubt has been tedious as well in regard of its length as subject.

CHAPTER XIV.

VERVELLE'S RETURN, ACCOMPANIED BY MONSIEUR LA
GARROUFFIÈRE. THE ACTORS AND ACTRESSES'
MARRIAGES ; TOGETHER WITH ANOTHER ADVEN-
TURE OF RAGOTIN'S.

ALL the company were extremely surprised to see Monsieur
La Garrouffière. As for Vervelle's return, it had been
long expected with impatience, and that chiefly by two
that were to be married. The company demanded of La
Garrouffière what news he had brought. He answered,
none ; but that Monsieur Vervelle having communicated
an affair of importance to him, he was glad of the occasion
to come and see them again, and to offer them a continuance of his services. Hereupon Vervelle made a sign to him
that that matter was to be talked of in private, and to break
off the discourse, presently presented the prior of St. Lewis
to him, who he told him was this particular friend, and
moreover a man of worth.

Then Star told them he had just concluded a story the
most entertaining that could be imagined, which caused
these two new arrived gentlemen to profess their concern
for not having come before to have had their share of it.
After this Vervelle went into another room, whither Destiny
followed him, when after they had continued there for
some time, they called in Star and Angelica, and afterwards Leander and Mrs. Cave, whom Monsieur La

Garrouffière followed without invitation. When they were all together, Monsieur Vervelle told them he had acquainted Monsieur la Garrouffière with the design of their inter-marriages, whilst he was at Rennes, and that he had presently resolved to go home by Alençon, to assist at their weddings. The two couple gave him a great deal of thanks, and returned him their acknowledgments of the honour he had done them. "But now I think on't," quoth Monsieur Vervelle to La Garrouffière, "had not we best have the man up that waits below?" "I think so," replied La Garrouffière, "if the company are willing." They answered, any friend of his or Monsieur Vervelle's would be welcome at any time to them. The man was thereupon sent for up. As he entered the room Mrs. Cave looked steadfastly upon him, and began to be moved, though she knew not at what. She was asked if she knew that man? She answered she could not remember she had ever seen him. Then she was desired to take more notice of his face, which she did, and began to find so many of her own features in him that she cried out, "It is not my brother, sure!"

Whereupon he immediately went to her, and embracing her, told her he was her brother, whom variety of misfortunes had kept so long from the sight of her. He afterwards saluted his niece and the rest of the company, and then assisted at the secret conference, where it was con-cluded that the two marriages should be speedily solemnized. All the difficulty at last was what priest should marry them. Then the prior, who had been called in to the conference, stepped up, and said he would talk about that with the parsons of the two parishes in the city, and of that of the suburbs of Monfort ; and if they made any difficulty about it, he would return to Sées, and obtain leave of that bishop, and providing he would not grant it, he would go and procure it from the Bishop of Mans, who was his intimate acquaintance, and within whose diocese his small concern lay. The company was very well pleased with his proposal, and desired him to take that trouble upon him. Then was a notary privately sent for, and the marriage contracts drawn. I don't tell you the particulars of them, because they never came to my knowledge ; but certain it is the parties were soon after married accordingly. Monsieur Vervelle, Monsieur la Garrouffière, and the prior of St. Lewis were witnesses to the contracts. This last went immediately to discourse the aforesaid parsons, but neither of them would marry them, alleging several reasons that the prior perhaps was unable to answer for want of capacity. This made him resolve according to his promise, to go to Sées. For this purpose he took Leander's horse, and one of his servants, and went to wait on the bishop of that diocese, who was very unwilling to grant his request. The prior urged that these people were of no diocese, being here to-day, and gone to-morrow, and yet could not be reputed vagabonds, as the three parsons would needs have them to be, by reason they had the king's licence, and by consequence were subjects of that diocese wherever they happened to come. Also, that those persons for whom he required a licence were at present in the diocese of Alençon, over which his lordship had jurisdiction, and that therefore he humbly requested the favour of a licence for them, they being very honest people.

Hereupon the bishop gave the prior liberty to have them married in what church he pleased. He would have called his secretary to have drawn up the licence in form, but the prior told him that a word or two under his own hand would be sufficient. Next day our solicitor returned to Alençon, where he found the betrothed parties making all manner of preparation for their nuptials. The other strollers who had not been admitted of the secret, wondered what all that provision meant, especially Ragotin, who was most concerned to know it. What obliged them to keep

it so secret related wholly to Destiny, for as for Leander
and Angelica, everybody knew they were to be married.
Another reason likewise was, their fear of not obtaining a
licence ; but no sooner were they secure of one than they
made the matter public, and having read the marriage
contracts before all the company, proceeded to appoint a
day for the solemnization.

This was a cruel blow to poor Ragotin, whom Rancour
whispered in the ear, " Did not I tell you what this would
come to ? I had always mistrusted it." Hereupon the
poor little man fell into a deep melancholy, which inclined
him to that despair, which you may read of in the last
chapter of this romance.   He became so disordered that
while he was walking one holiday before the great church
of Notre Dame, at the time of the ringing of the bells, he
fancied they were made to ring the following words on
purpose to affront him :

> " This-morn-ing-Ra-go-tine
> Got-drunk-by-too-much-wine :
> Go-home, go-home."

This made him to go immediately into the belfry, and
rattle the sexton, telling him he lied, for that he had not
drunk so much as he imagined.   " But," quoth he, " I
should not have been angry if you had made your bells to
cry—

> " ' The-mu-ti-neer-Des-ti-ny
> Has-got-thy-dear-Star-from-thee,
> Ra-go-tin, Ra-go-tin.'

for then I should have rejoiced to have found inanimate
bodies sensible of my wrongs.   But to call me drunkard,
a name I never deserved—I will be revenged of you and
your bells, if possible."   Having said this, and crowded
on his hat fast to his head, he mounted up a pair of
winding stairs, which he thought went to the place where
they were ringing, but which were indeed those belonging

to the organ. When he began to perceive that this was not the belfry staircase, he was somewhat troubled; nevertheless going on forwards, he at length met with a little low door, which went under the tiles.   Here he crept in ; and whereas other people would have been forced to creep on all-fours, by reason of the lowness of the place, he nevertheless afterwards had room to walk upright ; when coming at last to another door that opened into the ringing room, he went in, and found several persons at it, ding-dong, with such eagerness that they never looked behind them.   At his first entrance he saluted the fellow that stood next him with all the injurious language he could think of, calling him "villain, rascal, sot, puppy, blockhead, clown," and what not ; which, notwithstanding, the noise of the bells hindered that person (or any of the rest) from hearing.   At this Ragotin, believing himself not only affronted but despised, went up to the said fellow and gave him a good lusty thump on the back with his fist. The fellow feeling himself struck, turned about of a sudden, and cried, " What little t——d fly's this ?   I wonder who sent thee hither to strike me ? "

Ragotin was about to have given him a reason for what he had done, when the ringer holding his bell-rope in one hand, and catching him by the arm with the other, twirled him about, and at the same time gave him such a kick in the a—e, that he sent him headlong down a pair of stairs into the chime-room.   He tumbled so violently, with his head against some of the clockwork, that his nose gushed out with blood, besides the many other parts of his body that were extremely bruised.   This made him roar out like a bull, but perceiving no remedy, and fearing to go up again to the ringer, he ran down stairs as fast as he could drive, to complain to the lieutenant-criminal, who lived hard by.   This magistrate, seeing Ragotin in that pickle, was easily inclined to believe what he told him ; but after having heard the reason likewise from the sexton that followed him to his house; he could not forbear laughing immoderately, though he pitied him at the same time, well knowing the little man must needs have his brain out of order to be guilty of such extravagances; nevertheless to content him what he could, he told him he would do him justice, and consequently sent a footman for the ringer, who being come, he demanded of him why he had abused that little gentleman there with his bells. To which he answered, He knew not how he could abuse him, since he and his companions rung only after their wonted rate—

" Or-le-ans-Bois-gen-cy
No-tre-dame-de-Cle-ri :
Ven-dosme-Ven-dosme "—

but that indeed after he had once struck him he did kick him, which happening to be towards the top of the stairs, he could not help his falling to the bottom. The lieutenant-criminal bid the ringer be more cautious for the future how he bestowed his favours of that kind, and advised Ragotin to be wiser hereafter than to trust to his imagination, since it had so palpably deceived him.

Ragotin not finding it likely to have any farther justice done him in this case, went home as well satisfied as he could; when the actors perceiving his face bruised and bloody in many places, inquired of him what had been the occasion of it, but he would by no means tell them, yet they soon after came to know it by others, which caused them, together with Monsieur Vervelle and Monsieur la Garrouffière, to laugh exceedingly at him. The wedding-day being at length come, the Prior of St. Lewis told the parties he had made choice of his own church to marry them in, whither they went soon after, with as little noise as they could, and were married after a very pious exhortation. The business being ended, they returned to their lodgings, where they dined; after which they knew not how to pass their time till supper. As for plays,

interludes, and balls, they had been so used to them, that
they were not at all entertaining, and therefore they
proposed to hear some novel read. Vervelle said for his
part he knew none. If Ragotin had not been melancholy,
he had been the properest person to relate one, but he was
dumb. Then Rancour was desired to tell that of the poet
Roquebrune which he had promised the company to do
whenever occasion served, and none could happen better
than this. His answer was, he was not at all in humour ;
and besides that, he did nor care to bespatter his friend
Roquebrune with aspersions, since he had better deserved
of him of late than he had formerly done. At length
Monsieur la Garrouffière told the company that if they
would accept of such as he could entertain them with, he
would tell them some adventures he had been an eye-
witness of, and which you'll find in the following chapter.

CHAPTER XV.

THE TWO JEALOUS LADIES : A NOVEL.

"My father, who was a counsellor of the parliament of Rennes," said Monsieur la Garrouffière, "and who designed me for his successor, as I am, sent me to the college to qualify me for that purpose ; for whilst I continued in my own country he fancied I profited but little, and therefore resolved to send me to La Flêche, where, you know, the Jesuits have the best college throughout all France. It was in this little town that what I am about to tell you happened ; and moreover, at the same time I studied there, there were two gentlemen, the most accomplished in all that place, who although they were a little advanced in years, were nevertheless not married, as it often happens amongst persons of any quality, who according to the proverb, 'Between whom we would have, and whom we would not, we remain a long time unmarried.' This saying was nevertheless crossed at last by these two well-bred gentlemen. One of them, called Monsieur de Fons-blanche, married a daughter of the family of Chateau-d'un, who were a meaner sort of gentry, but very rich. The other, whose name was Monsieur du Lac, married a lady from the city of Chartres, who was not rich, but nevertheless exceeding beautiful, and of so good a family that she was related to several dukes, peers, and marshals of France.

"These two gentlemen, who could share the town

betwixt them, had been always good friends till after
their marriage, when their two ladies looking enviously on
each other, it quickly occasioned a rupture between the
husbands. Madame de Fons-blanche was not, it is true,
handsome in countenance, yet she had nevertheless a
graceful mien, well shaped, had a great deal of wit, and
was very obliging. Madame du Lac, as beautiful as she
was, yet wanted address ; she had wit indeed a great deal,
but so ill managed that she thereby rather rendered herself avoidable than acceptable. These two ladies were of
the humour of most women nowadays, who never think
they live great unless they have a score or two of beaux
after them. This caused them to employ all the arts they
had in making conquests, but therein Du Lac succeeded
much better than de Fons-blanche, for she had subdued all
the youth of the town ; I mean among the quality, for she
would by no means suffer any others to speak to her.
This pride and affectation occasioned a great many
murmurings against her, which at length broke out into
open detraction, but nothing harmed her, for it is thought
it rather contributed to than hindered her procuring new
lovers.

" Fons-blanche was not so desirous of having a great
number of sparks ; she nevertheless had some, which she
managed with a great deal of address, and whereof there
was one a very handsome young fellow, that had as much
wit as she, and was one of the bravest youths of his time.
This spark was her greatest favourite, but at length his
diligence caused him to be suspected by the neighbours,
and slander began to talk loud. It was here the rupture
began between these ladies, who before had visited each
other very civilly, nevertheless with a little jealous envy.
Du Lac began at last to slander Fons-blanche openly, to
pry into her actions, and do all that lay in her power to
ruin her reputation, especially about the aforesaid gentleman, whose name was Monsieur du Val-Rochet. This

soon came to Fons-blanche's ears, who was extremely
nettled at it, and said that 'If she had lovers, it was not
by scores, as Du Lac had, who every day gained new
conquests by her impostures.' Du Lac hearing this,
quickly returned her the like reflections. Whence you
may imagine that these two women lived together in
a town like a brace of demons. Some charitable people
did all they could to reconcile them, but which proved in
vain, for they could never be prevailed upon so much as to
see each other. Du Lac thought the only way to offend
Fons-blanche to the quick would be to get away her lover
Du Val-Rochet from her. She then caused Monsieur de
Fons-blanche to be acquainted underhand that he was no
sooner out of doors, which he was often, either hunting or
visiting, but that Du Val-Rochet lay with his wife ; and
farther, that several persons of credit were ready to testify
that they had seen him come naked out of her bed.
Monsieur de Fons-blanche, who had never yet had any
suspicion of his wife, was nevertheless inclinable to reflect
a little upon what he had heard, and in confusion, desired
his lady to oblige him so far as to entertain Du Val-Rochet's
visits no longer. She seemed all obedience, nevertheless
insinuated so many reasons why she might safely admit
him, that he gave her liberty, and suffered her to act as
before.

"Du Lac perceiving this contrivance of hers had not had
its desired effect, resolved to get some opportunity to talk
with Val-Rochet herself. She was both fair and subtle,
two qualities sufficient to surprise the wariest heart, though
it had been never so much engaged. De Fons-blanche
was extremely concerned at being like to lose her lover,
but much more when she heard that Val-Rochet had spoke
unhandsomely of her. This grief was augmented by her
husband's death, which happened a little while after. She
went into close mourning 'tis true, but still jealousy got
the ascendant of her outward concern. Her husband had

been scarce buried fifteen days before she had a secret conference with Val-Rochet. I know not the subject of their discourse, but the event makes me pretty well able to guess at it, for in little more than a week after, their marriage was made public, so that in less than a month's time she had two husbands, a living and a dead. This seems to me to have been the most violent effect of jealousy imaginable; for to deprive Du Lac of her lover she both forfeited her modesty by marrying so soon, and forgave the unpardonable affront Val-Rochet had offered her. Du Lac was almost ready to run mad when she first heard this news, and resolved forthwith to have him assassinated as he went on a journey to Brittany; but which he being made acquainted with, she was prevented in that design.

" Then she entered upon the strangest thought that ever jealousy could suggest, and that was, to set her husband and Val-Rochet together by the ears, which she brought about by her pernicious artifices. They quarrelled divers times, and at length came to a duel, which Du Lac encouraged her husband in, being none of the wisest men in the world, that Du Val-Rochet might have an opportunity to kill him, which she fancied no hard matter, and then she proposed to hang him out of the way for his pains. But as fortune would have it, it happened quite otherwise; for Val-Rochet, trusting to his skill in fencing, seemed to despise Du Lac, thinking he durst not make a thrust at him, but therein he was extremely deceived; for whilst he put himself out of guard, Du Lac made a home thrust at him, and run him through the body, whereof he instantly died. This done, Du Lac went home to his house, and acquainted his wife therewith, who was not only surprised, but concerned at so unexpected an accident. He after this fled away privately to a relation of his wife's, who as I have told you before, had several persons of quality to her kindred, who laboured incessantly to obtain her husband's

pardon from the king. Madame Fons-Blanche was not a
little astonished when she was first told that her husband
was killed; but coming afterwards to herself, she was
advised to bury him quickly and privately, to prevent his
body being arrested by the bailiffs. Thus in less than six
weeks' time Fons-Blanche had been a widow twice. Du
Lac not long after obtained his pardon, which was confirmed by the parliament of Paris, notwithstanding all the
opposition the deceased person's widow could make.

"This made her to entertain a wilder design than
Madame du Lac had done before, and that was to stab
Du Lac as he walked in the market-place with some of his
friends. For this purpose she provided herself a poignard,
and marching up to him, attacked him so furiously that
before he could get himself into a posture of defence, or
have any of his friends turn about to help him, she had
stabbed him mortally in two places, whereof he died three
days after. His wife immediately got this virago seized
and clapped up in prison. Her trial came on, and she was
condemned to die, but her execution was respited, by
reason of her being with child; nevertheless, not long
after the stench of the prison did the work of the hangman, for she died of a disease caused thereby, after having
been first delivered before her time, and her child being
baptised, died likewise soon after. Madame du Lac began
afterwards to reflect on what she had been the occasion of,
and therefore forthwith resolved to turn a nun, which she
did, after having put her affairs in order, in the nunnery of
Almeneche, in the diocese of Sées, where she now continues, if she be not yet dead of her austerities, which she
voluntarily inflicted on herself."

The actors and actresses continued their attention, even
while Monsieur la Garrouffière had done speaking, so well
they liked the story he had entertained them with. Roquebrune, starting up all of a sudden, told the company, after
his usual way, that this was a rare subject for a grave

poem, and he would make an excellent tragedy of it, which he would reduce to dramatic rules. The company took little notice of what he said, but all admired at the wondrous courage of the women, who being pushed on by jealousy, did not boggle at the most hazardous attempts. Then it was disputed whether jealousy were a passion or not; and all concluded that whatsoever it was, it ruined the noblest of passions—love. There was a good while yet to supper, when all the company agreed to go and walk in the park, which they did, and afterwards sat themselves down on the grass. Then Destiny said "he thought nothing so pleasant as novels," which Leander confirming, offered to relate another concerning a neighbour's daughter of his, which was accepted, and after three or four times coughing, he began as follows.

CHAPTER XVI.

THE CAPRICIOUS LADY: A NOVEL.

THERE lived in a small town of Brittany, called Vitray, an ancient gentleman, who had been married a great while to a very virtuous lady without having any children by her. Amongst other household servants, he had a steward and a housekeeper through whose hands most matters relating to the family passed. These two persons, as most servants do sooner or later, made love, and promised each other marriage. They had so well played their parts in their several stations, that both the good old gentleman and his lady died not long after, very much incumbered. As for the two servants, they became rich, and married, having little or no regard to their master's misfortune. Some years afterwards a certain ill accident fell out, that caused the steward to fly his country, which to do the more securely, he 'listed himself in a troop of horse, leaving his wife without children. She having waited for his return about two years, and hearing nothing of him, caused a report to be spread abroad that he was dead, and accordingly went into mourning for him. When this was a little over, she was sought after by several persons in marriage, and amongst the rest by a certain rich merchant, who married her, and at the year's end had a child by her, who might be about four years old when her mother's first husband returned home to his house. To tell you which was the most surprised, the two husbands or the wife, is

not in my power ; but certain it is, the first husband's
occasion of going away still continuing against him, he
was easily prevailed upon by the other husband to take a
small sum of money to be gone again. It is true, he every
now and then returned secretly for a little subsistence from
his wife, which was not refused him.

" In the meantime the daughter, whose name was
Margaret, grew up, and being rich, though she was not
handsome, did not want for sparks to court her. Among
the rest was a rich merchant's son, who did not mind his
father's business, but loved to frequent gentry's company,
where he often met with his Mistress Margaret, who was received among them on account of her riches. The young
man, whose name was Monsieur de Saint Germain, had a
good countenance, and courage enough to engage him
often in duels, which at that time were very frequent. He
danced gracefully, gamed with all the better sort of company, and was always well dressed. In the many meetings
he had with this young lass he took all opportunities to
let her know what a kindness he had for her, and how
desirous he was to be her husband. This she seemed to
approve of well enough, and consequently invited him to
come and see her at home, which he did by permission of
her father and mother, who extremely favoured the match.
But afterwards, when he was about to ask her of her
parents, he would by no means do it till he had her consent
first, not believing when she had yielded so far in other
things she would oppose him in that ; but to his great
surprise, upon putting the question, he found her to re-
pulse him furiously, both in words and actions. Hereupon
he went his way, and forbore visiting her for five or six
days, hoping thereby he might in some measure abate his
passion ; but to his disappointment found that it had
taken too deep root to be so easily removed, insomuch
that he was quickly forced to go see her again. He had
no sooner entered her house but she went out of it among
her companions in the neighbourhood, whither he followed

her, after having had a promise from her father and mother
to use their endeavours to make her more sociable.   This
nevertheless they durst not attempt to do with rigour,
she being their darling and only daughter, and therefore
chose rather to represent to her mildly what injustice she
did the young man, after having once professed to love him.
To this she gave no answer, and notwithstanding all was
said, continued in her ill humour ; for whenever he offered
to come near her she would still change her place.   Then
he would follow her, but she always flew from him.

"One day, as she was getting away, he caught her by
the sleeve ; she told him he rumpled it, and that if he offered
to come near her any more she would give him a box of
the ear.   In a word, the more he followed her, the more she
avoided him.   When she was at the ball, and he offered to
dance with her, she affronted him, telling him she was out
of order, and at the same time danced with another.   She
at length arrived to that pitch of ill-nature, that she occasioned him quarrels, and he above four times accepted
challenges on her account, in all which he nevertheless came
off safe, which she seemed to be very sorry for.   All this ill
usage did but inflame his passion the more, like oil thrown
upon the fire, insomuch that his visits were made the more
frequently for his being discouraged.   One day above the
rest he fancied his perseverance had wrought an alteration
in her, for that she suffered him to come near her, and
seemed to hearken attentively to what he said to her.   His
language was this : 'Why do you thus fly me, insensible
fair one! that cannot live without you ?   If I have not
merit sufficient to deserve you, yet consider at least the
excess of my passion, and the many indignities I have borne
from you with patience.' 'Very well,' answered she, ' you
may flatter yourself with that fancy if you please, but I
would have you to know, that the best way for you to win
upon me, is to get as far out of my sight as you can ; and
because you cannot well do so as long as you continue in
this town, I command you (which if you have that respect

you pretend for me, you will not fail to obey me in) to list yourself in the troops that are now raising ; and after you have made a few campaigns it may be you may find me more kind. This small pittance of hope which I afford you ought to incline you to obey me ; but if you will not do it, lose me for ever.' Then she drew off a ring from her finger, and gave it him, saying, 'Keep this ring to put you in mind of me, but remember I forbid you to come any more near me, though to take your leave of me.' This said, she suffered him to take a parting kiss of her, and so went into an adjoining chamber, locking herself up. Then this wretched lover went to take leave of her father and mother, who pitied him extremely, promising to continue always his friends, and next day he listed in a troop of horse that was raising to go to the siege of Rochelle. His mistress having enjoined him not to see her again till after his return, he durst not pretend to attempt it ; however, the night before his departure he gave her a serenade under her window, with this complaint at the end of it, which he sung to the melancholy strains of his lute.

THE WORDS OF THE SERENADE.

" ' Iris, inexorable fair !
    Whom neither lover nor friendship sway,
    Will you not pity my despair,
    Rather than innocence betray ?

" ' Will you for ever cruel prove,
    And must I think your heart of stone ?
    Will you not yet consent to love,
    But suffer me to be undone ?

" ' Alas ! fair nymph, at length I yield
    To fate, and take my last adieu :
    Never was lover surer killed,
    Nor mistress less concerned than you.

" ' When I am dead, some friend of mine
    Shall rip up this unhappy breast,
    And to your power my heart resign,
    But leave to earth and worms the rest.'

"The capricious creature at the sound of this serenade got out of her bed, and opening the shutters of the window, peeped through the glass, and set up so hearty a laugh as might well make the poor lover think he was not like to succeed in his design. Just as he was about to express his mind farther she clapped to the shutters, crying out to him aloud, 'Keep your promise, sir, for your own sake, and it may be I may not be worse than mine.' With this answer poor Saint Germain retired, and a few days afterwards set out with his troop for the siege of Rochelle.

"This town, as you may have heard, held out very obstinately for some time, till at length it was forced to surrender upon discretion. Then was it that the troop wherein Saint Germain rode was disbanded, and he consequently returned to Vitray. He no sooner arrived than he went to wait on his unkind mistress Margaret; who permitted him, it is true, to salute her, but afterwards told him he had returned too soon, and that she was not yet disposed to receive him, therefore desired him to be gone again. His answer was in these mournful words : 'You are certainly the most cruel creature of your sex, and I plainly perceive you desire nothing more than the death of him that has all along approved himself the most faithful lover in the world. You have put me four times upon single trials of my courage, and I have always had honourable escapes. You then would have me hazard my life in the army, and I have likewise come off safe there even where many a less unhappy wretch than I has met his end. But since I find you so ardently covet my ruin, I will go seek my fate in so many places, that it shall be out of the power of fortune to afford me any more deliverances ; it may be you will not be able to forbear repenting of having occasioned this, since my death shall be of that kind, as will not only surprise, but incline you to pity me. Adieu,' then added he, 'most cruel of your sex, adieu for ever.'

"Having uttered these words, he was rising to be gone,

but she would not suffer it till she had told him, that she did not by any means desire his death, and that what she had done by engaging him in duels, was only to be the better convinced of his courage, that he might be the more worthy of her. And lastly, she let him know, that she was not yet disposed to receive his addresses, but that time, for aught she knew, might make an alteration upon her to his advantage. With these words she left him and retired. The small hopes she gave him put him upon a stratagem which was like to have spoiled all, and that was to make her jealous. He considered with himself, that since she had showed some goodwill towards him, she would not fail to be jealous if she really loved him. He therefore sought out a comrade of his that had a mistress that loved him as much as his slighted him. He desired him to give him leave to make his addresses to her, and he would do the like to his, to the end he might observe how she would take it. His comrade would by no means grant his request till he had his mistress's consent, which nevertheless soon after demanding he easily obtained.

"The first time that these two ladies came together, which I should have told you they did almost every day, the two lovers made their exchange according to agreement, Saint Germain stepping up to and courting his comrade's mistress, whilst his comrade did the like to the haughty Margaret, who received him but very coldly. But as soon as she perceived her former spark and his mistress laugh, she began to fly out into a great passion, well knowing then that this exchange had been concerted on agreement, and therefore immediately flung out of the company with tears in her eyes. This caused the obliging mistress to go after and endeavour to appease her, telling her this stratagem of her lover's was only to know her mind the better, and not to either circumvent or affront her, and therefore earnestly entreated her to take no farther notice of it, but rather to favour the constant addresses of so sincere a lover as Saint Germain had long been to her. All this notwithstanding gained little upon the humoursome Margaret ; whereupon the unfortunate Saint Germain was driven to so fierce despair, that for the future he sought nothing so much as to show the violence of his love by some rash action, which he hoped might procure his death. This resolution, one night not long after, he had an occasion to put in practice ; for whilst he and seven of his comrades were coming out of a tavern half drunk, and with their swords by their sides, they chanced to meet three or four gentlemen, amongst whom was a captain of horse. With these they began to dispute the wall, and which they obtained by being the greater number ; but the gentlemen returning immediately after with four or five more of their company, pursued these persons that had so greatly affronted them, and overtook them in the high street ; when Saint Germain being the foremost, and having been the forwardest in the affront, the captain discovering him to be a trooper by his hat, stepped up to him, and gave him such a lusty blow with a backsword, that he cut through his hat, and cleft part of his skull. Having done this, and thinking themselves sufficiently revenged, the captain and his companions marched off, leaving Saint Germain for dead in the arms of his friends. He had little or no pulse left, and less motion, insomuch that they immediately carried him home, and sent for several surgeons, who found life yet remaining in him. These dressed his wound, stitched up his skull, and then bound it up.

"The noise of this contest had at first alarmed the neighbourhood ; but they were much more surprised when they heard a man had been so dangerously wounded. The thing was talked about from one to the other after a different manner ; however all concluded Saint Germain was a dead man. This report quickly got to his cruel mistress's house ; who though undressed, yet immediately

ran to see him, and whom she found in the condition I
have told you. As soon as she saw death begin to show
itself in his face she fell down in a swoon, and it was found
no easy matter to recover her. When she came to herself
the neighbours began to accuse her of being the cause of
this disaster, and that if she had not been so unkind to
him, he would never have been so desperately rash, this
being but the result of what he had frequently threatened.
Then began she to tear her hair, wring her hands, and
do all that mad people are wont to do. She afterwards
proceeded to serve him with that diligence, that all the
time of his illness she would neither undress herself, lie
down on the bed, nor permit any of his sisters to do anything about him. After he came to himself, and began to
know people, it was judged necessary she should absent
herself, which she was nevertheless with great difficulty
prevailed on to do. He at length was cured, and when he
came to be perfectly well, was married to his capricious
mistress Margaret, to the satisfaction of everybody, but
much the more of himself."

After Leander had finished this novel, the company
returned to the town, where having well supped, danced,
and the like, they put the new-married couples to bed.
These weddings had been kept so secret, that they had no
visitors for two days after, but on the third they were so
embarrassed with company that they had not leisure left
them to study their parts. After a little time they all
returned to their exercise as before, except Ragotin, who
was fallen into a perfect despair; as you will find in the
following chapter.

CHAPTER XVII.

RAGOTIN'S DESPAIR AND DEATH, WITH THE END OF THE COMICAL ROMANCE.

RANCOUR now perceiving that he as well as Ragotin had no more hopes left of his succeeding in his love to Star, got up betimes, and went to the little man, whom he found likewise risen and writing at the table. Upon his inquiry what he was doing, he told him he was writing his own epitaph. "How!" quoth Rancour, "do people use to make their epitaphs before they are dead? But what surprises me yet more," continued he, "is that you make it yourself."

"Yes, I have made it myself," answered Ragotin, "and will show it you." He thereupon opened a paper which was folded, and read these verses—

RAGOTIN'S EPITAPH.

" Here the unlucky Ragotin lies,
 Who lived a slave to fair Star's eyes,
  Yet Destiny him of her deprived ;
 Which made him take a journey straight
 To the other world, compelled by fate,
  For needs must where the devil drived.
 For her a stroller he became,
 And here with life concludes the same."

"This is fine indeed," quoth Rancour ; "but you will never have the satisfaction to read it on your own tomb ;

for it is the common opinion that dead people neither see nor understand anything they do that survive them."

"Ah!" answered Ragotin, "you have partly been the cause of my misfortunes, for you always gave me hopes I should succeed, and yet I am very well assured you all along knew the contrary."

Then Rancour protested to him that he knew nothing certainly of it, but confessed he had all along suspected it as he had told him before, when he advised him to stifle his passion, she being the proudest woman in the world. "But methinks," added he, "her profession of a stroller, which you know is none of the most honourable, might have somewhat abated her self-conceit ; yet it has always so happened, that these sort of women take much more upon them than belongs to them. But at length," continued he, "I must discover something to you that I have kept a secret till now, and that is, that I was as much in love with Madam Star as you, and I know not how a person that had so much conversation as I had with her could have well avoided it ; but now that I find myself out of hopes, as well as you, I am resolved to leave the company, especially since Mrs. Cave's brother is come to it, who can act all those parts I did ; and therefore I believe they will be the more willing to part with me. I will then go to Rennes, where the other company is, and whereinto I do not question I shall be received, because they at present want an actor."

"Then," quoth Ragotin, "since you were in love with the same person, I do not know how you should speak to her for me."

But Rancour swore like a devil he was a man of honour, and had done all that in him lay to promote his interest, but said he could never prevail to be heard.

"Well, then," quoth Ragotin, "you have resolved to quit the company, and so have I, but I have determined to make a larger leap, and forsake the world too."

Rancour made no reflections on his epitaph, thinking he meant only retiring to a convent, and therefore took no care to prevent his doing himself any harm.   As for the epitaph, he never spoke of it to anybody except the poet Roquebrune, to whom at his request he gave a copy. When Ragotin was alone he began to think what method he should make use of to rid himself of the world.   He took a pistol and charged it with a brace of bullets, to shoot himself through the head, but then he was afraid that way would make too much noise.   Then he took the point of his sword and put it against his breast, but as soon as he felt it prick it made him sick, and therefore that method was rejected.   At last he went down into the stable, where whilst the hostlers were at breakfast, he took one of the halters that he found lying there, and fastening one end to the rack, put the other with a noose about his neck ; but when he was about to let himself swing, he found he had not the heart to do it, and therefore waited till somebody came in, when he was resolved upon it.   At length a gentleman came, and then he let go the hold of his hands, but still kept one foot bearing on the manger.   However he might have been strangled had he continued so hanging for any while.   The boy that went to put up the gentleman's horse seeing Ragotin hang in that manner, thought verily he had been dead, and therefore began to bawl out like mad for help.   All the family came down, and seeing a man hanged, immediately took the rope from his neck, and brought him to himself; which you may imagine was not very easy to do.   Then he asked what made him to enter upon so strange a resolution, but no answer could be got out of him.   Afterwards Rancour took Madam Star aside, whom I might have called by the name of Destiny, but being so near to the end of this romance, it will be scarce worth while, and told her the occasion, as he believed, of this strange undertaking.   She seemed much surprised, but was much more when she heard this wicked man tell her

he was still in the same mind, to make away with himself
but would not attempt it any more by a halter.   To this
Star answered not one word, whereupon Ragotin took his
leave and departed.

Some little time after he made known to the company a
design he had to accompany Monsieur Vervelle to Mans.
The company was willing enough to part with him as
long as he had a companion, but would not have cared to
trust him alone.   Next morning they set out betimes, after
that Monsieur Vervelle had made a thousand protestations
of continued friendship to the actors and actresses, but
especially to Destiny, whom he embraced, professing
the great joy he had to see his designs accomplished.
Ragotin made a long harangue by way of compliment,
but which was so confused that I do not think fit to insert
it.   When they were ready to go, Vervelle inquired if the
horses had drunk.   The hostler told him it was too early
in the morning, but he might let them do it on the road if
he pleased.   Then having taken leave of Monsieur la
Garrouffière, they mounted and set forwards.   Monsieur la
Garrouffière mounted likewise to go home, to whom the
new-married couples returned abundance of acknowledgments, for coming so far to honour their nuptials with his
presence.   After a hundred protestations of service on
both sides, he set out, and Rancour followed him, who notwithstanding his insensibility could not forbear weeping.
Destiny wept also, calling to mind the many services
Rancour had done him, especially that upon the Pont-neuf
at Paris, when he was there set upon and robbed by La
Rappinière and his followers.   As soon as Vervelle and
Ragotin were got to a river, they immediately went therein
to water their horses, but it was Ragotin's peculiar ill
fortune to light on a place where the bank had been cut
down, which causing his horse to stumble, he threw the
little man violently over his head into the river, which was
exceeding deep in that part above others.   Poor Ragotin

knew not how to swim, and though he had, his equipage of carbine, basket-hilted sword, and cloak, would have sunk him in spite of his teeth. One of Vervelle's men immediately rode after Ragotin's horse to catch him, whilst another stripped himself and leapt in after the master to save him, but found him dead. The company was called and the body taken out and laid on the grass. Next the strollers were sent for, who mightily condoled poor Ragotin's fate; which having done, they took him and buried him in St. Catherine's Chapel, which is not very far from this river. This dismal event nevertheless verified the proverb, "That he that was born to be hanged would never be drowned." Ragotin experienced the reverse, for he could not strangle himself, and so might be drowned. Thus ended the life and adventures of this little comical advocate, who shall be remembered by the inhabitants of Mans and Alençon as long as they have any taste for strolling or relish for stage-plays. Roquebrune seeing Ragotin in his grave, said that his epitaph must be altered after the following manner :—

> " Here the unlucky Ragotin lies,
> Who lived a slave to fair Star's eyes,
>   Yet Destiny him of her deprived ;
> Which made him straight resolve to float,
> To the other world without a boat ;
>   For needs must when the devil drived.
> For her a stroller he became,
> And here with life he ends the same."

The actors and actresses returned home to their lodgings, and continued their exercise with their ordinary applause.

SCARRON'S NOVELS.

NOVEL I.

AVARICE CHASTISED;

OR,

THE MISER PUNISHED.

IT is not quite a thousand years ago since a pretty younker, who was full as ambitious as poor, and had a greater itch to be thought a gentleman than a rational creature, left the mountains of Navarre, and came in company with his father to find that at Madrid which was not to be got in his own country, I mean wealth and riches; which are sooner acquired at court than any other place, and indeed are seldom obtained there but by importunity and impertinence. He had the credit, I cannot inform you how it came about, to be received as a page by a certain prince, which quality in Spain is not so gainful as that of a lackey in France, and not much more honourable. When he first put on his livery, he was about twelve years old, and from that very moment might be termed the thriftiest page in the world. All his worldly stock, not to reckon his expectations, that were very big, consisted of a wretched bed set up in a garret, which he had hired in that quarter of the town where his master lived, and where he pigged every night with his venerable father, who may be said to have been rich in grey hairs, because by procuring him the charity of well-disposed persons, they helped to maintain him. At last the old gentleman trooped off, at which his unrighteous son rejoiced, fancying himself already enriched by that which his father did not spend. From that very hour he enjoined himself so severe and strict an abstinence, and practised so wonderful a frugality, that he spent not a farthing of that little money his master gave him to keep body and soul together. It is true he did this at the expense both of his belly, which often grumbled at him for it, and of all his acquaintance. Don Marcos (for that was our hero's name) was of a stature a little below the common pitch ; and for want of due repairing the decays of his pigmy carcass, became in a short time as slender as a lath, and as dry as a deal-board. When he waited on his master at table, he never took away a plate with any meat in it but he dexterously whipped the better part into his pocket ; and because it could not so well contain soups and such-like liquids, he made money of a great number of torches' ends, which he had scraped together with much industry, and thereby bought him a pair of tin pockets ; by the help of which he soon began to perform miracles for the advancement of his fortune.

Misers are for the most part careful and vigilant, and these two good qualities, joined to the furious passion which Don Marcos had to become rich, made his master to take such a fancy to him, that he was resolved never to part with so excellent a page. For this reason he made him wear a livery till he was thirty years old. But at last this phœnix of a servant, being obliged to undergo the tonsor's hands too often to clear him of his ungodly beard, his master metamorphosed his page into a gentleman, and thus made him what heaven never designed him to be. Now you must know his revenues were hereby augmented by the addition of several reals a day ; but instead of increasing likewise his expenses, our spark shut his purse so much the closer, as his new employ, one would have thought, might have obliged him to open it. He had heard stories of some of his profession, who for want of a valet would call up your fellows that cry brandy about streets in a morning, to make their beds and sweep their chambers, under pretence of buying some of their liquor ; and of others, who in the winter got themselves undressed at night by your criers of grey peas, or link-boys. But as this was not to be done without some sort of injustice, and in regard our Don Marcos made a conscience of wronging every one but himself, he thought it much better to shift as well as he could without a valet. He never burnt but an inch of candle in his chamber but what he stole ; and to manage it with more economy always began to unbutton himself in the street at the very place where he lighted it, put it out as soon as he got to his lodgings, and so tumbled in to bed in the dark.

But still finding there was a cheaper way of going to bed, his busy inventing genius set him upon making a hole in the wall which divided his room from that of his neighbour, who no sooner lighted his candle but our Don immediately opened his hole, and by that means received light enough to do anything he had occasion for. Being not able to dispense with himself from wearing a tilter at his breech, by reason of his noble descent, which required it of him, he clapped a lath into a scabbard, wore it one day on the right, and the next on the left side, in order to use his breeches to some sort of symmetry, and because his trusty whinyard would wear them out the less, being equally divided between the right and the left. At break of day he stood at the street-door, begging in God's name for a cup of water of every tankard-bearer that passed by, and thus furnished himself with enough of that element to serve him several days. He would often come into the common hall, where his master's other servants used to take their repasts, and whatever he saw them eat was sure to commend it to the skies, to give him some sort of privilege to taste it. He never laid out a farthing in wine, yet drank more or less every day, either by sipping of that which was publicly cried about streets, or else by stopping porters that were carrying some to the taverns, whom he would ask to give him a taste of their wine, that if he liked it he might know where to send for it. Once riding towards Madrid upon a mule, he so dexterously cheated the eyes of his inn-keepers, that he fed trusty Dapple with the straw of the beds where he lay ; but the very first day of his journey, being weary of paying for his servant's dinner, who was the first he ever had, he pretended he could not drink his landlord's wine, and therefore sent the poor fellow to find out better, a full league at least from the inn where he then was. The servant accordingly beat the hoof thither, relying upon his master's honour, who nevertheless fairly gave him the slip, and so the wretch was forced to beg all the way to Madrid. In short, Don Marcos was the living picture of avarice and filching, and was so well known to be the most covetous devil in Spain that at Madrid he advanced himself into a proverb, for they there called a pinching miser a Don Marcos. His master and all his friends told a thousand merry stories of him, and that even before his face, because he understood raillery to perfection, and would stand a jest as well as a managed horse will fire. It was a usual saying with him, that no woman could be handsome if she loved to take nor ugly if she gave money, and that a wise man ought, never to go to bed, unless for the satisfaction of his conscience he had turned the penny the same day.

His excellent theory, seconded by a most exact practice, had brought him together by that time he was forty years old, above 10,000 crowns in silver, a prodigious sum for a grandee's gentleman to get, especially in Spain. But what may not a man save in the compass of many years who steals all he can both from himself and other people ? Don Marcos having the reputation of being rich, without being either a debauchee or a gamester, was soon courted in marriage by abundance of women, who loved the money

more than the man, and whose number in all parts of the
world is great. Among others that offered to carry the
marriage yoke with him, he met a woman whose name was
Isidore, who passed for a widow, though in truth she had
never been married, and appeared much younger than she
was, by patching, painting, and tricking up herself, in all
which mysteries she was skilled to admiration. The world
judged of her wealth by her way of living, which was
expensive enough for one of her condition ; and those who
frequently guess at random, and love to magnify matters,
bestowed on her at least three thousand livres a year and
some ten thousand crowns in plate, jewels, and the like
convenient moveables. The fellow that proposed her to
Don Marcos for a wife, was a notable sharper, one that
trucked in all sorts of merchandise, but his principal subsistence was selling of maidenheads, and making of
matches. He spoke to Don Marcos of Isidore in such
advantageous terms that he set him upon the tenter-hooks
to see this miracle (a curiosity he had never expressed for
any woman before), and so effectually persuaded our un-
thinking cully that she was rich, and the widow of a
certain cavalier, descended from one of the best families
in Andalusia, that from that very instant he had an itch
to be married to her. The same day this proposal was
made to him, our marriage-pimp, whose name was Gamara,
came to call upon him, to introduce him into Isidore's company. Our covetous hunks was ravished to see the neat-
ness and magnificence of the house into which Gamara
conducted him, but he was much more so when this
master of the ceremonies assured him it belonged to
Isidore. He was perfectly transported at the richness of
the furniture, the alcoves, and rooms of state, and a pro-
fusion of sweet scents, that rather seemed proper for a
lady of the highest quality than one that was to be a
wife to a grandee's gentleman and no better. Then as for
the mistress of this enchanted castle, he took her for a

goddess. Don Marcos found her busy at work between a damsel and a chamber-maid, both so beautiful and charming, that whatever aversion he had to expensive living, and a great number of servants, yet he resolved to marry Isidore, were it only for the vanity to be master of two such charming creatures. Whatever Isidore said to him was uttered so discreetly that it not only pleased but perfectly ravished him ; and what contributed to make an entire conquest of his heart, was a collation as nice as neatly served up, where the clean linen and the silver plate were all of a piece with the other rich movables.

There sat down to this entertainment a young gentleman very well dressed and well made, whom Isidore pretended to be her nephew. His name was Augustine, but his good aunt called him Augustinet, although the pretty baby was above twenty years old. Isidore and Augustinet strove who should make Don Marcos most welcome, and during the repast helped him to all the choicest bits. Now whilst our trusty miser laid about him like a harpy, and crammed his half-starved guts with victuals enough to have lasted him eight days, his ears were charmed by the melodious voice of the damsel Marcella, who sung two or three passionate airs to her harpsichord. Don Marcos lost no time, but fell on like a devil, it being at another's expense. The collation ended with the day, whose light was supplied by that of four large candles in silver sconces, of admirable workmanship and weight, which Don Marcos at that moment designed within himself to reform into one single lamp, so soon as he was married to Isidore. Augustinet took a guitar and played several sarabands and other tunes, to which that cunning jilt Marcella, and Inez the chamber-maid danced admirably well, striking their castanets exactly to the time of the guitar. The discreet Gamara whispered Don Marcos in the ear, that Isidore never sat up late ; which hint our civil gentleman taking immediately, rose from his seat, made her a thousand compliments and protestations of love, more than he had ever done to any female, wished her and the little Augustinet a good night, and so left them at liberty to talk of him what they thought fit.

Don Marcos, who was up to the ears in love with Isidore, but much more with her money, protested to Gamara, who accompanied him to his lodgings, that the charming widow had entirely gained his affections, and that he would give one of his fingers, with all his soul, that he were already married to her, because he never saw a woman more made to his mind ; although in sober truth he confessed, that after marriage he would retrench somewhat of that endless ostentation and luxury of hers.

" She lives more like a princess than the wife of a private man," cries the prudent Don Marcos to the dissembling Gamara ; "and she does not consider," continued he, "that the movables she has, being turned into money, and this money being joined to mine, we may be able between us to purchase a pretty handsome estate, which by God's blessing and my own industry, may make a considerable fortune for the children Providence shall bestow on us. And if our marriage," proceeded he, " should prove without issue, then since Isidore has a nephew, we will leave him all, provided I like his behaviour, and find him no way addicted to ill husbandry." Don Marcos entertained Gamara with these discourses, or somewhat of the like nature, till he came before his own door. Gamara took leave of him after he had given him his word that next morning he should conclude his marriage with Isidore, by reason, he said, affairs of this nature were soon broke off by delays, as by the death of either of the parties. Don Marcos embraced his worthy marriage-jobber, who immediately after went to give Isidore an account in what disposition of mind he had left her lover. In the meantime our amorous coxcomb takes an end of a candle out of his pocket, fixes it to the point of his sword, and having lighted it at a lamp, which burnt before a

public crucifix hard by, not without dropping a few hearty
ejaculations for good success in his affair, opened the door
of the house where he lodged, and repaired to his wretched
bed, but that rather to think of his amour than to sleep.

Gamara came to visit him next morning, and brought
him the agreeable news that his business was done with
Isidore, who wholly left it to his discretion to appoint the
day of marriage. Our besotted lover told Gamara he was
upon thorns till it was over, and that if he were to be
married that very day, it would not be so soon as he
wished. Gamara replied, it lay solely in his own power to
conclude it whenever he pleased ; when Don Marcos
embracing him, conjured him to use all his diligence to get
the contract dispatched that very day. He appointed
Gamara to give him a meeting after dinner, while he went
to his master's levee, and waited on him at table. Both
met exactly at the time of assignation, and then immediately
went to Isidore's house, who received them much better
than the day before. Marcella sang, Inez danced,
Augustinet played upon the guitar, and Isidore, the principal actress of this farce, gave her spouse that was to be a
noble repast, for which she knew well enough how to make
herself full amends afterwards. Gamara brought a notary,
who perhaps was a counterfeit one. The articles of marriage were signed and sealed. It was proposed to Don
Marcos to play a game at *primera* to pass away the time.
" Heaven bless me ! " cried the astonished Don Marcos, " I
serve a master who would not let me live a quarter of an
hour with him, if he knew I was a gamester ; but, God be
praised, I don't so much as know the cards."

" How much does it delight me," replies Isidore, " to
hear Signor Don Marcos talk after this manner. I daily
preach the same doctrine to my nephew Angustinet here,
but your young fellows are not a farthing the better for all
the good advice that is given them. Go, foolish, obstinate
boy," says she to Augustinet, " go and bid Marcella and

Inez make an end of their dinner, and come and divert us with their castanets."

While Augustinet went to call up the maids, Don Marcos, stroking his whiskers with admirable gravity, thus carried on the discourse ; " If Augustinet," says he, " has a mind to keep in my favour, he must renounce gaming and staying out late at nights. If he'll keep good hours, I am content with all my heart he should lie in my house ; but I'll have my windows barred, and doors locked and bolted before I go to bed : not that I am in the least jealous in my temper, for I think nothing can be more impertinent, especially where a man has a virtuous wife, as I am going to have ; but houses, where there is anything to lose, cannot be too well secured against thieves ; and for my part I should run distracted if a villain of a thief, without any other trouble than that of carrying off what he found, should rob me in an instant of what my great industry had been scraping together for many years ; and therefore," continues Don Marcos " I forbid him gaming and rambling at nights, or the Devil shall roast him alive, and I will renounce the name of Don Marcos."

The choleric gentleman uttered these last words with so much vehemence and passion, that it cost Isidore abundance of fair speeches to put him in a good humour again. She conjured him not to trouble himself about the matter, assuring him that Augustinet would not fail to answer his expectation in all points, because he was the most tractable and the best-conditioned boy that ever was known. The coming in of Augustinet and the dancers put a stop to this discourse, so they spent the greatest part of the night in dancing and singing.

Don Marcos being loath to give himself the trouble to walk to his lodgings so late, would by all means have persuaded Isidore to give her consent that they might live together from that time forward like man and wife, or at least that she would suffer him to lie at her house that night. But our widow, putting on a severe countenance, protested aloud that ever since the unhappy day on which her widowhood commenced, no man living had put his leg within her chaste bed, which she reserved to her lord and master, nor should do so till the rites of the Church were performed ; adding, that in her present circumstances her reputation would not suffer her to let any man, but only her nephew Augustinet, lie in her house. Don Marcos gave her his humble thanks for her civilities, notwithstanding his amorous impatience. He wished her a good repose, returned to his own lodging, accompanied by Gamara, took his end of a candle out of his pocket, fixed it to the point of his sword, lighted it at the lamp of the crucifix, and in short, did everything else that he had done the night before ; so punctual was he in every respect, unless it were that he omitted to say his prayers, because he thought his affair as good as concluded, and so did not want the assistance of heaven to further it. The banns were soon published, a cluster of holidays coming together. In fine, this marriage, so much desired on both sides, was celebrated with more expense and formality than one would have expected from so sordid a miser, who for fear of touching his six thousand crowns had borrowed money of his friends to defray the charges of that day. The chief servants belonging to his master were invited to the wedding, who all concurred in commending the happy choice he had made. The dinner was sumptuous and noble, though provided at the expense of Don Marcos, this being the first time he had ever bled in his pocket, and to do him justice, out of his excess of love he had bespoke very fine wedding clothes for Isidore and himself.

All the guests departed in good time, and Don Marcos with his own hands locked the doors and barred the gates, not so much to secure his wife, as the coffer wherein his money lay, which he had ordered to be set by his bedside. In short, the married couple went to bed, and Don Marcos, not finding all he expected, began even then perhaps to repent of his marriage : Marcella and Inez were grumbling together at their master's humour, and blamed their mistress for being so hasty to be married. Inez swore by her Maker she would sooner choose to be a lay-sister in a convent than endure to live in a house that was shut up at nine.

"And what would you say were you in my case ? " says Marcella, " for you have the pleasure of going sometimes to market to buy provisions for the family ; whereas I, who am my lady's waiting-woman, forsooth, must never peep abroad, but live a solitary life with the chaste wife of a jealous husband ; and as for the serenades we used to hear so often under our window, I now expect to hear them no more than the music of the spheres."

"Yet for all this," replied Inez, we have not so much reason to complain as has poor Augustinet. He has spent the best part of his youth in waiting upon his aunt, who has disposed of herself as you see ; she has set a formal pedagogue over his head, who will reproach him a hundred times a day with every bit he eats, and with his fine clothes, which God knows whether he came honestly by or not."

"You tell me news," says Marcella, " that I never heard before, and I don't wonder that our mistress has made so foolish a bargain on't, when her nephew *ad honores* is forced to pass his time with us. If I would have believed his fair promises, I might easily have carried off the young spark from his aunt before this, but she has kept me from my childhood, and I ought in conscience to be faithful to those whose bread I have all along ate."

"To tell you truth," continued Inez, " I have no aversion to the poor boy, and must own I have often pitied him, to see him sad and melancholy by himself, while other people are making merry and diverting themselves."

After this manner did these servants entertain each

other, and reason upon their mistress's marriage. The
good Inez soon fell asleep, but the virtuous Marcella had
other things to mind. No sooner did she find her bed-
fellow fast, but she steals out of bed, dresses herself, and
packs up in one bundle the wedding clothes of Isidore, and
some of Don Marcos's things, which she had dexterously
conveyed out of their chamber before the provident master
had locked the door. This having done, away she
marches, and because she had no design to return, she left
open the doors of the apartment which Isidore had hired
in that house. Inez awaked not long after, and missing
her companion, had the curiosity to inquire what was
become of her. She listened at Augustinet's door, not
without some little suspicion and spice of jealousy; but
hearing not the least noise there, she examined every
place elsewhere she thought it probable to find her, but
missed of her aim. At length seeing the doors wide open,
she ran upstairs, and rapped at the chamber-door of the
new married couple as hard as she could drive, whom she
strangely alarmed by this noise. She told them Marcella
was gone, that she had left the doors open, and that she
was afraid she had carried off some things, which she
never designed to restore. Don Marcos leaped out of
bed like a madman, and ran to his clothes, but found
them gone as well as those of Isidore's; when turning
suddenly about, to his inexpressible mortification, he saw
his dear spouse of so different a figure from what had
charmed him before, that he thought he should have sunk
through the floor. The unfortunate lady being awakened
so on the sudden, had taken no notice that her tower was
not upon her head. She saw it lying on the ground near
the bed, and was going to take it up; but alas! we do
nothing orderly when we go rashly to work, and in confusion she put the back part of it before; and her
visage, which had not received its usual refreshment so
early in the morning, the gloss of her paint and washes

being gone, appeared so ghastly to Don Marcos, that he
fancied he saw a spectre. If he cast his eyes upon her, he
beheld a terrible monster, and if he carried his sight elsewhere, he found his clothes were missing.

Isidore, who was in a strange disorder, perceived some of
her teeth hanging in the large, long, and well provided
mustachios of her husband, and went about in this consternation to recover them ; but the poor man, whom she
had so dismally affrighted, not being able to imagine she
stretched out her hands so near his face with any other
design than to strangle him or pluck out his eyes, retired
some paces backward, and avoided her approaches with so
much address that, not being able to come up to him, she was
forced at last to tell him, that some of her teeth were
lodged in his whiskers. Don Marcos directed his hands
thither, and finding his wife's teeth, which formerly belonged to some elephant, a native of Africa or the East-
Indies, dangling in his beard, flung them at her with a
great deal of indignation. She gathered them up, as likewise those that were scattered in the bed, and up and down
the chamber, and then retired to a little closet with this
precious treasure, her painting brush, and some other
necessaries she had placed upon her toilet. In the meantime Don Marcos, after he had heartily renounced his
Maker, sat him down in a chair, where he made sorrowful
reflections upon his being married to an old beldame,
whom he found by the venerable snow, which sixty long
winters had strewed upon her bald skull, to be at least
twenty years elder than himself, and yet was not so old
neither, but that he might expect to be plagued with her
twenty years more. Augustinet, who upon this noise had got
up in haste, came half dressed into the room, and endeavoured all that lay in his power to appease the worthy
husband of his aunt by adoption. But the poor man did
nothing but sigh and beat his thighs with his hands, and
sometimes his face. He then bethought himself of a fine

gold chain he had borrowed to set himself off on the day of his marriage, but to complete his vexation, there was nothing but the remembrance of it left him, for Marcella had taken care to secure it among the other things she had carried off. He looked for it at first with some tranquillity, yet as carefully as might be ; but after he had wearied himself to no purpose in looking for it all over the chamber, he found it was lost, and his labour likewise, when certainly no despair could equal his. He gave such terrible groans as disturbed all the neighbourhood where he lived. Upon these doleful cries, Isidore bolted out of her closet, and appeared so much renewed, and beautiful, that the poor man thought this was the third time they had changed his wife. He looked upon her with admiration, and did not express himself angrily to her. At last he took out of one of his trunks the clothes he wore every day, dressed himself, and attended by Augustinet inquired in every street after the perfidious Marcella. They looked for her in vain till dinner, which was made up of what they had left the day before. Don Marcos and Isidore quarrelled with one another, like people that had a desire to dine, and dined like people that had as good a stomach to quarrel. However, Isidore sometimes endeavoured to bring back Don Marcos to his peaceable humour, speaking to him in as submissive and humble terms as she could think of ; and Augustinet used his best entreaties to reconcile them to each other ; but the loss of the gold chain was more to Don Marcos than a stab with a dagger. They were ready to rise from table, where they had done little else but quarrel, while Augustinet all alone by himself, employed his teeth to the best purpose ; during which there came into the room two men from the steward of the Admiral of Castile, who desired the Lady Isidore to send the silver plate he had lent her for fifteen days only, and which she had kept above twenty. Isidore could not tell what other answer to make, but that she would go and fetch it. Don

Marcos pretended the plate belonged to him, and that he was resolved to keep it. One of the men stayed still in the chamber, lest they should remove that which they made such difficulty to restore, while the other went to find out the master of the house, who came, and reproached Isidore with her unjust dealing, took no notice of the opposition Don Marcos made, and in spite of all he said to him, moved off with the plate, and left the husband and wife quarrelling about this new disaster.

Their dispute, or to speak more properly, their quarrel, was in a manner concluded, when a pawnbroker, accompanied by his porters and followers, came into the room and told Isidore that since he was informed she was married to a man of bulk and substance, he was come to fetch away the movables she had hired of him, and the money due for the loan of them, unless she was minded to buy them. Here Don Marcos lost all patience, he called the broker saucy rogue and rascal, and threatened to belabour him lustily. The broker told him he valued not his big words, that every honest man ought to restore what did not belong to him, and fell foul upon Isidore with unmannerly language, who was not wanting on her side to give him as good as he brought. He struck her, she returned the blow, and the floor was in a minute covered with the counterfeit teeth and hair of Isidore ; and with the cloak, hat and gloves of Don Marcos, who interposed to defend the virtuous rib of his side.

While the combatants were gathering up their things that were fallen ; while the broker removed the movables, and paid himself as honest brokers use to do ; and while all of them together made a noise as if hell were broke loose, the landlord of the house, who lodged in an apartment above, came down into Isidore's room, and acquainted her that if they designed to make such a noise as that every day, they must go seek out another lodging.

" 'Tis you, you impertinent puppy, that must seek out

another lodging," replies Don Marcos, whose anger had
made him look as pale as a ghost. Upon this the landlord
answered him with a box on the ear, and our angry Don
was looking for his sword or poignard, but Marcella had
carried them off; Isidore and Augustinet interposed in the
scuffle, and with much ado appeased the master of the house,
but not Don Marcos, who beat his head against the walls,
calling Isidore a hundred times cheat, strumpet, and thief.
Isidore, with tears in her eyes, answered that a poor woman
ought not to be blamed for setting her brains to work to
get a man of such merit as Don Marcos was, and therefore
he had more reason to admire her for her wit, than to beat
her as he did ; adding, that even in point of honour, a man
ought never to lay hands on his wife. Don Marcos, swearing most heroically, protested his money was his honour,
and that he was resolved to be unmarried, whatever it cost
him. To this the meek Isidore replied with a world of
humility, that she would still be his loving wife, that their
marriage had been celebrated in the usual forms, and 'twas
impossible to dissolve it, for which reason she advised him
to sit still and be patient. When this point was pretty
well over, the next question was, where they should take
another lodging, since this was too hot for them. Don
Marcos and Augustinet walked out to find one, and in this
interval Isidore enjoyed a little breathing time, and with
the trusty Inez, comforted herself for the ill humour of her
husband, so long as she saw his trunks full of money still
in the chamber. Don Marcos took a convenient lodging
in his master's neighbourhood, and sent Augustinet home
to sup with his aunt, not being able, as he said, to bring
himself as yet to eat with such an impudent cheat.
Towards the evening he came home as surly as a baited
bear, and as fierce as a tiger. Isidore endeavoured with all
her arts to soften him into a better temper, and next morning
had the boldness to desire him to go to his new lodging and
stay there to receive the movables, that Augustinet and

Inez were going to carry to a cart which they had newly hired. Don Marcos accordingly went, and while he expected their coming, the ungrateful Isidore, the knavish Augustinet, and the jilting Inez, with all expedition conveyed the whole substance of this unfortunate man into a cart, drawn by four lusty able mules, went into it themselves, quitted Madrid, and took the road to Barcelona.

Don Marcos, who had exhausted all his patience in waiting for their coming, went back to his former lodging, found the doors shut, and was informed by the neighbours that they had removed from thence with their goods several hours before. Upon this he returned to the place from whence he came but did not find what he expected. Immediately he went back to the old place, suspecting the misfortune that had happened to him. He breaks open the chamber door, where he could see nothing but a few wretched wooden platters, an old rusty pair of tongs, a battered pair of bellows, the broken leg of a crippled andiron, and such like precious ware which they had left behind them, as not thinking it worth their while to encumber the cart with them. Now he was convinced into what treacherous hands he was fallen : he tears off his beard and hair, buffets his eyes, bites his fingers till the blood came ; nay, was sorely tempted to kill himself, but his hour was not yet come. The most unfortunate men sometimes flatter themselves with vain hopes. Thus he went to find out the fugitives in all the inns of Madrid, but could hear no tale nor tidings of them. Isidore was not such a fool as to employ a cart by which she might be betrayed, but had hired one in an inn near Madrid, and to secure herself from being pursued, had articled beforehand with the owner that he should stay no longer in the city than was sufficient to take up her, her company, and her goods.

More tired and weary than a dog that has coursed a hare and missed her, our poor gentleman was returning

home, after having fruitlessly inquired at all the inns in the
city and suburbs, when by mere accident he popped full
butt upon Marcella. He caught hold of her by the throat,
and cried out, "And have I met thee, thou traitorous
baggage ? I will keep thee fast till thou hast restored every
farthing thou hast stolen from me."

"Oh ! good heavens," says this subtle dissembler, without changing countenance for the matter, " how did I
always mistrust that this would one day fall upon me.
Hear me, dear master, for the love of the blessed Virgin ;
hear me, before you ruin my reputation. I am a woman of
virtue and honesty, I thank my good God for it ; and
should you disgrace me never so little before my neighbours here, it would be my utter undoing, for I am upon the
point of marriage. Let us step a little to yonder corner,
and if your lordship will but give me the hearing, I will tell
you what are become of your chain and clothes. I knew
well enough the blame would be laid upon me for what has
happened, and told my mistress as much beforehand,
when she forced me to do what I did, but she was mistress,
and I a poor servant. Well, how wretched is the condition
of those that serve, and what pains do they take to get a
sorry livelihood ? "

Don Marcos had little malice in his nature ; the tears
and eloquence of this dissembling cockatrice inclined him to
listen to her, and even to believe whatever she told him.
He walked with her therefore under a porch belonging to a
great house, where she informed him that Isidore was an
old battered strumpet, who in her time had ruined several
persons that were smitten with her, but had saved nothing
out of all her gettings by reason of her profuse and riotous
living. She likewise told him what she had learned from
Inez, that Augustinet was not nephew to Isidore but a sort
of a bravo, the bastard of another whore, and that she
caused him to pass for her nephew, only to give her some
authority among women of her own profession and to

revenge her quarrels. She acquainted him it was he to whom she had given the gold chain and the clothes that were stolen, and that it was by his order she went away in the night, without taking leave, that thereby she might alone be suspected of so wicked an action.

Marcella told all these fine stories to Don Marcos not at all regarding what might be the consequence, either to get clear of his hands, or perhaps to keep up a good old custom long ago observed by servants, which is to lie boldly, and tell their masters all they don't know, as well as all they do. She concluded her discourse with an exhortation to him to be patient, giving him hopes that his things might be restored to him when he least expected it.

"And perhaps never," replies Don Marcos very discreetly ; "there is little likelihood that a traitress, who has robbed me of my goods, and is gone off with them, will ever return to restore them to me."

He afterwards told Marcella all that had befallen him with Isidore ever since she had been gone. "Is it possible she should have so little conscience with her ? " says that wheedling devil Marcella. "Ah! dear master, it was not without good reason I pitied your hard usage, but I durst not say anything to you of it : for that very evening you were robbed, taking the boldness to tell my mistress that she ought not to touch your gold chain, she beat me black and blue, God knows, and called me all the whores in the world."

"But thus the case happened," says Don Marcos, fetching a deep sigh ; "and the worst of it is, I see no remedy to help me."

"Hold a little," cries Marcella interrupting him, "I know a cunning man, a friend of mine, who will shortly be my husband, I trust in heaven, and he will tell you where you may find these people as plainly as if he saw them He's an admirable man, that's certain, and can make the devil fetch and carry for him like a spaniel."

The credulous Don Marcos conjured her to let him see
this son of art. Marcella promised him to do it, and told
him she would certainly meet him next day in that very
place. Don Marcos came accordingly, nor was Marcella
forgetful of her appointment, telling our unfortunate spark
that the magician she had spoke to him about, had already
begun his operations to help him to his stolen goods, but
that he wanted a certain quantity of amber, musk, and
other perfumes to make a fumigation for the demons
whom he intended to invoke, who were all of the first
order, and of the best families in hell. Don Marcos, without deliberating farther on the matter, carries Marcella to
a perfumer's shop, buys as much of those scents as she told
him would be necessary, nay, and presented her besides
with some essences and oils she begged of him, so much
did he fancy himself obliged to her for helping him to a
magician. The wicked Marcella carried him to a house
of a very scurvy aspect, where in a low room, or rather a
nasty dog-hole, he was received by a man in a cassock,
whose beard reached down to his girdle, and who accosted
him with a world of gravity.

This villainous impostor, on whom Don Marcos looked
with a great deal of respect and fear, two qualities that
generally go together, lighted two black-wax tapers, and
gave them to the affrighted Don Marcos to hold one in
each hand. He ordered him to sit down upon a little low
stool, and exhorted him, but his exhortations came too
late, not to be afraid. After this, he asked him several
questions concerning his age, his way of living, and about
the goods that were stolen from him ; and having looked a
while in a mirror, and read half a score lines in a book, he
told Don Marcos, who was ready to expire with fear, that
he very well knew where his things were, and described
them one after another so exactly to him, that Don Marcos
let the candles drop to go hug and embrace him. The
serious magician blamed him extremely for his impatience,

and told him the operations of his infallible art demanded
a great deal of circumspection and care; giving him to
understand, that for actions less hardy and indiscreet the
demons had sorely buffeted, nay, sometimes strangled
people.

At these words Don Marcos looked as pale as a criminal
after sentence, and taking the candles again in his hands,
sat down on his stool as before. The conjurer then called
for his perfumes that Don Marcos had bought, and which
the perfidious Marcella immediately gave to him. Hitherto
she had been a spectatress of the ceremony, but now he
commanded her to quit the room, because, says he, the
devils don't like the company of women. Marcella at her
going out made a profound reverence, and the magician
drawing near a little pan of coals, made as if he threw
Don Marcos's perfumes upon the lighted charcoal, but
indeed cast a noisome composition into it, which raised so
thick and dismal a smoke that the magician, who im-
prudently leaned over the pan, had like to have been
suffocated by it. He coughed several times to expectorate
the steams he had sucked in, and that with so much
violence, that his long venerable beard, which was not of
the growth of his chin, and had been ill-fastened on, fell
down, and discovered him to be the pernicious Gamara.
Don Marcos caught hold of him by the throat and gripped
and squeezed him like any Hercules, crying out at the
same time "thief, thief," in a shrill, terrible voice. As it
happened, a magistrate was going down the street at that
time, who entered the house, from whence such dismal
cries proceeded that alarmed all the neighbourhood ; for
you must know, Gamara, whom Don Marcos held all this
while by the throat, roared out as loud as he could for the
heart of him. The first person the officers seized was
Marcella, and after breaking open the door of this magical
apartment, found Don Marcos and Gamara very lovingly
hugging and tugging one another about the room. The

L 2

provost knew Gamara at first sight, whom he had been
hunting after a good while, and had ordered to be apprehended for a pick-pocket, a cock-bawd, and above all, a
notorious thief. He hurried him away to prison together
with Don Marcos and Marcella, took an inventory of all
the goods in the house, and saw them carefully locked up.
Don Marcos was enlarged, upon his master's security, that
he should appear next day. Accordingly he came as
evidence against Gamara and Marcella, who were plainly
convicted of having robbed him of his goods, that were
found safe and untouched among several other things that
had been set down in the inventory. Some of these
Gamara had stolen, and the rest were pawned to him, for he
was a Jew by religion, and consequently an usurer by
profession. When he was apprehended he was just upon
marrying Marcella, who was to have brought him by way
of portion, besides the things she had stolen from Don
Marcos, a dexterity in stealing little inferior to his, a pliant
wit, capable of learning anything that could be shown her ;
nay, even of surpassing it : and lastly, a wholesome, juicy
young carcass, considering it had been so often bought and
sold, and had endured so many heavy shocks and fatigues
in the mansions of fornication. The case appeared so
plain on Don Marcos's side, who was supported by the
credit of his master, that he had his goods immediately
restored him. Gamara was sent to the galleys for the
remainder of his life ; Marcella was soundly whipped and
banished ; and moreover, all people thought that both the
Jew and his wife elect had been too favourably dealt by.

As for Don Marcos, he was not so well pleased with
having his things again and being revenged on Gamara
and Marcella, as vexed that this great impostor did not
prove a magician. The loss of his ten thousand crowns
had almost turned his brain. He went every day to
inquire at all the inns in Madrid after those darlings of
his, and at last met with two muleteers lately returned

from Barcelona, who told him that about four or five days'
journey from Madrid they had met a cart upon the road
laden with goods, with two women and a man riding
behind, and that they had been forced to make a halt at
an inn by reason that two of the fellow's mules had been
killed with being over-laboured. They described this man
and the two women so well to him, and the marks they
gave them so fitted Isidore, Inez, and Augustinet, that
without farther deliberation he disguised himself in the
habit of a pilgrim, and having obtained from his master
letters of recommendation to the viceroy of Catalonia, and
from the bench of justice a decree for his fugitive wife, he
took the road towards Barcelona, sometimes beating it
upon the hoof, sometimes on horseback, and arrived there
in a few days. He went towards the harbour to take a
lodging there, where the first thing that greeted his sight
were his own coffers, that were carrying to a boat, with
Augustinet, Isidore, and Inez attending them, which was
to convey them to the vessel that waited for them in the
road, wherein they designed to embark for Naples. Don
Marcos followed his enemies, and threw himself like a lion
into the long-boat. They did not know him by reason of
his huge flapping pilgrim's hat, that eclipsed his little
countenance, but took him to be some pilgrim going to
Loretto, as did the seamen to be one of Augustinet's
company. Don Marcos was in the strangest perplexity of
mind imaginable, not so much to think what would become
of him, as of his dear, dear trunks. All this while the
long-boat made the best of her way to the merchantman,
and sailed so swift, that Don Marcos being puzzled with
what his brains were hammering, found himself directly
under the vessel, when he thought himself at a great
distance from it. The sailors now began to heave up the
trunks, which awakened Don Marcos out of his contemplations, who always kept his eye upon the dearest of his
trunks, wherein his money was lodged. A seaman at last

came to take up this very individual trunk, and began to fasten it with a thick-cord that was let down from the vessel in a pulley. Now it was that Don Marcos forgot himself, for he saw his trunk tied up just by him, and did not stir ; but at last seeing it mount in the air, he caught hold of it with both hands by one of the iron rings that served to lift it from the ground, being resolved not to part with it. And perhaps he had accomplished his ends, for what will not a covetous wretch do to preserve his pelf? had not by ill fortune this trunk parted from the rest, and falling plumb upon the head of this unlucky gentleman, who for all that would not quit his hold, beat him down to the bottom of the sea, or if you please to the regions of Erebus. Isidore, Inez, and Augustinet knew him just at the very minute he sunk with the dear trunk, the loss of which troubled them infinitely more than any apprehensions they had from the revengeful Don Marcos. Augustinet, enraged at the loss of his money, and not being able to master his passion, struck the seaman, who had tied the trunks so carelessly, with all his force. The tar, in requital, gave him a heartier blow, which threw him headlong into the sea. As he fell over-board he took the unfortunate Isidore with him, who held by nothing, and so accompanied her beloved Augustinet, who against his inclination accompanied Don Marcos. Inez embarked in the vessel with the rest of the goods, which she spent in a short time after at Naples, and when she had for a long while exercised the laudable profession of a whore there, went off like one, that is to say, died in a hospital.

THE USELESS PRECAUTION.

A GENTLEMAN of Granada, whose true name I don't think fit to discover, but will call him Don Pedro de Castile, Arragon, Toledo, or what you please, courteous reader, since after all one name costs a man no more than another. For which reason perhaps the Spaniards, not content with their own names, bestow upon themselves the most magnificent ones they can think of, and sometimes tack two or three together, that are as long as a Welsh pedigree. But to quit this digression, the above-mentioned Don Pedro, at the age of twenty, found himself without either father or mother, and moreover exceeding rich; which circumstances, when they meet in the same person, very often help to spoil him, if he be born with no great stock of brains; but if otherwise, put him in a capacity of making what figure he pleases. During the year of mourning, he discreetly abstained from most of those diversions to which young gentlemen of his age are addicted, and wholly employed his time in taking an exact survey of his estate and settling his affairs. He was well made as to his person, had abundance of wit, and behaving himself, young as he was, with the prudence and circumspection of an old man, there was not a fortune in all Granada which he might not justly pretend to, nor a

father that thought so well of his daughter but would be
glad with all his heart to accept him for a son-in-law.

Among several handsome ladies, who at that time
disputed the empire of hearts in that city, there was one
that had charms enough to conquer that of Don Pedro.
Her name was Seraphina, beautiful as an angel, young,
rich, and of a good family ; and although her fortune was
not altogether so great as that of Don Pedro, yet everything considered, there was no such mighty difference
between them. He did not question but that at the first
proposal of marriage he made to her parents he should
find them ready to comply with him ; however, he rather
chose to owe his success to his merit, and resolved to court
her in the gallantest way, that he might make himself
master of her affections before he was so of her person.
His design was generous and noble, if fortune, that often
delights to break the measures of the wisest politicians,
had not raised him a rival, who had already taken
possession of the town he designed to invest before he had
so much as made his approaches. 'Tis to no purpose to
tell you his name, but he was very near Don Pedro's age,
and perhaps was as handsome, but all historians agree he
was much more beloved. Don Pedro was soon sensible he
had a competitor to remove, but this did not much alarm
him, knowing few were able to dispute estates with him.
He gave concerts of music in his mistress's street, while
his happy rival had the pleasure to hear them in her
chamber, and perhaps was revelling in her arms, while our
poor lover was cooling his heels, and making melancholy
reflections below.

At last Don Pedro was weary of throwing away so much
powder in the mines, that is to say, of making all this
bustle and courtship without advancing his affairs. However, his love did not slacken upon his ill success, but made
him so impatient, that he thought fit to lay aside his first
design of winning his mistress's heart before he demanded

her of her friends. In short, he asked their consent, which they granted him upon the spot, without deliberating farther on the matter, being extremely pleased to be asked that which they so earnestly desired, and indeed could hardly hope for. They acquainted Seraphina with the good fortune was offered her, and prepared her to give Don Pedro a kind reception, in order to marry him in a short time. She was troubled at this news, that ought to have given her all the satisfaction in the world ; and not being able to conceal her surprise from them, dissembled the occasion of it, pretending it grieved her to part from persons so dear to her as they were. She managed this point so dexterously, that they wept out of mere tenderness, and much commended the sweetness of her temper. She conjured them to put off her marriage for four or five months, representing to them that she had been a long time indisposed, as her looks sufficiently discovered, and that by her good-will she would not marry till she was perfectly rid of her illness, that so she might come more agreeable to her husband's bed, and not give him any occasion to be disgusted at the beginning of their marriage ; and consequently to repent of his choice. 'Tis true indeed, she had looked somewhat sickly of late, which made her friends well enough satisfied with her request, and they took care to acquaint Don Pedro with it ; who, for his part, was so far from taking it ill, that he liked her the better for giving so good a proof of her discretion. In the meantime the articles of marriage were proposed, examined, and agreed on.

However, Don Pedro did not think himself excused from any of his usual gallantries, which every man is obliged to observe that courts his mistress in the common forms. He entertained her often with letters, and did not miss a day to write to her. She returned him such answers as were at least very civil, if not altogether so passionate as his own ; but she would receive none of his visits

in the day-time, excusing herself upon her indisposition, and
at night appeared very rarely at the window, which made
Don Pedro exceedingly to admire her reserved temper.
He thought too well of his own merit to doubt the success
of his courtship, and questioned not to be beloved by his
mistress when she came to know him better, although she
should have even an aversion for him, now he was a
stranger to her.   Hitherto his affairs went well enough, but
at last it so happened that he could not get a sight of his
mistress for four or five days following.   He was extremely
afflicted at it, or at least pretended to be so.   He composed
several verses upon the occasion, I mean, either hired or
bought them, and had them sung under her window.

But though he omitted nothing that the most zealous
lover could practise, yet all the favour he could obtain was
only to speak with her maid, who informed him her lady was
more indisposed than ever.   Upon this his poetic faculty
was strangely perplexed, or at least the gentleman poet
whom he employed ; for upon the strictest search I find
versifying was never his talent.   He caused an air to be
made upon Aminta's being sick, or Phyllis, or Chloris, no
matter whether ; and besides his offensive and defensive
arms, taking a guitar with him, which we must suppose to
be the best in the whole city ; he walked furiously in
this equipage towards his mistress's quarters, either to make
her weep out of pure compassion, or else to set all the dogs
in the neighbourhood a barking, in order to complete the
concert.   Now any one, I believe, would say, that 'twas a
hundred to one but our gentleman must do one of the two
or perhaps both ; but alas! he did neither.   Within fifty
paces of the thrice happy mansion of his divinity he saw
the door open, and a woman go out, who had much of the
air and shape of his invisible angel.   He could not imagine
why a woman alone, and so late at night, should so
resolutely turn up into a large spacious house, lately
destroyed by fire.   To inform himself better, he walked

round the ruins, which one might enter at several places,
that he might get nearer the person whom he dogged. He
believed this might be his mistress, who had made an
assignation with his rival to meet her in this strange place,
not daring to do it at home, and not thinking fit to
communicate this business to a third person, which it so
much concerned her to keep secret ; he therefore resolved,
within himself, that in case what now he only suspected
happened to prove true, he would kill his rival upon the
spot, and revenge himself upon Seraphina, by giving her
the most opprobrious language he could think of. Being
thus resolved, he crept along as softly as he could, till he
came to a place whence he could plainly see her ; for it was
she, sitting upon the ground, groaning so piteously, as if she
was going to give up the ghost, and, in short, after most
severe pangs, delivered of a small squalling creature, which
we may suppose did not give her altogether so much pain in
the begetting. She was no sooner safely delivered, but her
courage giving her strength enough, she returned the same
way she came, without troubling her head what would
become of the poor brat that she had brought into the
world.

I will leave you to judge how great Don Pedro's surprise
was. He now found out the true reason of his mistress's
indisposition ; his head almost turned round to think what
a precipice he had escaped, and he thanked heaven most
devoutly for preserving him from the danger ; but being
generous in his temper, he scorned to revenge himself upon
the faithless Seraphina by exposing the honour of her
family ; neither in his just resentment would he suffer the
innocent babe to perish, which he saw lying at his feet
exposed to the first dog that had the luck to find it. He
wrapped it up in his cloak for want of something else, and
making all the haste he could, called upon a discreet woman
of his acquaintance, to whom he recommended the care of
the child, putting it at the same time into her hands, and

giving her money to buy it all sorts of necessaries. This discreet woman finding herself nobly paid, acquitted her charge very well. Next day the infant had a nurse, was baptized, and named Laura, for you must know it was a female.

In the meantime Don Pedro went to a relation of his in whom he mightily confided, and told her he had changed his design of marrying to that of travelling. He desired her to manage his estate for him in his absence, and to receive into her house an infant, which he said belonged to him, to spare nothing in her education, and for certain reasons, which he would acquaint her with at some other time, to send her to a convent as soon as she was three years old ; and above all, to take particular care that she should know as little as might be of the affairs of the world. He furnished her with necessary instruments to look after his estate, provided himself with money and jewels, took a faithful and trusty servant ; but before his departure from Granada writ a letter to Seraphina. She received it just at the time she had acquainted her friends that her illness should retard her marriage no longer. But Don Pedro's letter, which gave her to understand he knew what had so lately befallen her, put other thoughts into her head. She devoted herself to a religious life, and soon after retired to a convent, with full resolution never to stir thence, and could not be induced to alter her mind by all the entreaties and tears of her parents, who used all the arguments they could think of to dissuade her from this resolution ; which appeared so much the stranger to them, as they could not divine the occasion of it.

Let us leave them to weep for their daughter's turning nun, who on her part wept heartily for her sins. Let us likewise leave her little daughter Laura to grow in bulk and beauty, and return to meet Don Pedro on the road to Seville, who could not drive this last adventure out of his head, and was now as much disgusted at marriage as once he was desirous to taste the pleasures of it. He is afraid of all women ; and not considering there are both good and bad of that as well as of his own sex, he concluded within himself that a wise man ought to be diffident of all women, and particularly of the witty more than the foolish ; being, it seems, of the opinion of those worthy gentlemen, who think a woman knows more than comes to her share if she knows a jot more than stewing prunes, preserving fruits, dressing her husband's dinner, or mending his stockings.

Tainted with these heretical doctrines he arrived at Seville, and went directly to the house of Don Juan the Lord knows what, a man of wealth and quality, who was his relation and friend, and would not suffer him to lodge anywhere else but with him. The magnificence of Seville gave him a desire to make a longer stay there than he at first designed ; and his cousin Don Juan, to make his stay more agreeable to him, showed him all the most remarkable curiosities of that place. One day as they were riding on horseback through one of the principal streets of the city, they saw in a coach, that was driving towards a stately house, a young lady in a widow's habit, so beautiful and charming, that Don Pedro was exceedingly surprised, and set his cousin a laughing by the many vehement exclamations and oaths he made, that he had never seen anything so lovely in his life. This angel of a widow restored the whole female sex to his good opinion, whom the unhappy Seraphina had rendered odious to him. He desired Don Juan to go back through the same street, and frankly owned that he wanted little of being wounded to the heart by her. " Your business is done," replies the other, " and I am very much mistaken if the little god has not shot his arrow so deep, that there is no plucking it out but heart and all must come together."

" Alas ! " says the amorous Don Pedro, " I will conceal nothing from you. How happy should I reckon myself if I could pass my days with so charming a lady ! "

"You must go this way then," replied Don Juan, "and travelling so fast as you do, you may in a few minutes arrive at the place, where you expect to find so much happiness. Not but that such an enterprise," continued he, "will give you difficulty enough. Elvira is a woman of quality, and very rich ; her beauty is such as you have beheld it, neither is her virtue any ways inferior. During the two years of her widowhood, the best matches in Andalusia have not given her the least inclination to change her condition ; but a man so well made as yourself may perhaps succeed where others have failed. She is related to my wife, and sometimes I make her a visit. If you please, I will propose your design to her, and I have good hopes to succeed in my negotiation, since I now see her in her balcony, which is no small favour, let me tell you, in so nice and reserved a lady. She might have shut her lattices and windows, and so have balked our expectation."

These words were no sooner out of his mouth, but our two cavaliers made each a reverence after the Spanish mode, which gave them no little trouble before they could recover themselves. Especially Don Pedro made his so profoundly low, and with that contortion of his body, that he had like to have tumbled off his horse. The lady in the balcony returned them a handsome courtesy, upon which Don Pedro and his companion bowed again.

"And when the bright charmer did leave the balcony,
One spurred on his horse, t'other gaped like a Tony."

"Alas! my dear cousin," says Don Pedro to Don Juan, "what probability is their that a stranger can be able to gain that heart, which has defended itself against all the men of quality and merit in Seville. However," continues he, "since my despair would otherwise give me my death's wound, I had as good receive it from her refusal and contempt. Therefore let me conjure you to speak to her as soon as you can, and don't so much enlarge upon my estate and quality as upon the violence of my passion."

Don Pedro could not talk of anything but his love, and Don Juan was sensible he could not oblige him more effectually than by taking the first opportunity to make this overture to Elvira. He accordingly did so and not without success. The charming widow received the proposal he made for his friend so well, that she confessed she did not dislike him. But withal she acquainted him, that having obliged herself by vow to stay three full years from the death of her first husband before she took a second, nothing in the world should prevail with her to break it. She added, that because she had resolved to pay this respect to the memory of her late spouse, she had hitherto refused all the offers that had been made her, but that if Don Pedro had courage and constancy enough to serve her a whole year, in which time they might know one another's tempers much better, she gave him her word to choose no other husband.

Don Juan came to give Don Pedro an account of his negotiations, and made him the most satisfied as well as most passionate of all men breathing. He was not in the least deterred by the long time he was to stay, and resolved to employ it in all the refined gallantry of a nice lover. He bought him a fine coach and horses, made his house and liveries as sumptuous as might be, set all the embroiderers and tailors of Seville at work, and the musicians into the bargain. He offered to regale Elvira, but she would not suffer it. Her servants were nothing near so difficult, for they accepted his presents as heartily as he gave them. In a short time he was more master of Elvira's domestics than she herself, whom her damsels persuaded to appear in the balcony, even when she had no mind to it, and that as often as Don Pedro exerted his lungs in the street, for I have been told he sang to admiration. Don Pedro had now spent six tedious months in

courting Elvira, without being able to obtain a private conversation with her all the while, which daily increased his
esteem and love for her. At last, by dint of prayers and
presents, a damsel bolder than the rest, or rather more
covetous, promised to introduce him one night into her
mistress's apartment, and place him in a corner, where he
might see her undress before she went to bed, take two or
three turns in her shift to cool herself, and sing and play
upon her lute, which she did to a miracle.

Don Pedro gave this trusty maid a better reward than he
promised her ; and when night came, our Granada adventurer, following the abigail's instruction, slipped into
Elvira's house, stole up to her apartment, and there from
a gallery, which was over against the chamber door, saw
her lying upon a couch reading a book of devotion, whether
with much attention is more than I am able to tell you, all
the while her maids undressed her. She had only a light
gown on, and was ready to go to bed, when Don Pedro's
pensionary damsel, who designed to give him as much
reason to be satisfied with her as she was with him
entreated her mistress to sing. Her companions joined in
the same petition ; but Elvira denied them a good while,
telling them she was very melancholy, nay, and assuring
them she had occasion to be so. But the damsel, whom
Don Pedro's presents had gained, putting a lute into her
mistress's hand, Elvira was so complaisant as to sing,
which she did in so charming and graceful a manner, that
Don Pedro was within an ace of throwing himself at her
heavenly feet, and acting there the ravished lover. The
song was soon over, and then she went to bed. The maids
retired to their own apartments, and Don Pedro, who
made the best of his way towards the street, was strangely
surprised to find the great gate locked. He had nothing
now left to do but to stay there till day, which would soon
appear. He sat upon the side of a well, which was in a
corner of the court, strangely perplexed lest he should be

discovered, and incur his mistress's displeasure for so bold an attempt. He had not been here long, but he made a thousand attempts, and wished as often, to no purpose, that he was safe in the street, when he heard a door open in Elvira's apartment. He immediately turned his head towards the place whence the noise came, and was strangely surprised to see the beautiful widow come into the court, whom he thought to be fast asleep. By the light of a wax-taper she carried in a little silver candle-stick, he saw her nightdress was nicely adjusted, her breasts open and unguarded, a fine necklace of pearl about her neck, and that over her smock, which had more lace than linen about it, she wore nothing but a rich simarre. She carried in her hand a great phial full of jelly, comfits, and conserves ; and in this surprising equipage appeared so charming, that Don Pedro had like to have preferred the pleasure of discovering himself to her, to all the ill effects which so bold a presumption might have drawn upon him. But he was wise in his love, and hid himself behind the well, though he kept his eyes upon his mistress all the while, flattering himself sometimes that it was he she came to look for. She walked directly towards the stable ; Don Pedro followed her at some distance, and saw her go into a little room.

At first he was of opinion his pious and charitable mistress went to visit one of her domestics that was sick there, though without doing any wrong to her charity she might have left that affair to any of her women. He crept behind a horse that stood not far from the chamber-door, and from thence observing his dear widow, saw her put the candle-stick and glass phial, and in short all she carried in her ivory hands, upon a little table. In a sorry bed, which in a manner took up all the room, he beheld a sick negro, who seemed to be above thirty years old, but so deformed and ghastly, that he was frightened at the sight of him. His face was as meagre as that of a skeleton, and the poor fellow had much difficulty to fetch his breath.

Don Pedro admired the unparalleled goodness of the beautiful Elvira, who took off all the negro's blankets, and having made his bed, sat down by the sick wretch, and put her hand upon his forehead, that was all over in a cold sweat. The negro cast a dismal look upon the charitable angel that came to comfort him, and seemed to pity him with her eyes brimful of tears. Don Pedro could not tell what to think of so unexampled a strain of charity, and after he had first admired it, began to alter his opinion, and concluded it was carried too far. But as yet he had seen nothing. The charming widow first broke silence, and weeping at such a rate as if it were to be her last, asked the black how he found himself.

"My dear Antonio," says she to him, in a voice interrupted with frequent sobs, "art thou then resolved to die, and wilt thou make me die too for company? Thou dost not speak to me, my life, my jewel. Take courage, if thou wouldst have me live, and eat a little of this jelly for my sake. Thou wilt not so much as afford me one kind look, cruel creature; me, I say, that love thee, me that adore thee. Kiss me, my dear angel, kiss me, and get well, if thou wouldst not have me attend thee in thy death, after I have so passionately loved thee during thy life." As she spoke these tender words, she joined her angel face to the diabolical visage of the Moor, which she moistened with her tears. I fancy any man that had seen so odd a sight would have presently thought he had seen an angel caress a devil. As for Don Pedro, he now began to think the beautiful Elvira as ugly as her negro; who at last casting his eyes upon his importunate lover, whom he scarce vouchsafed to look upon before, and with his lean bony hand turning away her face from his, thus spoke to her in a low feeble tone:

"What would you have me to do, madam? Will you not let me die in quiet? Is it not enough that you have brought me to the condition I am in, but must you force

me, now I am just dying, to throw away the little snuff of
life that is left me, to satisfy your libidinous appetite ? Take
a husband, and expect no more drudgery from me. I will
see you no more, nor eat anything you have brought me,
but am resolved to die, since I am good for nothing else."
When he had said this, he sunk down in his bed, and the
unfortunate Elvira could not draw the least word from
him in answer to all the tender things she spoke ; whether
he was already dead, or refused to speak to one whom he
believed the cause of his death, I can't determine. Elvira
wept like a church spout when it rains, and afflicted at the
sad condition wherein she left her beloved negro, but much
more at his unkindness, took back with her everything she
had brought, and walked towards her chamber, though with
so sorrowful and sad an air, that it was her great misfortune
her future cuckold did not see her in that pickle. In the
meantime Don Pedro hid himself in the obscurest part of
stable, so confounded, that he was not half a quarter so
much when he was witness of Seraphina's happy delivery.
He saw this monstrous hypocrite go back the same way
she came, afflicting herself like any widow at the funeral of
her dear husband ; and some time after hearing the great
gate open, he got into the street, not at all caring whether
he was seen or not, since he thought it not worth his while
to have any regard for such a woman's reputation as
Elvira's. However he treated her like a gentleman of
honour, and did not discover what he had seen to his friend.
The next day he happened to pass by Elvira's gate at the
very instant the Moor was carried out to be buried. Her
women told him their mistress was sick ; and for four or
five days following, as he passed to and fro before her
windows, she was not to be seen there according to her
custom, so inconsolable had the death of her lovely African
made her. Don Pedro was mighty desirous to know how
she fared. One day as he was discoursing with Don Juan,
one of Elvira's slaves delivered him a letter from his

mistress. He opened it with impatience, and read what follows.

THE LETTER.

"Two persons, who are minded to marry, don't need a third to put them in mind on't. You would persuade me you don't dislike me; and I must own, you please me well enough to grant you this moment what I did not promise you till the year was ended. You may make yourself, as soon as you please, master of my person and estate; and I request you to believe, that although I cannot deliberately embark in such an affair as this, yet your merit and my love will render it easy to me, and make me break through all difficulties whatsoever.

"ELVIRA."

Don Pedro read over this letter twice or thrice, and could hardly believe he was awake. He bethought himself that this was the second time he had run the danger of being married as ill as any man in Spain, and thanked heaven with all his heart for having delivered him from two such imminent misfortunes, by discovering to him two secrets of so great importance. As the negro's death had put Elvira upon this sudden resolution to be married, Don Pedro as suddenly resolved to get out of her sight as soon as he could. He told Don Juan that it nearly concerned his life and honour to leave Seville within an hour, and that he would only take one servant with him, that he had brought from Granada; he desired him to sell his coach and horses, and to pay his servants with the money, and conjured him not to ask the reason of so sudden an alteration and a journey so hurried, promising to write to him the very first town he stopped at. He writ to Elvira while they went to hire two mules for him; he gave his letter to the slave, and when the mules came, took the road to Madrid; being confirmed more than ever in his first opinion, and resolving to stand upon his guard against all witty women, nay, even to detest them. While he jogged gently on, full of these virtuous resolutions, Elvira opened his letter and read the following lines.

THE LETTER.

"As violently in love as I am with you, yet I always prefer the care of preserving your honour to the pleasure of possessing you. Thus you could not but observe with what discretion I always managed my gallantry. I am somewhat scrupulous in my own nature, and therefore cannot in conscience ask you to marry me so soon, since you are a widow of but a day's standing. You owe more than that comes to, madam, to the memory of the poor negro defunct, and you cannot take less than a year to lament the loss of a person who did you so considerable services. In the meanwhile, you and I shall have time enough to consider what we have to do.

"DON PEDRO."

Elvira had like to have run distracted when she read this letter, and it touched her more to the quick than even the loss of her Guinea lover had done ; but considering that Don Pedro had left Seville, and another gallant, that had all the qualifications to please her, had offered at the same time to marry her, she took him to supply the negro's room. Not but that she could have found negroes enough to have done her business, but somebody had told her there was a difference in negroes, as well as other folks, and that everything is not the devil, though it be black. In the meantime Don Pedro and his trusty mule got to Madrid, where he went immediately to an uncle's house, who received him very courteously. This uncle of his was a rich cavalier, that had an only son, that was betrothed to a young cousin that was an only daughter likewise and who being but ten years old, passed her time in a convent, till she came to be of age to marry him. His name was Don Rodriguez, and who possessed all the good qualities that can make a man amiable. Don Pedro entered into a stricter league of friendship with him than men usually do with relations, though they love them never so well ; for they are not always our relations whom we love best. Don Rodriguez seemed to be disturbed in his mind, and Don Pedro perceiving it, related all his adventures to him, that he might oblige him by this confidence to communicate his to him, and if he had any occasion for his service, to let him see that he was much more his friend than his relation. After this, he told him he had observed that somewhat sat uneasy upon him, and therefore begged him to let him know what it was ; otherwise he must believe his friendship was not so hearty as his. Don Rodriguez desired nothing more, hoping to receive some relief in his inquietude when he had once communicated it. He therefore acquaints Don Pedro that he was passionately in love with a damsel of Madrid, who was promised to a kinsman, whom she expected every hour from the Indies, but had never seen him, like as he was engaged to a cousin, and waited till she was of age, of whom he had but little knowledge.

"This conformity of adventures," said he to Don Pedro, "has very much contributed to increase the affection we have for one another, although at the same time it keeps us both in our duty whenever our passion advises us to prefer our satisfaction to those engagements, wherein the interests of our families have linked us. Hitherto my love has made as fair a progress as I could wish, though I have not as yet been able to compass my desires, which she puts off till her husband's arrival, when her marriage may secure both of us from any ill consequences that may follow upon an assignation, when we may probably do something more than discourse and talk. I will say nothing to you of the beauty of Virginia, since it is impossible to say too much of it, and because I should be apt to say so much of it that you would not believe me. However, this I am certain of, that when you have seen her and her cousin Violante, who lives with her, you will readily own, that all Spain cannot show anything more beautiful than this incomparable pair ; and when you have conversed a few moments with them, I will leave you to tell me whether you ever saw wittier women in your life."

" 'Tis this that makes me pity you," says Don Pedro to him.

" And why so ? " replied Don Rodriguez.

" Because a woman of wit," cries he, " will most infallibly jilt you either sooner or later. You cannot but know," continues he, " by the recital I have made you of my own adventures, what has happened to myself ; and I seriously protest to you, that if I could hope to find woman as foolish as I know some of them are witty, I would employ all arts to gain her, and prefer her even to wisdom itself, if she would but choose me for her gallant."

" You are much in the wrong," replies Don Rodriguez, " for I never met a man of tolerable sense in my life but was soon weary of a woman's company if she was a fool. Indeed 'tis not reasonable, that whilst our eyes, our hands, and in short all our body finds something to divert it, our soul, which is the noblest part of the composition, should be forced to endure a tiresome insipid conversation, as that of all persons must certainly be that have no wit to support it."

" Let us not carry this dispute as far as it will go," cries Don Pedro to him, "for a man may say too many things upon so copious a subject. Only let me see this miracle of a woman and her cousin as soon as you can, that if I don't dislike her, I may have something to amuse myself with during my stay in Madrid."

" I don't believe it will be worth your while," cries Rodriguez.

" And why so ? " replies Don Pedro.

" Because," says the other, " she is the only woman in the world that is least a fool."

" I will however suit myself to the time," says Don Pedro.

" To tell you the truth," answers Don Rodriguez, " I don't know after what manner Madam Virginia will receive us. For these eight days last past she has used me most unmercifully ; she has sent back all my letters without so much as opening them, and in short has given me to understand that she would never admit a visit from me, by reason she saw me some time ago talking with a young lady at church, in whose company she had seen me the same day at the playhouse ; and this is the reason why I have been of late so melancholy."

" It signifies nothing," says Don Pedro ; " let us go and see them, and take my word for it, you'll sooner reconcile matters by justifying yourself to her face, than by writing her a cart-load of whining letters."

Thus our two gentleman-cousins went to visit the two lady-cousins, and the beautiful Virginia gave Don Rodriguez leave to clear himself, which was easily done. Don Pedro thought both of them to be the handsomest women he had ever seen, not excepting either the imprudent Seraphina or the hypocritical Elvira. Violante, who had dressed herself that day in her finest clothes, because she was to sit for her picture, charmed Don Pedro so effectually, that he immediately broke the vow he had made, never to love anyone but a fool. This did not displease Violante, but he said so many pretty engaging things to her upon the occasion of her picture, that she was no less satisfied with his wit than his gallantry ; and here I am obliged to make a short digression, to acquaint those that knew it not before, that your mighty retailers of compliments and fine expressions generally deal in whipped cream, and are justly accused of bombast by men of wit and sense. If this small advice had been considered by the public, they would have found

it no less useful than a receipt against flies in the summer,
and stinking breaths all the year round. Don Pedro, who
had solemnly sworn by his Maker that he would marry
none but a fool, was now fully convinced that oaths made
by gamesters and lovers signified just nothing. He was
so ravished with Violante's wit, no less than her beauty,
that finding he could obtain no other favours from her
than such as she might grant without any prejudice to
her honour, he resolved to marry her, if she did not forbid the banns. He frequently gave her occasion to explain
her mind upon this article, but either she did not, or
would not understand him ; whether it was because she
loved her liberty, or had an aversion to matrimony, I
don't tell you.

Thus all things went smoothly on between these four
young lovers, and they only waited for the critical minute
to consummate. One day, when these two young sparks
had spruced themselves up like Castor and Pollux, and
made no question to be masters at least of all the out-
works they attacked, a servant maid, whose appearance
boded worse luck than that of an owl, came to acquaint
the two cousins that the Indian husband of the fair
Castilian was arrived at Madrid, without so much as
sending her advice of his coming from Seville, where he
landed. The two cousins concluded from hence that he
had a mind to surprise them, and therefore desired our
lovers to fortify themselves with patience, till such time as
Virginia had found out the humour of her Indian spark ;
and in the meantime requested that they would not only
forbear to visit them, but even to walk before their windows,
till they received new orders. Thus all their tricking up
and powdering that morning was thrown away, and the
next two days they had no more mind to dress than a
criminal condemned to be hanged. They learnt, among
other news of the town, that the Indian and Virginia were
married in private, that he was very jealous in his temper,

that he was a man of experience, having seen forty years ; and in fine, that he had so ordered his family, and kept so strict a watch over all Virginia's actions, that her gallants, if she had any, must never expect to see her so much as at her window.

The new orders, which had been promised, did not come, and they were impatient with expecting them.　They daily walked through the street where their mistresses lived, and took their usual turns before the house, without seeing any but unknown faces go in or out, and without being able to meet with the least man or maidservant of their acquaintance.　They saw the husband go into his house one day, accompanied by his brother, who was handsome and well made, and so young, that he was still at the college.　This increased their ill humour.　They went out early in the morning, and came not home till it was very late, and lost both their time and their labour.　At last, upon a certain holiday, they saw Violante's maid going to mass by break of day ; they stopped her at the church-porch, and by the never-failing rhetoric of money, Don Rodriguez persuaded her to carry the following billet to her mistress :

" Your forgetting me does not disoblige me, more than my jealousy torments me, since it is without remedy, now you are under the government of a husband.　However, you are not totally freed as yet from my importunities, although you have discarded me from your remembrance.　The last favour I have to beg of you, is to inform me whether I have any reason still to hope, or whether I must prepare to die."

They followed Violante's maid at a distance.　She delivered the letter according to her promise, and making a sign to them to draw near, dropped the following answer from the window into the street :

" A jealous man so newly married is never out of his wife's company, and watches all her motions.　He talks of taking a journey to Valladolid shortly without me ; I will then justify myself and pay my debts."

This billet, which they kissed a hundred times, by the same token that they strove which should out-do the other, gave them fresh encouragement, and made them easy enough for a few days. But at last, hearing no news from their cruel mistresses, they began after their old laudable custom to walk to and fro a hundred times a day before their windows ; they passed whole nights in the street, but could not see a soul stir out of the house, no more than if it had not been inhabited. One day, as these despairing lovers happened to be at church, they had the good luck to see our young bride come towards them. Don Rodriguez kneeled down by her, under the very nose of an old gentleman-usher that had squired her to church. He made his complaints to her in few words, she excused herself in like manner, and at last told him that her husband was not to go to Valladolid, although he daily talked of it ; that she was impatient to have a private conversation with him, and that she only knew one way of bringing it about, which wholly depended upon Don Pedro. " My husband," says she, " sleeps as sound as if he took opium every night, and we have not exchanged a word for these four or five days, by reason of a small quarrel between us, which is not yet made up. I had prevailed on my cousin Violante to take my place, but she's unhappily sick, and since none are privy to our amour but she and Don Pedro, for I would not for all the world have it communicated to more, you must even get him (if you think he loves you well enough to venture it) to supply her room, and go to bed to my husband.

" This attempt seems somewhat dangerous at first sight ; but if you consider my good man and I are at odds, as I have already told you we are, and that he does not easily wake, I don't question but it will succeed to our expectation, and this is all I can do for you." This happy love stratagem, which Don Rodriguez so earnestly desired to know, cooled him in a minute when he heard it. He not only doubted whether his cousin would take upon him to act this dangerous part, but likewise, whether he ought so much as to propose it to him. His mistress continued inflexible in her resolution, and as she took leave of him protested that in case the proposal she had made him was not well received, and executed after the manner she had directed, he had no more to hope from her; nay, she gave him full leave to banish her out of his remembrance, although at another time she would have as soon consented to her own death. Neither the time nor place would permit Don Rodriguez to talk any longer with his mistress. She went home, and Don Rodriguez repaired to his companion, who could not get a word out of him, so much confounded was he at the unhappy dilemma wherein he found himself, either to make so unreasonable a request to his friend, or else to live without enjoying that happiness which is ever more esteemed before possession than after. At length, shutting themselves up in their chamber, Don Rodriguez, after he had for a while refused to declare his grievance, opened the above-mentioned proposal to Don Pedro, gilding the pill as well as he could, to make it go down with him the better. At first Don Pedro thought he had a mind to banter him, but his cousin protesting the contrary with a very serious air, and confirming it by so many oaths, that he could no longer doubt of it, he must needs turn the thing into raillery, and therefore told him he was exceedingly obliged to his mistress for designing him such good fortune with so lovely a bed-fellow, and that it was undoubtedly the effect of Violante's gratitude, who, not being in a condition to reward his services, because she was sick, and being pressed to pay her debts, turned it over to her cousin's husband, with whom he should certainly pass the night very agreeably. He talked much to the same purpose, and jested a long while, sometimes well, and sometimes but indifferently. But Don

Rodriguez was not in a humour to be merry, for he appeared so dejected and melancholy to his cousin, that he heartily pitied him, and was afraid his despair would carry him to some dangerous resolution. Don Pedro was bold in his temper, a great lover of intrigues, and no man so ready as he to engage in any extravagant adventure ; he loved Don Rodriguez tenderly, insomuch that all this joined together made him resolve to supply the room of the beautiful Virginia, whatever her jealous husband might do to him. Being therefore fully determined upon the matter, he embraced his cousin, and put fresh life into him, and at the same time assured him he would hazard all, that he might enjoy his beloved mistress. "You will not, however," added he, "be so much obliged to me as you think. I consider it is an honourable action, whereby I pretend to get as much reputation as if I should signalize myself at a breach."

Word was sent Virginia that her proposal was accepted ; she appointed that very evening to put it in execution. The two cousins went to her house, and were introduced with as little noise as possible. Don Pedro was obliged by the fair lady of the enchanted castle to undress himself before her, being resolved that her orders should not be transgressed in the least. Don Pedro having nothing on now but his shirt, was conducted by her with all the care and circumspection imaginable to the fatal room, where opening the curtains, she softly put the bold champion between the sheets, who perhaps at that moment repented for having gone so far, and one may swear did not put himself into the middle of the bed. She went away and locked the chamber-door, which put Don Pedro into cruel apprehensions, while she repaired to Don Rodriguez, to whom I suppose she paid, like a woman of honour, all that she owed him, or at least as much as he demanded of her. In the meantime Don Pedro was in different circumstances from those of his cousin, who lay in the arms of his charming mistress, while our too charitable and adventurous friend feared nothing so much as the embraces of a detestable man, whom to his great sorrow he was like to find a very uncomfortable bed-fellow. He then began to consider, but it was somewhat of the latest, to what hazards his foolish rashness had carried him. He blamed himself, called himself fool a thousand times in his thoughts, and was sensible that to transgress thus against any husband was an unpardonable crime, though even he himself were to be judge of it.

These melancholy reflections were disturbed, and his just fears increased, by a huge villainous arm which his bed-fellow threw over him, drawing still nearer and nearer, pronouncing some few inarticulate words, as people are wont to do when they are asleep, and making as if he was going to embrace his wife. Don Pedro was terribly affrighted, and removed this arm, that lay heavier on him, he thought, than the greatest burthen, as gently as he could, for fear of awaking him, and when he had so done, with all the precaution of one in danger, crept to the bed-side, thrusting half his body out, insomuch that he had like to have fallen upon the floor, cursing his stars and his own folly for exposing him to such dangers, to serve the passion of two indiscreet lovers. He had hardly begun to breathe again, when his troublesome bed-fellow laid his leg over his ; which last action, as well as the former, had like to have made him die with fear. In short, the one still drawing nearer, and the other getting off as far as he could, the day appeared just at the nick when the unfortunate Don Pedro was no longer able to keep his ground against a man who still drove him farther and farther. He arose as softly as might be, and went to open the door, which he found locked, a greater misfortune than any had yet befallen him.

As he was endeavouring in vain to thrust the lock back, it flew open all of a sudden, and had like to have broke his nose. Virginia came boldly into the chamber, and asked him aloud whither he was going in such haste. Don Pedro conjured her in a low voice not to make such a noise, and asked her whether she had not lost her senses to venture thus the waking of her husband, and desired her to let him go.

" How ! go ? " says the lady aloud to him ; " I am resolved my husband shall see whom he has lain with to-night, to the end he may know what his jealousy has brought him to, and what I am capable of doing when provoked.' Having said this, as bold as a lioness she took Don Pedro by the arm, who was so confounded that he had not strength to get loose from her, opened the window-shutters without quitting her hold, and pulling him to the bedside, drew the curtains, and cried out aloud, " See, jealous master of mine, see whom you have lain with to-night." At this Don Pedro turning his eyes towards the terrible bed, instead of an ugly fellow with a beard, beheld his charming Violante, who had lain by his side all night, and not the jealous husband of Virginia, who had been gone into the country about eight days before.

The two pretty cousins pelted him with considerable raillery ; and never did man of wit so lamely defend or say so little for himself. Violante, who was naturally gay, and rallied with a grace, had like to have made her cousin die with laughing when she pleasantly exaggerated to her what bodily fears she had put poor Don Pedro in as often as she had pretended to be awake, and drew nearer to him. It was a long time before Don Pedro could recover out of his confusion and set his countenance in order. At last Virginia took compassion on him, and left him alone with her cousin, with whom you may suppose he had affairs of great importance to settle, because he was shut up with her till noon. From this happy hour, all the while the husband stayed in the country, the two gentlemen-cousins and the two gentlewomen-cousins met frequently

together, and made the best use of their time. When the
husband came to town again Rodriguez was the less
happy of the two, for Don Pedro, by the charitable
assistance of the servants, whom his presents had brought
over to his interest, made a shift for two or three months
to pass most of the nights with Violante, who was mistress
of her own actions, and ever since the marriage of her
cousin lodged in a separate building, which had a door
into another street. He became so passionately in love
with her that he earnestly desired to marry her; but
whenever he made any such proposal she always turned
the discourse so dexterously, that he could not positively
tell whether she did it out of design or because she did
not care to listen to him. In short, as there is nothing
permanent in this transitory world, Violante began at
length to slacken in her passion, and grew cold by little
and little, insomuch that Don Pedro could not forbear
complaining of it, and not knowing better how to account
for this alteration, accused her of infidelity, and reproached
her with having some other gallant more happy than
himself. Instead of mending matters by this procedure
he utterly ruined them, and made himself at last so
insupportable to Violante, that she not only refused to see
him a nights, but likewise to admit his visits in the daytime. This treatment did not in the least discourage him;
he gained by virtue of his money one of her maids, who
was so treacherous as to inform him that her mistress was
passionately in love with her cousin's brother-in-law, who
had just left the college; that he was a very handsome
youth, and no less in love with Violante than she was
with him.

To complete her perfidious treachery, this ill-conditioned
devil advised him to pretend himself sick, to acquaint her
mistress with his illness, and complain of her being the
cause of it, which was likely enough; and in short to feign
it so well, that her mistress might be no longer upon her

guard, as she had hitherto been, ever since she knew herself guilty of infidelity to him. Don Pedro played his
part to admiration. Violante fell into the trap, and our
treacherous damsel had no sooner introduced her mistress's
new Adonis, but she opened the door to the jealous Don
Pedro. He bolted very furiously into Violante's chamber,
who by that time was got to bed, and her young gallant
undressing to prepare for the encounter. He came with
his sword in his right hand towards his rival, perhaps with
an intention only to frighten him ; but our young spark
was not to be daunted so, for holding out one of his shoes
which he had just plucked off, after the same manner as
you do a pocket pistol, he aimed it at Don Pedro's head
in so formidable a manner, that he who little expected
such a welcome, and did not doubt but he would fire at
him, ducked his head, and turned the other way, which
gave our youngster time enough to get to the door.
Violante, who was desirous to break with Don Pedro,
immediately fell a laughing, and told him he was the first
man that had ever been afraid of being killed by a pistol
made of an old shoe. He was so nettled at this jest, that
he gave her a box on the ear, she took him by the beard,
they tugged and grappled, and at last the discourteous
Granada spark, after he had used her so very ill that she
had nothing but cries to have recourse to, just got into the
street at the very moment that Virginia, her husband, and
all the servants, expecting a military scuffle, came into
Violante's chamber. He immediately went to acquaint
Don Rodriguez with what had happened to him, and
without losing any more time, offered his service to the
Duke of Ossuna, who went the next day for Naples, of
which kingdom he was made viceroy. Don Pedro waited on
him to the harbour, where he took shipping with him,
leaving his dear cousin very much afflicted for his absence.
He stayed about six or seven years in Naples, being
exceedingly beloved by the viceroy, who allowed him a

considerable pension. He likewise received great returns from Spain, through which means no one made a handsomer figure than he, which made him be so much the more considered in Italy, by reason the generality of the Spaniards go thither to make their fortunes, as the French do to spend them. He made a voyage into Sicily, visited its most remarkable cities, and then returning into Italy, lived two or three years at Rome, as many at Venice, saw all the considerable towns, and at last, having been fourteen or fifteen years out of Spain, always up to the ears in love, or if you please, in fornication, ever a mighty intriguer, and still confirming himself in his heretical opinion that it was not safe for a man to marry a woman of wit, he at length resolved to put an end to all his rambles, and re-visit Granada, and the friends he had left there.

What principally contributed to make him leave Italy was his want of money, through the negligence of his correspondents, or at least he had so little left, that he had scarce enough to defray his charges to Barcelona. He was forced to sell some of his movables there, wherewith he bought him a mule, and only reserved his best suit of clothes to ride in. Thus equipped he took the readiest road towards his dear native country, without so much as a valet to keep him company, the servant whom he had brought along with him from Spain being dead, as we may reasonably suppose, of the Neapolitan disease ; and his small fund being not sufficient to maintain another. He left Barcelona by break of day to avoid the heat and flies of the month of August, and by nine in the morning had got about five or six leagues. He rode through a large town, where a Catalonian duke had passed part of his summer, in a noble castle that faced the road. This duke was well stricken in years, and had married a fine young lady not above twenty years old. This day, as it happened, he was gone a hunting, and was not expected home till the next.

The young duchess saw our Granada gentleman moving forward, from a balcony she had that looked towards the great road. His good mien made her desirous to view him nearer, besides, she was naturally very curious, and would not by her goodwill suffer any strangers to pass through her town, without sending to speak with them. Although our Granada hero could have been very willing to have travelled a few miles farther before he dined, yet could he not in good manners refuse to wait on the duchess, who sent a page to let him know she would be glad of his company. She was as beautiful as an angel ; and our Don for his part had no aversion to pretty women, although they were not duchesses. He was well shaped and tall, and the duchess took a peculiar delight to gaze upon handsome young fellows like him, to make herself some amends for the penance she did in her husband's conversation, who was so exceedingly fond of her, and so pleased with her cheerful temper, that he thought he did not see her enough, although he was seldom from her.

Don Pedro, who was a man of wit as well as judgment, diverted the duchess extremely with the recital of his travels, and fancied at first dash that she was a lady that had no aversion to pleasure. She informed herself particularly of the gallantry of Naples, desired to know whether the women there were allowed any liberty, and whether the Italian gallants carried on their amours as bravely as those of Spain. At last Don Pedro confirmed himself by the questions she put to him, that if she did not go to the bottom of an intrigue it was not for want of goodwill. She made him dine with her, to the mutual satisfaction of both. Our Granada adventurer would have taken his leave of her after dinner, but she would not suffer it, telling him that since the duke her husband would not come home that day, she desired him to be her guest ; adding obligingly, that persons of merit were very rare in Catalonia ; and therefore whenever she had the happiness to meet them, no wonder if she coveted to enjoy their conversation as long as she could. She led him into a large closet, very cool and refreshing, adorned with fine pictures, china, and other rich furniture. It wanted not, since we are obliged to be particular, a noble alcove, embroidered cushions, and a convenient couch, with a rich satin quilt thrown over it. Here our traveller recounted to her all his adventures at Granada, Seville, and Madrid, together with those of Italy, which are not as yet come to my knowledge. The duchess listened very attentively; at last he told her he was resolved to marry, if he could but find a woman from whom he should have no reason to apprehend any of those ill offices which witty women are always able to do their husbands.

" I have an estate," continues he, " that is far from being contemptible ; and though the woman I marry does not bring me a farthing, yet provided she has been well educated, and is not deformed, I shall make no scruple to choose her; although to deal ingenuously with you, I would much sooner pitch upon a woman that is deformed, and fool enough, than one that is handsome and not so."

" You are certainly wrong in your notions," replies the duchess; " but what do you mean by being well educated ? "

" I mean a woman of virtue," answered our traveller.

" And how is it possible for a fool to be a woman of virtue," cries the duchess, " if she neither knows what virtue is, nor is capable of being taught it ? Besides, how can a fool love you, that has not sense enough to know your merit ? She will trespass against her duty, without knowing what she does ; whereas a woman of wit, although she should distrust her honour, will know how to avoid those occasions where she may run any risk of losing it."

They argued a long while *pro* and *con* upon this subject ; our Don maintaining that all the knowledge required in a woman was to love her husband, to be faithful to him, and

carefully to look after her family affairs and children ; and
the duchess endeavouring to convince him that a fool was
not capable of doing it ; nay, though she were beautiful,
would certainly disgust him at last. They mutually gave
several proofs of their wit, and the good opinion they had
of each other soon improved into esteem, nay, and somewhat better. Our Spaniard did not only differ from the
duke in age, wit, and person, but was also one of the
handsomest, best-shaped men in the world, and if he
appeared such to the duchess, he likewise thought her the
loveliest woman he had ever beheld.

He was as bold as a lion, and never found himself alone
with a woman but he immediately offered his service to
her. If she accepted it, he did his best to acquit himself ;
and if she took snuff at it, would fall down on his marrow
bones, and terming himself the horridest sinner in the
world, ask pardon so ingenuously, and with so much hypo-
crisy, that the lady must needs forgive his transgression,
or perhaps by way of atonement made him transgress again.

" I could never have imagined," says he to the charming
duchess, " that anyone was able to make me throw up an
opinion the truth of which so many experiments have confirmed to me ; but it was never yet opposed by so extraordinary a person as yourself, whose soul, without being
beholden to her beauty, which however is not to be matched
in the universe, may acquire her as large an empire as she
pleases, over all those that have wit enough to discover that
she has a greater share of it than all her sex put together.
You have cured me of an error," added he, " but you leave
me troubled with an illness, which is so much the more
dangerous and hard to cure, as I am pleased to have it, and
by suffering it to gratify the noblest ambition that a mortal
is capable of having."

I cannot possibly tell how many more hyperboles he
shot at the duchess's virtue, and whether he did not speak
abundance of pathetical impertinences, for upon such

occasions as this a man is most terribly given to be impertinent. Neither do I know after what manner the duchess received a declaration of love her gallant delivered in due form at the same time ; I mean, whether she seemed to like it by an answer suitable to the occasion, or whether by answering nothing, she made good the old proverb, " Silence gives consent." But this is certain, that a maid of hers, who died of the king's evil in France, often owned before several credible gentlemen, that the closet door was shut for some two hours upon them, that they were together till supper time ; and although this maid, whom I suppose to have been an Andalusian, had never told me this, yet do I know full well that opportunity makes a thief. The night came, that favourable goddess to stolen love, but neither was Don Pedro nor the duchess the better for it, for partly out of good manners, and partly not to give the servants an occasion to guess, who generally do so beyond the truth, to which they have a natural antipathy, they called for candles, which were almost eclipsed by the brighter eyes heaven had bestowed upon the duchess, and which at that moment twinkled prettier than any pair of stars in the firmament. The vermilion of her cheeks was double to what it used to be, which made her appear more glorious than the sun on a fine summer's day to Don Pedro, whose visage too was a little inclined to scarlet. Thus they merrily passed away the time in exchanging glances with one another, when the servant came to acquaint the duchess that his grace her husband was below in the court. All that she could do in this surprise, was to shut up the thrice astonished Don Pedro in a large gilt cupboard, where she kept her perfumed waters, which done she put the key in her pocket, and threw herself upon the bed. The duke, who was at least threescore years old, came into his wife's closet, and found her as gay and fresh as a rose upon the stalk. He told her he had just received a letter from the king, which obliged him to return sooner than he thought.

He was very hungry, and therefore ordered the servants to bring whatever they had ready in the house into the same closet ; and the duchess, who had no great stomach to eat, while her traveller perhaps wished himself ten feet under ground, took a chair near the table. She was exceeding cheerful and brisk, and of a gaiety that bestowed new youth upon her old husband, so much did it revive his spirits. It was a customary thing for her to lay extravagant wagers with him, especially when she wanted money, which her good man always took a pleasure to lose to her, being perfectly charmed with so agreeable a wife. He never fancied her more beautiful than now ; she told him a hundred merry stories, by the same token, that our duke had like to have choked himself with laughing at them ; for eating heartily and laughing heartily at the same time, a bit of meat happened to go down the wrong way, but heaven be praised it did him no harm.

At last the duchess, who was of a humour to turn everything into merriment, had a mind to divert herself at the expense of her gallant in the sweating-tub. Says she to the duke, "Methinks it is a long while since we laid a wager last ; now I would fain lay a hundred pistoles, that I have occasion for, upon the first subject that offers itself. The duke told her he was ready, and that he would leave it to her to propose the subject. The duchess proposed several, which she knew he would not accept, and at last asked him whether he would lay that he could reckon up all the things in a family that are made of iron. The duke agreed to do it, though he thought it a very foolish thing to lay a wager on, and calling for paper and ink, so soon as the cloth was removed and his chaplain had said grace (for the duke you must know kept a good decorum in his family), he writ down the names of all the iron utensils he could think of ; but it fell out luckily for the duchess that he forgot to mention a key. She got him to read over what he had written two or three times, and when he had so done, asked him if he was satisfied with it, and whether he had anything to add. She then folded the paper, telling him she would examine it at her leisure, and in the meantime relate to him one of the prettiest adventures he ever heard.

" A little after you were gone upon your sports, I was," continues she, " looking out of one of our windows that faces the high road, when I saw a man of an extraordinary mien mounted on a mule, who pricked and spurred his beast to make all the haste he could. I had the curiosity to know whither he was going in so much haste, and dispatched one of my pages to tell him I would speak with him. To be plain with you, I never in all my life saw a man better shaped, or more likely to make even a woman of virtue dispense with a conjugal vow. I asked him whence he came and who he was. He answered me so genteelly, and with so much wit, that I was desirous to have more of his conversation. So I engaged him to stay with me the remainder of the day, and to acquaint me with all his adventures, which I imagined must needs be very curious and entertaining. He performed what I desired to my expectation, and I must frankly own I was never better diverted with any history in all my life, and am resolved," quoth she, " to divert your grace likewise with it." Then she recounted to the duke all that had happened to Don Pedro at Granada, Seville, and Madrid, and her good man, who was as merry a wight as is possible for a duke to be, fell a laughing, as if he would have burst his hoops, which made the duchess and some of his chief servants, whom he allowed to be familiar with him, to join in this merry concert. After this she acquainted him with all that had befallen our Granada gentleman in Italy, which was very pleasant as I have been told, for I could never yet inform myself what the particulars were. All I know is, that the duke laughed heartily at them, and Don Pedro himself could not forbear doing the like in the chest. In short, after she had very well diverted herself with making her husband laugh, and all the company, and even Don Pedro into the bargain, who till now had had his share in the mirth, she told her husband that our traveller, after he had recounted all his adventures, was so hardy as to make love to her, and did it with so much address, that she could not find it in her heart to be angry with him for carrying his gallantry so far, and who could not but perceive that he was by no means displeasing to her. "But why should I multiply words in vain," continued the duchess; "a gentleman so well made as he may attempt anything without danger. We spent the greatest part of the day together to our mutual satis- factions, and had done so still, but that you came home when I little expected you. Not to mince matters, your return both afflicted and surprised me. My lovely stranger seemed to be in a greater consternation than myself, so I hastily shut him up in my chest of perfumed waters, from whence he must needs hear me, if he is not already dead with fear. But knowing what an ascendant I have over you, and being in my own temper incapable of dissembling even those very things where my too great freedom may do me harm, I was resolved to divert you at the expense of this poor gentleman, whom I will draw out of his hole as soon as you are gone to your own apartment, and leave him to pursue his journey to Granada, where he is going, as he tells me, to find out a woman who is fool enough, it seems, to deserve to be his wife." The duchess gave such air of probability to this true story, that the duke quitted his good humour, and turned serious all on a sudden. He looked pale, was afraid that what his wife had told him was true, and could not forbear asking for the keys of the chest, wherein, as she pretended, the stranger was shut up. She changed the discourse, and by that means increased both his suspicion and fears. He asked her once more for the keys, which she refused him. He was resolved to have them, and arose from his seat in a passion.

"Very well, sir, very well," quoth the duchess, "before you ask me for the keys in such haste, pray be pleased coolly and calmly to read over your catalogue; you have forgot to set down keys in it, you cannot deny but that they are made of iron, and that you owe me a hundred pistoles upon the wager. Pray give them me now, as you are obliged in honour, and take notice that if I have told you a merry story, it was only to put you in mind of what you had lost, and at the same time to divert you, that you might part the freer with your money. The next time I would have you to be wiser than to take an invented story for a truth. It was not probable that so many extraordinary adventures should befall one single man, and much less that I would have told you such a story if it had been true." He laughed as if he had been distracted, admired the prodigious wit of his wife, and commended it before his servants, who were perhaps as arrant fools as himself.

"See now," cries he as loud as he was able, and laughed at the same time, "see now by what a cunning fetch the gipsy has given me to understand I have lost."

The duchess had liked to have killed herself with laughing, her woman seconded her, and Don Pedro was half dead with stifling his laughter in the chest. At last the duke, after he had ordered the steward to pay his wife a hundred pistoles, leaves her to go to his own apartment, often saying to himself that she was a true devil, and sometimes that she had the wit of a devil. The duke's servants repeated the same words after their master, so that all the while the duke was going towards his chamber you could hear nothing else upon the stairs but different voices, crying, "My lady duchess has the wit of a devil," "My lady duchess is a true devil." In the meantime the steward paid the duchess her hundred pistoles and went his way. The duchess shut her chamber-door, and having freed Don Pedro out of his little ease, who had scarce recovered of his fright, she endeavoured to convince him that a woman of wit could disengage herself with honour out of a scurvy business, the very thoughts of which would have made a fool to die with fear. She would have had him take part of a collation, which her women had just then set upon the table ; but he begged her pardon, and desired her to let him go. She gave him the hundred pistoles she had won of her husband, together with a gold chain and her picture that were worth as much more, conjuring him withal not to forget her, but to let her hear from him now and then. After this she tenderly embraced him, and put him into the hands of her maids, who let him and his mule out privately by a back-door. He did not think convenient to lie in that place, but rode two leagues farther till he came to the town where he intended to have dined the day before if the duchess had not stopped him. This odd adventure with the Catalonia duchess ran perpetually in his head. He could not enough wonder at her falling in love with him so on the sudden before she knew him, at her rashness in relating to the duke a story so nice, but so true, and last of all at her great address in applying it to her wager. He likewise admired the good temper of the duke, pitied his condition, and fortified himself more than ever in his opinion, that a woman of wit was hardly worth looking after ; and doubted not but that if the duchess had not too much relied upon the goodness of her invention, she durst never have carried on her intrigue so far nor had the boldness to communicate it to her husband. He promised himself that he would never run any such risk of being ill married, because he would either take no wife at all, or if he did, pitch upon one that was so foolish, that she should not be able to distinguish between love and aversion. As he was making these wise reflections he arrived at Madrid, where he found his cousin Don Rodriguez had inherited his father's estate, and was married to his kinswoman. He was informed by him that Violante had disposed of herself in matrimony, and that the beautiful Virginia was gone to the Indies with her husband. From Madrid he arrived at Granada. The first visit he paid was to his aunt, who welcomed him with a thousand embraces. Told him that Seraphina lived like a saint, and that her lover had died of grief, because he could not persuade her to quit the cloister to marry him.

Next day he went in company with his aunt to see young Laura, Seraphina's daughter. She had been put into a convent when she was but four years old, and now might be about fifteen. He found her as beautiful as all the angels put together, and as foolish as all the nuns that come into the world without brains, and are taken out of it in their infancy, to be buried alive in a convent. He gazed upon her, and was charmed by her beauty ; he made her talk, and admired her innocence. He now flattered himself he had found what he had been so long looking after ; and what made him take the greater fancy to Laura was that she much resembled Seraphina, with whom he had once been passionately in love, though the copy infinitely exceeded the original. He told his aunt she was not his daughter, and acquainted her with his resolution to marry her. The old gentlewoman approved his choice, and communicated the good news to Laura, who neither rejoiced nor was sad at it. Don Pedro furnished his house, and looked out for the most foolish servants he could find. He likewise endeavoured to get a set of maids full as simple as Laura, which however gave him no small trouble. He presented his mistress with the richest clothes and the finest things that Granada could afford. All the persons of quality in that city were invited to the wedding, and were as much pleased with Laura's beauty as they were disgusted at her simplicity. The company broke up betimes, and our new-married couple were left alone to themselves. Don Pedro sent his servants to bed, and having ordered his wife's maids likewise to retire so soon as they had undressed her, he shut the chamber-door ; and now the devil put it into his head to execute the most nonsensical frolic that ever one was guilty of, who had passed all his lifetime for a man of sense. He sat down in a chair, making his wife to stand all the while before him, when he spoke the following words to her, or others much more impertinent :

" You are my wife, and I hope I shall have reason to bless God for it, so long as we live together. Be sure you remember what I tell you, and carefully observe it while you live, lest you otherwise offend God and displease me."

At these words the innocent Laura made him many profound courtseys, whether seasonably or not, signifies nothing, and with her two little roguy blinking eyes, looked as fearfully upon her husband as a new-come scholar does upon an imperious pedagogue.

" Do you know," continued Don Pedro, "how married people ought to live ? "

" Not I, forsooth," replied Laura, dropping him a courtsey much lower than she had done before ; " but if you'll teach me, I'll remember it better than my *Ave Maria ;* " and then she dropt him another. Don Pedro thought himself the happiest man upon earth, to find more simplicity in his wife than he durst to have hoped. He took from his armoury a very rich but light suit of armour, which he had worn formerly at a magnificent reception the city had made the King of Spain. With this he equipped his pretty idiot, put a little gilt murrion on her head, finely adorned with plumes, girt a sword by her side, and putting a lance into her hand, gravely told her it was the duty of all wives, who had a mind to be thought virtuous, to watch their husbands while they slept, armed in all points as she was. She answered him with her usual courtseys, and kept on court-seying, till he bid her take two or three turns about the chamber, which she happened to perform with so good a grace, her natural beauty and military habit not a little contributing to set her off, that our too refined politician of

a husband was perfectly charmed with her. He went to
bed, and Laura continued in motion till five o'clock in the
morning. Our gentleman, who was the most considering
and discreet of all husbands in the universe, or at least
thought he was such, got up, dressed himself, disarmed his
wife, helped her to pluck off her clothes, put her to bed,
which he had just quitted, and kissed her a thousand times,
weeping for mere joy, that he had at last found so ines-
timable a jewel. He then wished her a good repose, and for-
bidding his servants to awake her, went to mass and about
his other affairs. For I had forgot to inform the courteous
reader that he had purchased a place in Granada, much
like to that of our *maires*, or provosts of the merchants.
The first night of their marriage passed after the manner I
have related, and the husband was such a confirmed sot as
to employ the second no better. Accordingly heaven
punished him for his stupidity. An unlucky business
happened, which obliged him to take post that very day
and ride to court. He had only time to change his
clothes and take leave of his wife, enjoining her under pain
of offending God and displeasing him to observe exactly
in his absence the duty of a married woman.

Those that have business at court, let them be as good
astrologers as they please, cannot assign the precise time
when it shall be concluded. Don Pedro did not think of
staying there above five or six days at farthest, but however
was forced to wait five or six months. All this while the
simple Laura did not fail to pass her nights in her armour,
and to spend her day in working at her needle, which she
had learnt in the convent. A gentleman of Cordova came
to Granada at this time about a lawsuit. He was no fool
as to his intellectuals, and was well made as to his person.
He often saw Laura in her balcony, thought her exceeding
pretty ; passed and repassed before her windows a hundred
times a day at least, after the mode of Spain ; but Laura let
him fairly pass and repass without knowing what it meant, or

so much as desiring to know it. There lived over against Don Pedro's house a poor sort of woman, but charitable in her nature, and ready to relieve the wants of her neighbours, who soon perceived both the stranger's love and the small progress he had made on the charming Laura's affections. She was a woman of intrigue, and her chief business was that of bringing good people together, for which she was admirably fitted for her trade, which lay in commodes, towers, washes, essences, elixirs, and some fine secrets for beautifying the skin and taking off freckles; but what recommended her most for this virtuous employment was her being supposed to be skilled in the black art. She so punctually bowed to the Cordovan gentleman and good-morrowed him so often as he passed before Laura's window, that he fancied she did not do it for nothing. He accosted her, and all at once struck up an acquaintance and friendship with her; he discovered his passion to her, and promised to make her fortune if she could but serve him in his amour. This old agent of Lucifer loses no time, gets herself introduced by the foolish servants into the company of their foolish mistress, under pretence of showing her some fine curiosities. She commended her beauty, lamented her being so soon forced to lose her husband's company, and when she found herself alone with her, spoke to her of the fine gentleman that passed so often before her window. She told her he loved her more than his life, and that he had a violent inclination to serve her if she thought fitting.

" In truth, I am very much obliged to him," replied the innocent Laura, " and should like his service well enough, but our house is so full of servants, and should any of them go away, I durst not receive him in my husband's absence. However, I will write to him about it if the gentleman desires it, and don't doubt but I shall obtain what I ask of him."

This was enough to so experienced a bawd as ours, to

convince her that Laura was simplicity itself. She therefore
endeavoured to explain to her as well as she was able after
what manner this gentleman desired to serve her. She
told her he was full as rich as her husband, and that if she
had a mind to see any proofs of it, she would bring her
from him the finest jewels and the richest clothes that
could be.

"Alas! madam," says Laura, "I have so much of what
you talk of, that I don't know where to put them."

"Since 'tis so," answered the ambassadress of Satan, "and
you don't care that he should present you, suffer him at
least to visit you."

"He may do that," says Laura, "whenever he pleases;
no one will hinder him."

"That is as much as can be desired," replies this venerable
bawd; "but yet it would be much better still if your footmen and maids knew nothing of it."

"That's easy enough," answered Laura, "for my maids
don't lie in my chamber. I go to bed without their help,
and that very late. Take this key along with you," continued she, "which opens all the doors in the house, and
about eleven at night he may come in at the garden-door,
where he will see a little staircase, that will lead him to my
chamber."

This old beldame took her hands and kissed them a
hundred times, telling her she was going to bestow new life
upon a poor gentleman, whom she had left a dying.

"And how came that about?" cries Laura, all in a
fright.

"Why 'tis you that have killed him," replies this dissembling gipsy. Laura hereat looked pale as if she had
been convicted of the murder, and was going to declare her
innocence, if this wicked woman, who did not think it convenient to abuse her ignorance any longer, had not left her,
throwing her arms about her neck, and assuring her the sick
man would not die. You may imagine she understood her

trade too well to forget the miraculous key that could open all the doors.

Some malapert critic now will fall upon my bones about this key, and tell me, 'tis all over witchcraft, and smells of a fable ; but let him know from his most humble and most obliged servant, that the gentlemen in Spain have such sorts of keys, which they call mistresses, and that in the days of yore people were better bred, and more civil than to find fault with what they did not understand. Let him maul me fore-stroke and back-stroke, all that lies within the compass of his little capacity, but I should be reckoned as great a coxcomb as he, to trouble my head any more about him. To return then to our old matron. She went to find out the impatient lover, and told him, with an infernal sneer, what progress she had made in his business. He rewarded her like a liberal gentleman, and expected the night with impatience. The night at last arrived, he opened the garden-door, and stole up as softly as he could to Laura's chamber, at the time when this silly creature was walking up and down in her room armed *cap-à-pié* with a lance in her hand, according to the salutary instructions of her extravagant husband. There was only a small light in a corner of the room, and the door stood wide open without question to receive the Cordovan gallant. But our spark seeing a person all in armour, did not doubt but he designed to get him into his clutches. His fear then prevailed over his love, as violent as it was, and away he fled faster than he had come, fearing that he should not get into the street time enough. He went to his trusty goer-between and informed her what a hazard he had run, who being mightily concerned at what had happened, went directly to Laura's house, to discourse her about the matter. Our silly innocent no sooner saw her, but she asked her why the gentleman did not come, and whether he was still sick ?

" He is not sick," replies old iniquity, " but came to wait on you last night, and saw an armed man in your chamber."

At this Laura made a long-winded laugh, then fell into a second fit, and then into a third, all which while the old woman could not tell what to make on't. At last, when she had fully satisfied herself with laughing, and was at liberty to speak, she told the reverend beldame that it was plain the gentleman was not married, and that it was she who had walked in armour in her chamber. Our virtuous matron could not tell what to make of these words, and for a pretty while thought that Laura was a downright natural, but after she had put her several questions, she came to understand what she could not otherwise have imagined, as well the great simplicity of a girl of fifteen, who ought to have known what was what at that age, as the extravagant precaution her husband had used to secure his wife's chastity. However, she thought it was best to leave Laura in her error, and instead of showing any surprise at the novelty of the thing, fell a-laughing with Laura at the great fright the gallant had been in.

A meeting was appointed that night. The old woman encouraged the gallant, and admired as well as he at the strange stupidity of our husband and wife. The night came, he got into the garden, crept up the little staircase, and found his lady again in armour, performing her conjugal duty, as she thought. He embraced her all covered as she was with iron, and for her part she received him as if she had known him from her cradle. At last he enquired what she designed to do in this armour. She fell a-laughing, and told him she durst not take it off, nor pass the night in any other equipage ; and informed him withal, since it seems he knew it not before, that it was a mortal sin to do otherwise. Our charitable wheedling Cordovan took abundance of pains to undeceive the poor creature and persuade her that she was abused, and that married persons passed their time after another manner. At last he prevailed upon her to disarm, and learn a more easy and pleasant way of performing the duties of matrimony than her rigid husband had taught her, which Laura owned to be a cruel fatigue. He was not long in getting off her armour, he likewise helped her to unrig, finding she was too long about it herself, and then threw himself into the bed by her side, where he made her confess that chalk and cheese were not more different than his precepts of matrimony, and those of her husband. In short, he taught Laura all he knew, who for her part was not backward to learn, while her husband danced attendance at court. At last she received a letter from him, wherein he sent her word that, his business being now over, he was preparing to come home : and at the same time our Cordovan having dispatched his affairs at Granada, returned to Cordova, without so much as taking leave of Laura, being, as I suppose, not very much concerned to part with her, since nothing is so short-lived as our love for a fool.

Laura was not much mortified at it, and received her husband with as much joy, and as little concern for the loss of her gallant, as if she had never seen him. Don Pedro and his wife supped together, to their mutual satisfactions. The night was now pretty well spent : Don Pedro went to bed according to custom, and you may judge what a surprise he was in when he saw his pretty consort in her smock coming to lie by him. Being much disturbed in his righteous spirit, he asked why she was not in her armour.

"Oh," says she, "I now know a much better way of passing the night with one's husband, which my other husband taught me, I thank him."

"What, have you got another husband then?" replies Don Pedro.

"Yes," says she, "and so fine and handsome a husband too, let me tell you, that you'd be pleased to see him ; but in truth I don't know when we shall see him again, for ever since the last letter you sent me he has not been here."

O 2

Don Pedro dissembling his vexation, asked her who he was? but she could not resolve him, and like a loving tit proposed to Don Pedro to show him what a pretty game her other husband had taught her. Our unfortunate gentleman pretended to be sick, and perhaps was really so, at least in mind. He turned his back, and chewing the cud upon the blessed choice he had made of a wife, who had not only violated the honour of his bed, but had not sense enough to conceal it from him, bethought himself of the wholesome advice of the Catalonian duchess, detested his errors, and owned (but it was somewhat of the latest,) that a woman of wit knows how to preserve the laws of honour; or if out of weakness she breaks them, knows at least how to keep her transgression private. At last he comforted himself as well as he could for a calamity that was not to be redressed : he feigned to be indisposed for some time, to see whether the instructions of his deputy would have any other effect than just teaching her a lesson, which he had done better to have taught her himself. He lived several years with her, had always a watchful eye over her actions; and when he died left her all his estate, upon condition she would take upon her the habit of a nun, in the same convent where Seraphina lived, who was at the same time informed by him that Laura was her daughter. He sent all the particulars of this history to his cousin Don Rodriguez at Madrid, and confessed to him how finely he had found himself mistaken in his erroneous opinion. He died; Laura neither rejoiced nor grieved at his death. She entered herself in the same convent where her mother lived; who finding what a great estate Don Pedro had left her daughter, founded a religious house with it. The history of Don Pedro was divulged after his death, and convinced all those people, who doubted of it before, that virtue cannot be perfect without good sense ; that a witty woman may be honest of herself, but that a fool cannot be so without assistance and good looking after.

NOVEL III.

THE HYPOCRITES.

IT was in that lovely season of the year, when Flora and Apollo—no, I beg your pardon, Apollo and Flora—dress the earth in her gayest livery, that a woman arrived at Toledo, the most ancient and most renowned city of Spain. She was fair and young, as subtle as the old serpent, and so great an enemy to truth, that for several years she never suffered that virtue to approach her lips; and what is more wonderful, did not find herself a jot the worse—at least she never complained of it. Thus she trafficked in lies, and generally made a good market of them; for nothing is more certain, than that a cheat of our heroine's complexion has sometimes stole herself into the approbation even of those persons who have a mortal aversion to falsehood. She had a magazine of fiction large enough to furnish all the poets, heralds, vision-mongers, quacks and astrologers in Christendom. In short, this natural qualification, which she had taken care to cultivate from her infancy, joined to the charms of her face, had got her in a short time a fine parcel of pistoles. Her eyes were black, lively, brilliant, large, as fine as fine could be, but withal most notorious killers, convicted of some four or five murders, suspected of fifty more that were not sufficiently proved; and as for the wretches they had wounded, their numbers could not be computed, nor even imagined. No woman in the universe dressed finer; the least pin fixed by her hand carried a peculiar charm with it. She advised with no other counsellor as to her dress than her looking-glass, which was her chief minister of state, her treasurer, and father confessor. She was a most dangerous woman to look upon, that's certain ; for a man could not for the heart of him help loving her, and yet could not be long her gallant, without being her slave as long.

Well, our lady, such as I have described her, arrived at Toledo towards the evening, just at the very nick when all the cavaliers of the city were preparing a masquerade for the wedding of a young gentleman of the neighbourhood, who was to marry a lady descended of one of the best families in that city. The windows were illuminated with torches, but much more with the brighter eyes of the fair ladies, and the incredible number of wax lights triumphed o'er the vanquished night, and restored the foregoing day. Women of the least quality showed all their finery upon this occasion. A world of beaux had most nicely spruced up their fine persons with a felonious intention to murder the ladies. I mean those empty fops that all great cities are plagued with, who don't care a farthing whether they make real conquests or not, provided they can but have the reputation or scandal of them : who never attack but in a troop, and that always with insolence, and who by virtue of a handsome face, red stockings, a gilt snuff-box, and a fine periwig, think they can command the lives of all they meet, and murder all the women with love and all the men with fear. Oh! what a fine time had the men of compliment that day to show the fruitfulness of their imaginations ; and how much glittering rhetoric was thrown away upon goddesses, who had not been deified a full hour. Among the rest a dapper younker, who from a school-boy had advanced himself to the dignity of a page, surpassed himself in talking magnificent nonsense before

our heroine, and never was better pleased with his dear
person than then. He had seen her alight out of the stage
coach, by the same token he was terribly smitten with her ;
but resolving not to stop there, followed her to the very
door of the house where she hired a room, and from thence
to all the several places where her curiosity led her. At
last our stranger stopped at a certain place, where she
might behold the masks at her ease ; and our eloquent
page, who had put on his best linen that day, and was
finer than ordinary, immediately entered into a conversation
with her, and began to display his talent. She was a
woman that understood the world very well, and loved
dearly to banter and laugh at your forward young prigs,
that think they are born with a patent to be troublesome.
Judge therefore if, finding our page an everlasting talker,
that cared not what came uppermost, she did not soon
carry the shallow sot out of his depth, and manage him as
she pleased. She intoxicated him with her praises, so that
both his heart and soul were at her service. He told her
that he waited on an ancient cavalier of Andalusia, uncle
to the young gentleman that was to be married, for whom
the city made all this rejoicing ; that he was one of the
richest men of his quality, and that he had no other heir
but this young nephew, whom he loved exceedingly,
although he was one of the most extravagant young fellows
in Spain, a lover of all the women he saw, and, besides, of a
little army of whores and other women whom he had in-
veigled, either by fair speeches or money ; and lastly, that
he had committed several rapes, without respect either to
age, degree, or condition. He added, that his follies had
been very expensive to his old uncle ; who was the more
desirous to link him in matrimony, that he might see
whether he would not alter his manners with his condition.
While the page discovered all these affairs and secrets of his
master, she made him giddy with her flatteries, commending
every word he spoke, bidding the company to observe

with what a grace he told his story ; and, in short, omitting nothing that might help to turn the head of a young fop. who had already but too good an opinion of his own parts.

The commendations and applauses that proceed from a fair mouth are dangerous and deceitful. Our indisceet page had no sooner informed Helen that he was a native of Valladolid but she began to express herself very much in favour of that city and its inhabitants ; and after she had put herself to the expense of some hyperboles in praising them, assured our young coxcomb that of all the fine gentlemen she had known of that country, she never yet saw one so well made and accomplished as himself. This was the finishing compliment, that pinned up the basket. Just as our page was going to take his leave of her, she invited him to conduct her to her lodgings, and you must not ask the question why she gave her lily-white hand to him rather than another. This unexpected favour made his heart to leap within him, so that he was perfectly out of his little senses ; and he concluded within himself that a man ought not to despair of his good fortune, although he were never so miserable. When our charming flatterer came into her room, she placed the page in the best seat. He was so confounded at this kind treatment, that for want of taking due care, he came souse with his breech to the ground : his cloak fell one way, his hat and gloves another, and besides, he had like to have run himself through with his poignard, which dropped out of the scabbard as he fell. Helen went to help up our poor spark, and seemed to be mightily concerned at his mischance. She put up his poignard and told him she could not see him wear it any more that day, after the slippery trick it had played him. The page picked up the scattered remains of his ship-wreck, and made several wicked compliments suitable to the occasion. All this while Helen made as if she could not recover herself from her late fright, and began to admire the fine workmanship of the poignard. The page gave her to understand it belonged to his old master, who had formerly bestowed it upon his graceless nephew, with a sword and other accoutrements belonging to it, and that he had chosen it among several more, that were in his master's wardrobe, on purpose to make a better figure upon a day of such public solemnity.

Helen made the page believe she had a mind to go out in disguise, to see after what manner people of quality were married at Toledo. The page told her the ceremony would not be performed till midnight, and offered her a small collation in the apartment of the master of the house, who was his friend. He railed at his unpropitious stars, that he was forced to quit the most agreeable company in the world to wait upon his master who kept his bed by reason of his illness. He added, that his gout was the reason why he did not assist at the wedding, which was to be kept in a great house in the city, at a good distance from his own, that was called the hotel of the Count of Fuensalida. He was pumping his brains to make some pretty compliment at parting, when he heard somebody knock very hard at the door. Helen seemed to be strangely discomposed at it, and desired the page to retire into a little closet, where she shut him up longer than he imagined. He that made such a rapping at the door was Helen's gallant, half pimp and half bully, whom, to stop the mouths of the wicked, she was pleased to call brother. He was the trusty accomplice of all her rueful actions, and drudge in ordinary to her private pleasures. She told him how she had disposed of the page, and discovered to him besides her design to finger some of his old master's pistoles, which required as much speed as dexterity in the execution. The mules, though very well harassed, were immediately put into the coach that had brought them from Madrid ; when Helen with her company (which was composed of the terrible Montafar, the venerable Mendez, and a small lackey) embarked in this foundered vessel, which carried them to a sort of Long Lane, where a parcel of

Christian Jews lived, whose faith was as threadbare as the
secondhand clothes they sold. The maskers ran still about
the streets ; and it so happened, that the bridegroom, who
was masked as well as the rest, met Helen's coach, and in
it beheld our dangerous stranger, who seemed to him to be
Venus in disguise, or the sun hurrying about the streets.
He was so strangely tempted by this bewitching sight,
that he was within an ace of leaving his bride elect in the
lurch to run after this unknown fair ; but at that time his
prudence had power enough to stifle this growing passion,
he followed his companions in the masks, while the stage-
coach drove furiously on towards the aforesaid street, where
the brokers lived, and here, without much haggling and
making of words, Helen soon equipped herself in mourning
from top to toe, together with the ancient Mendez,
Montafar, and the little boy.

After this, getting into the coach again, she ordered the
fellow to stop at the hotel of the Count Fuensalida. Our
diminutive lackey went in first, enquired out the apartment
of the Marquis of Vallafagnan, and told him that a lady
from the mountains of Leon was at the door, who had some
business of great importance to communicate to him. The
good gentleman was surprised to hear of a visit from such
a lady, and at such an hour : he raised himself up in his
bed as well as he could, adjusted his wrinkled cravat,
and ordered two cushions to be put under his back, to
receive so important a visit with the better grace. He kept
himself in this posture, with his eye still fixed upon the
chamber-door, when he saw enter the room (not without
the greatest admiration of his eyes, and as great a palpitation of his heart) the sorrowful Montafar, muffled up in as
much black crape as would serve half a score hearses,
followed by two women in the same habit, the youngest of
whom he led by the hand, and who covering part of her
face with her veil, seemed to be the most sorrowful and
considerable of the two. A lackey held up her train, which

was so enormously prolix, that when it was spread out it covered the whole floor. At the door they saluted the sick old gentleman with three profound reverences, not reckoning that of the little lackey, which is not worth mentioning. In the middle of the room with three other reverences all at the same time, and three more before they took their seats, which were brought them by a young page, comrade to him whom Helen had locked up safe in the closet ; but these three last reverences were so extraordinary, that they effaced the remembrance of the former.

The courteous soul of our old gentleman was strangely surprised at so odd a scene, the ladies took their seats, and Montafar and the little lackey retired bare-headed towards the door. The gouty cavalier was at his wits' end to find them compliments, and afflicted himself at their mourning before he knew the cause of it, which he entreated them to be so kind as to let him know, as likewise the reason why they did him the honour of that visit at so unusual an hour for persons of their quality to be abroad. Helen, who needed not to be informed what a strange efficacy and persuasion there was in tears that came from beautiful eyes immediately poured out a torrent of them, intermixed with violent sobs and sighs raising and falling the tone of her voice as she saw most proper. She discovered ever and anon her lily-white hands, with which she wiped her eyes, and sometimes showed her face, to let him see she was as beautiful as afflicted. The old gentleman expected with impatience when she would open, and began now to hope it since that impetuous flood of tears, which had overflowed her charming field of lilies and roses, was in a manner stopped ; when the venerable Mendez, who judged it convenient to reassume this mournful harmony, which the other had just finished, began to weep, sob, and lay about her with that violence, that it was equally a misfortune and shame to Helen that she had not grieved enough. The old matron stopped not here, but resolving to outdo Helen, thought that to tear off a handful or two of her hair would not have an ill effect upon the audience. It was no sooner thought of but done : she committed most horrible ravage upon her locks, but in truth this was no mighty loss to her since there was not one single hair of the growth of her head.

After this manner did Helen and Mendez strive who should exceed the other, when Montafar and the lackey, at a signal concerted between them, began a doleful concert at the door, and wept and sighed so cruelly, that one would have thought they had designed to outrival the two pensive ladies near the bed ; who by this new striking up of the chorus, began to play their parts again so furiously, as if they had been too remiss before. The old gentleman was almost distracted to see them weep so immoderately, and yet could know nothing of the occasion. He wept however to keep them company, sobbed as strenuously as the best of them, and conjured the afflicted ladies by all that was good and sacred, by their seraphical eyes, and their celestial charms, to moderate their afflictions a little, and to acquaint him with the cause of them ; protesting, that his life was the least thing he would hazard for their sakes, and regretting the loss of his youth, which hindered him from showing the sincerity of his heart by his actions.

At these words the sky began to clear up a little, their countenances were not so overcast as before, and they thought they had wept enough in all conscience, since they could weep no longer without spoiling the jest. Besides, they were good husbands of their time, and knew that they had not a minute to lose. Our old matron therefore, lifting up her veil above her head, to the end her venerable looks might give her all the credit she wanted on this occasion, declaimed in the following manner. "God of His Almighty power and goodness preserve and shield my Lord Marquis of Villafagnan from all harm, and restore him to his former health. Although, to speak truth, the tragical story we are going to tell him is not very proper to give him joy, which is the elixir of health : but our misfortune is of that nature, that we must communicate it."

At this the poor Marquis of Villafagnan, striking himself with the palm of his hand upon his thigh, and fetching a deep sigh from the bottom of his heart, cried, "Heaven grant that I am mistaken, but my foreboding mind tells me that this is some foolish frolic, or rather some extravagance of my nephew. Go on, madam, go on, and excuse me for interrupting you."

Our old matron fell a-weeping, instead of returning an answer, when the pensive Helen took up the discourse thus : " Since you know by sorrowful experience," says she "that your nephew is a slave to his extravagant appetites, and have been but too often troubled to compound his outrages, you will make no difficulty to believe his brutal usage of me. When you unhappily sent him to Leon last spring, he saw me at church, and at this interview said some things to me which, had they been true, neither of us ought to have stirred off from that holy ground ; myself, for fear of justice, as being his murderer, and he as a dead man and fit to be put in his grave. He told me a hundred times that my eyes had killed him, and omitted none of those insinuating wheedling tricks that lovers employ to abuse the simplicity of poor virgins. He followed me home to my lodgings, rode before my windows every day, and serenaded me every night. At last, finding all his amorous arts signified nothing, he by his money corrupted a black wench, a slave of ours, to whom my mother had promised her liberty, and by her infernal treachery surprised me in a garden we have in the suburbs of the city. I had none but this perfidious maid with me : he was accompanied by a man as wicked as himself, and had bribed the gardener to go to the other end of the town under pretence of business. What need I say more ? he clapped his poignard to my throat, and finding that my life was less dear to me than my honour, by the help of the companion of his crime, he took that by force which he could never have obtained by fair promises. The black acted the part of a distracted woman, and, the better to hide her perfidy, wounded herself slightly in the hand, and then vanished. The gardener returned : your nephew, affrighted at the blackness of his crime, leapt over the garden wall with so much precipitation, that he dropped his poignard, which I took up. However, this insolent young man had nothing then to fear ; for not being in a condition to stop him, I had command enough over myself to dissemble the inexpressible misfortune that had befallen me. I did all I could to appear no more concerned than I used to be. The wicked slave was not to be seen from that moment.

" Soon after I lost my mother, and I might say I lost everything in her, if my aunt, whom you see there, had not been so kind as to take me to her own house, where she makes no difference between her two beautiful daughters and myself. There I came to be informed, that your nephew was so far from designing me reparation for the injury he had done me, that he was upon the point of marrying in this city. Upon this I flew hither with the greatest haste I could, and expect, before I go out of your chamber, that you will give me in money or jewels, the value of two thousand crowns, to settle me in some convent ; for after what I have known by fatal experience of the temper of this cavalier, I can never bring myself to marry him, although he and all his relations should endeavour to persuade me to it by all sorts of offers and entreaties imaginable. I know well enough that he is to be married to-night, but I'll soon stop all proceedings, and raise such a hurricane, as shall make his heart ache as long as he lives, if you don't comply with my proposal. And to let you see," continued this dissembling hypocrite, " that what I have told you of your nephew is so true, that nothing can be more, see the fatal poignard which he clapped to my throat ;

and would to God he had done something more, than only
threatened me with it."

She began to weep afresh at the conclusion of her story.
Mendez took it in a higher key, and the harmonious concert
at the door, of which the little squeaking lackey made the
treble, and Montafar the bass, tuned their pipes to admiration. Our old gentleman, who had already but too easily
believed what the greatest cheat of her sex had told him,
no sooner saw the poignard, but he immediately knew it to
be the same he had formerly bestowed upon his nephew.
Therefore all his care was to prevent this story's taking
air, lest it should hinder his match.

He would have sent for him with all his heart, but he
was afraid lest some people should be so curious as to
enquire into the occasion ; and as 'tis natural for us to fear,
where we desire, he no sooner saw our afflicted ladies rising
from their seats, and making as if they were going to break
this marriage to pieces, which he so earnestly desired, and
had taken so much pains to bring about, than he ordered
his page to bring him his cabinet, and bid him tell out two
thousand crowns in four pistole pieces. Montafar received
them, counting them one by one ; and the old marquis
having made them promise to honour him with a visit next
morning, excused himself a hundred times to the ladies, for
not being able to wait upon them to their chariot. Away
they went very well satisfied with their visit, and ordered
the coachman to drive back to Madrid, concluding with
themselves, that if they were pursued, it would be on the
road to Leon. In the meantime their landlady finding her
lodgers did not come home, went into their chamber, where
she found the page in the closet, who could not imagine
why they had shut him up there, and whom she let go
about his business, by reason she knew him, or rather
because upon enquiry she found none of her movables
missing. Those people that make a trade of robbing, and
wholly subsist by it, though they don't fear God, yet always

fear man.   They are of all countries, and yet are of none,
as having no settled habitation.   As soon as they set foot
in one place, they make the most on't they can, and when
they have grazed it bare, remove to fresh quarters.   This
cursed occupation, which is learnt with so much pains and
danger, differs from all others in this respect, that whereas
we leave the rest when we grow old, purely for want of
strength to follow them, that of robbing generally leaves a
man in his youth, and yet 'tis for want of living longer.
One would think that the gentlemen that follow it must
needs find some unaccountable charms in it, since for its
sake they venture a great number of years, which are sooner
or later concluded by the hangman.

   Helen, Mendez, and Montafar, had none of these pious
reflections in their heads, but rather were in perpetual fears
lest they should be pursued.   They gave the coachman
double his fare to make the more haste, who, without
question, did all he could to please his passengers that had
paid him so liberally ; so that we may reasonably conclude,
never did any leathern vehicle make more haste to Madrid.
Montafar was very uneasy, and showed by the many sighs
that escaped from him, that he was rather in a penitential
than a merry strain.   Helen, who had a mind to divert
his melancholy by recounting the particulars of her life,
which till that moment she had carefully concealed, began
thus :

   " Since I find thou art in such a musty humour," said she
to him, " I will satisfy the great longing thou hast always
expressed to know who I am, and what adventures have
befallen me before we came acquainted.   I could tell thee
I am descended from a noble family, and, according to the
vanity now predominant, give myself an illustrious name as
easily as any of my neighbours ; but I will be so sincere,
as to acquaint thee, even with the least faults of those who
sent me into the world.   You must know then, my father,
of happy memory, was a Gallician by birth, a lackey by

profession, or to speak more honourable of him, a footman. He held the memory of the patriarch Noah in singular veneration, for his noble invention of the vine ; and were it not for his particular respect to the juice of the grape, one might say of him that he cared but little for the vanities of this wicked world.

" My mother was of Granada, to speak frankly, a slave ; but you know there's no contending with one's destiny. She answered to the name of Mary, which her masters gave her at her baptism ; but was better pleased to be called Zara, which was her Morisco appellative : for since I am to tell you the truth, the whole truth, and nothing but the truth, she was a Christian in complaisance and fashion only, but a Moor in reality. Nevertheless she frequently confessed, but that rather the sins of her master than herself ; and as she amused her confessor not with her own failings, but the things she was forced to suffer as a servant, and showed him of what a meek, humble, and patient spirit she was, the charitable old father, who was a godly man, and judged of others by himself, believed her upon her word, and commended instead of reproving her, so that any one that stood near enough, would have heard nothing but praises on both sides. Perhaps you are in pain to know how I came acquainted with so particular a secret, and may very well imagine my mother never disclosed it to me : but I must inform you, that I am very inquisitive in my nature, and as young as I was at that time, my mother never confessed herself, but I got as near as I could to overhear her confession. But to proceed, as tawny, or to express myself more properly, as black as she was, her face and shape were not disagreeable, and there were more than six cavaliers, commanders with red and green crosses, that were her humble admirers, and strove who should be most in her good graces. She was of so charitable a temper, that she granted them all they asked of her, and her gratitude to her masters was so great, that to make them some amends

for the pains they had been at in rearing her from her
childhood, she did all that lay in her power to bring them
every year a little slave, male or female : but heaven did
not second her good intentions, for all her motley progeny,
her chequered issue, I mean all the squalling demi-negroes
of her making, died as soon as they were born. She was
happier in bringing up the children of other people. Her
masters that had lost all their own in the cradle, got her to
nurse a young child, despaired of by the physicians, who in
a short time, by her good looking after it, and the good
qualities of my mother's milk, was perfectly recovered. For
this piece of service, my mother's mistress gave her her
liberty when she died. Being now at her own disposal, she
set up for washing and whitening of linen, and succeeded
so well that way, that in a short time there was hardly a
beau or courtier in Madrid, that thought his linen well
washed unless it had passed her hands.

" And now she began to practise over those lessons again
which her mother had formerly given her, I mean to renew
her acquaintance with her correspondents in the other
world. She had laid aside this ticklish employment rather
out of modesty, and because she was tired with the en-
comiums that were given her for being so well skilled in
this art, than for any fear of justice, or apprehension of the
magistrate. In short, she applied herself afresh to it, only
to oblige her friends, and in a little time made so great a
progress in this noble science, and acquired such credit in
the kingdom of darkness, that demons of the highest reputation were not thought to be worth a farthing if they
were not in league with her. I am not vain, neither do I
love to tell lies," added Helen ; " for which reason I will not
bestow any good qualities upon my mother which she did
not possess, but am obliged at least to pay this testimony
to her virtue. The secrets which she told, those which she
revealed, and her oracles, which made her pointed at in the
streets, were vulgar talents among those of her nation, in

comparison of what she knew in the mystery of maiden-heads. That incomprehensible flower was much better after she had lent it a lifting hand, than before it was gathered, and bore a greater price as its second edition, with my mother's corrections and amendments, than at the first.

" She might be about forty years old when she married my father, the good Rodriguez. All the neighbourhood wondered a man who loved wine so well would marry a woman that never tasted it, as if she still continued a disciple of Mahomet, and who had her hands always in water, being a laundress by profession. But in answer to this, my father worthily replied that love cleared all diffi-culties, and made everything easy. Some time after, her belly swelled to her chin, and she was happily delivered of me. But this joy did not last long in our family. I was about six years old, when a certain prince clothed a hundred lackeys in his own livery against a bull-feast. My father was one of the number, drank a large morning's draught, and being pot-valiant, must needs encounter a wild bull, who tossed him two or three story high, and tore out his guts. I remember they made ballads upon my father's death, and the burthen of the song was, ' That two of a trade can never agree.' I did not understand the meaning on't then, but have since been informed, that it alluded to his being a cornuted animal ; but you know 'tis impossible to stop people's mouths, if they have a mind to prate, and vent their ill-natured mirth. My mother was afflicted at my father's misfortune, and so was I ; she was comforted, and so was her daughter. When I was grown up, my beauty began to make people talk of me ; and lord ! what pressing and thronging there was to carry me to the park, to the play-house, and to give me collations on the banks of the Manzanares.

" My mother watched me like a second Argus, insomuch that I grumbled to be so confined ; but she soon made me sensible it was for my advantage. Her severity, and the high price she set upon me, enhanced the value of her merchandise, and raised a terrible competition among those that pretended to my favours. I was as it were put up by auction, each man thought he had the better of his rival, and each fancied he had found that which was long gone and vanished. A rich Genoese merchant, who courted me in private, so dazzled the eyes of my prudent mother with his yellow metal, and bled so plentifully, that she favoured his good intentions. He possessed the first place in my affections, but this superiority proved very expensive to him. We continued faithful to him so long as we believed he doubted us : when we found him no longer upon his guard, we fairly duped him. My mother was too tender-hearted and sensible of the pains of love, not to be touched with the continual complaints of these gentlemen, who were all topping cards at court, and as rich as Crœsus. 'Tis true, they did not throw their money about so plentifully as the Genoese, yet my mother, as she knew how to set a value upon great gains, so did not despise the smaller ; and besides, was obliging rather out of a principle of charity than interest. The Genoese in short was declared bankrupt, and I don't know but we might lend a helping hand to his breaking. He was engaged in several scuffles and quarrels about me. The magistrates came to visit us more out of civility than any other reason ; but my mother had a natural aversion to the gentlemen of the long-robe, and no less hated your bullies and rakehelly red-coats that began to besiege us. She therefore thought convenient to remove to Seville, turned all her plate and furniture into ready money, and took me along with her in the stage-coach. We were betrayed by our villainous coachman, robbed and stripped of all we had, and besides my mother was so bruised and battered, by reason she defended her own goods as long as her little strength would give her leave, that before I could drag her to a wretched inn, she gave up the ghost at the foot of a rock. I armed myself with resolution, although I was but very young. I bundled up every rag belonging to the old gentlewoman, but our thieves had been so careful, that they had left me but little to carry off. Thus I left her to the discretion of the next passengers, not doubting, but that upon so great a road as that between Madrid and Seville, some charitable Christians would come by, and take care to see her corpse interred. I arrived at Madrid ; my lovers were acquainted with my misfortune, and in a short time I was equipped with new rigging and furniture. About that time I happened to meet with thee at one of my female companion's, and I was perfectly charmed with thy good qualities. What has happened since I need not relate to thee, since we have never been asunder. We came to Toledo ; we left it in haste, but made so good a market there, that if thou art a man of that courage I take thee to be, thou wilt be merrier than thou art. But since this long story has made thee inclinable to take a nap, as I find by thy yawning and nodding thou art, lay thy head upon my lap and sleep ; but know, that if there is anything either good or useful in fear, 'tis before we have committed a crime, for 'tis the vilest and most dangerous quality in the world afterwards. Fear always discomposes the minds of the guilty, in such manner, that instead of flying from those that pursue them they frequently throw themselves into their hands."

Montafar fell asleep, and the morning awaked, so beautiful and charming, that the birds, the flowers, and fountains saluted her each after its manner ; the birds by singing, the flowers by perfuming the air, and the fountains by smiling or murmuring, no matter which, for one is as true as the other. And now the nephew of the Marquis of Villafagnan, the sensual Don Sancho, was getting up from his new bride, tired enough in all conscience, and perhaps already glutted with the pleasures of matrimony. He could think of nothing but the pretty stranger, I mean the dangerous Helen, whom he had seen the night before in the stage-coach, and fancied to be the Phœnix of her sex ; but in which particular he was guilty of great injustice to his own lady, who was very beautiful, and so amiable, that several lovers in Toledo died for her, while at the same time she sighed for her ungrateful husband, and that monster of inconstancy did the like for an infamous mercenary strumpet, that would have licked the devil's cloven foot for half-a-crown. But nothing is so irregular as our appetites. A husband that has a pretty wife runs after a draggle tailed nasty servant wench. A nobleman that has his ragouts and ortolans, despises what he sees before him and calls for the sturdy beef and pottage that his footmen dine on. All the world has a depraved taste in many things, but your men of quality more than any. As they have more wealth than they know what to do with, and fondly perplex themselves in searching after what is never to be found, so they choose coarse ordinary things, only for variety's sake. Thus we see they spare neither pains nor money to purchase trifles ; and sometimes court some common jilt a twelvemonth before they can obtain those favours of her which she flings away upon others without asking. Heaven permits this, on purpose that they may punish themselves with an evil of their own seeking. Wretched man ! on whom Heaven has bestowed those two things that contribute to make life happy, riches in abundance, and a lovely wife. Riches to support and relieve those that deserve, but have them not, and to secure thee from stooping to those meannesses to which poverty often exposes the most generous souls ; and a wife that equals thee in quality, beautiful both in body and mind, wholly perfect in thy eyes, but much more so in those of others, who see farther into the affairs of their neighbour than their own ; and, in short, possessed of those shining qualifications, moderation, chastity, and virtue.

What is it thou art looking for elsewhere ? Hast thou not at home thy other half, thy wife, whose wit can divert thee, who yields her body entirely to thy pleasure, who is jealous of thy honour, frugal of thy fortune, careful to preserve thy estate, who gives thee children to divert thee in their childhood, to support thee in thy old age, and to keep up thy name after thou art dead ? What is it, I say, thou art looking after abroad ? I will tell thee in few words, to ruin thy estate and reputation, to enfeeble thy body, to lose the esteem of thy friends, and, in a word, to create thyself abundance of enemies. Thinkest thou that thy honour is safe, because thou hast a virtuous wife ? Alas ! thou hast little experience of the things of this world, and art little acquainted with human frailty. The most tractable and quiet horse grows restive under an ill rider, and throws him to the ground. A woman may now and then resist a temptation to do ill, and yet commit a crime of much greater consequence, when she fancies herself most upon her guard. One fault draws many after it, and the distance between virtue and vice is sometimes not above a day or two's journey. And now methinks I see a malapert critic cock his hat, toss his wig over his shoulders, look fierce, and ask how these moral aphorisms come to be thus brought in hand over head. Why, pray, sir, don't be so choleric, make use of them or let them alone, as you shall see fit ; 'tis all a case to your humble servant, I'll assure you ; but under favour, sir, methinks you ought to thank the man who gives you them for nothing.

But to return to our story : Don Sancho was ready to rise from his young wife, when his uncle's steward brought him a letter, wherein the old gentleman sent him word of the strange lady who had visited him the night before, and whom he suspected to have cheated him, because she was not to be found in any of the inns in Toledo, whither he had sent to inquire after her. He desired him in the same letter to lend him one of his servants to pursue this

notorious cheat to Madrid, whither he supposed she had
steered her course, because he had sent his people upon all
the great roads from Toledo to the neighbouring cities, and
could hear no news of her. Don Sancho was not made of
brass or marble. He found himself attacked in the
weakest part of his soul, and was wondrous fierce and
uppish to be once in his life wrongfully accused of a fault,
who had been found guilty of so many before. The loss
of so great a sum, and the sham that had been put upon
his uncle equally incensed him. He told the story to his
wife, and some of his relations, who came to give our new-
married couple the good-morrow; and being not to be
dissuaded from his resolution by the entreaty of his spouse,
or the advice of his friends, dressed himself in a minute,
ate a little breakfast, and ran to his uncle's house as hard
as he could drive. The page, who had introduced Helen
into the old marquis's chamber, described the coach to
him, informed him how many they were in company, and
by what marks they might be discovered. He took post
from Toledo to Madrid, attended only by two footmen
whose courage was not unknown to him. He rode four or
five stages so fast, that he had no leisure to think of the
beautiful stranger; but when his indignation was a little
evaporated by his journey, Helen took place again in his
fancy, so beautiful and charming was she in his imagination, that he was in the mind once or twice to return
to Toledo to find her out. He wished himself a hundred
times at the devil, for concerning himself so far about his
uncle's robbery; and called himself sot, blockhead, and
enemy to his own pleasure as often, to fatigue himself thus
in riding post, whereas he might have employed his time
to much better purpose, in seeking a happiness, the
possession whereof, in his opinion, would have made him
the happiest man in the world. While these amorous
reflections took up his thoughts, he often talked to himself,
as fools do, and that so loud, that his servants who rode

before often stopped short, and turned back to inquire what he would have. "Why," would he often say to himself, "did I leave the place where I first beheld her, and shall not I be the most unhappy of men, if this stranger leaves Toledo before my return? Well, 'tis no more than what I deserve, who must needs take the office of a thief-catcher upon me unasked, unsought; but," continued he, "if I return to Toledo without doing anything, what will my friends say, who would have dissuaded me from this enterprise, and ought I to leave those villains unpunished that have robbed my uncle after so unheard of a manner, and besides, have so perfidiously wounded my reputation?" These different agitations employed the mind of our young extravagant, when near Xetaffe his footmen discovered Helen's coach by the tokens that had been given of it. They cried out with one voice to their master, "Yonder are the thieves," and without staying for him, rode up to the coach with their swords drawn. The coachman stopped, being terribly affrighted, and Montafar was much more than he. Helen ordered him to let down the glasses, and looked out to see how she could prevent so dangerous a storm. She saw Don Sancho riding towards her with sword in hand, whose angry countenance boded no good; but our amorous gentleman no sooner cast his eyes upon those two bewitching stars, which had so terribly wounded him, than his wounds bled afresh, and he immediately believed his servants had mistaken; for we have always a good opinion of the person we love; and as if he had known Helen from her cradle to have been a lady of unblemished virtue, laid about his footmen with his sword, like a distracted man. "You dogs," cried he, "you villains, did not I bid you have a care you did not mistake; and don't you deserve to have your throats cut for offering this rudeness to a lady who deserves respect from all mankind?"

The poor footmen, who had fallen so hastily upon the

coach, seeing it had all the marks the page had given them, and found within it a lady of so much beauty, which commands veneration even from the most brutal clowns kept off at a distance to avoid their master's fury, who thought he had reason on his side for what he had done, and that he was kind to them not to cut them to pieces. Don Sancho begged Helen's pardon, and acquainted her with the occasion why those sons of a thousand whores, his footmen, had attacked her so rudely, which she knew as well as himself. "See, I beseech you, madam," says he, "in what premunires these rascals may engage their masters; had not I happened to be with them, these blockheads upon a few foolish marks might have set the whole country in an uproar, raised the mob, and by mere force have carried you to Toledo for a thief. Not but that you are one," cries our gentleman, smoothing his countenance, "but, madam, you steal hearts, and nothing else."

Helen thanked Heaven within herself for giving her a face that stood her in such stead by clearing her from the wicked actions she used to commit, and recovering out of her fright, answered Don Sancho with a great deal of modesty, and in few words, knowing that to take a world of pains to clear one's self of a thing that is laid to one's charge, rather increases than lessens the suspicion. Don Sancho was surprised to find that treasure by mere accident which he had so violently longed to see, and was such a fool as to think that Heaven favoured his passion, since it had hindered him from going back to Toledo, as had been in his thoughts, which had he done, he had missed this happiness. He asked Helen what her name was, and where she lived in Madrid, and, moreover, begged her to give him leave to wait on her, that he might by his actions confirm the services he offered her. Helen told him both false: adding, she should think herself very happy to be honoured with his visits. He offered to see her safe home, but she would by no means consent to it, representing that she was married, and that her husband was to meet her on the road, therefore whispered him in the ear, that she was afraid even of her domestics, but much more of her husband's jealous temper.

This small confidence she seemed to repose in him made Don Sancho believe she did not hate him. He took his leave of her, and being carried swifter by his hopes than his trusty steed (if I may be allowed so to express myself) made the best of his way to Madrid. He no sooner arrived there, but he enquired after Helen, and her habitation, by the marks she had given him. His footmen were foundered in looking after her, nay, he employed all his friends upon this occasion, but to no purpose. When Helen, Montafar, and the venerable Mendez came to Madrid, their first care was how to get out of it. They knew well enough it would be impossible for them to escape the Toledo cavalier, and that if they stayed to give him a more particular knowledge of their merits, they should find him as dangerous an enemy as they took him now to be their humble servant. Helen disposed of all her movables, and next day after her arrival bought pilgrims' habits for herself and companions. In this equipage they beat the hoof towards Burgos, where Mendez was born, and where she had a sister of her own profession still living. In the meantime, Don Sancho, having lost all hopes of meeting with Helen, returned to Toledo, but so confounded and ashamed, that he did not speak one word from his setting out of Madrid till he came to his own house. After he had saluted his wife, who gave him a thousand caresses, she showed him a letter from his brother, who lived in one of the finest cities in Spain, where he had very good preferment in the cathedral church, and was one of the richest clergymen in all the country, wherein he sent him word that he was at the point of death. He stayed but a night at Toledo, and next morning betimes took post, either to contribute to his brother's recovery, or in case he died, to take possession of his estate.

In the meantime Helen pursued her journey to Burgos, being as much dissatisfied with Montafar as she had formerly loved him. He had shown so little bravery when Don Sancho and his footmen stopped their coach, that she did not question but he was a rank coward. This rendered him so odious to her, that she could scarce endure the sight of him ; her thoughts were wholly employed how to deliver herself from this domestic tyrant, and she flattered herself with hopes that she should soon get out of his clutches. It was the venerable Mendez that first put it into her head, and fortified this pious resolution, with all the reasons her prudence could suggest. This industrious matron was vexed to the very heart to see a lazy, useless lubber command her, govern Helen, and enjoy all the fruit of their labour, while he did nothing to obtain it. She incessantly represented to Helen the unhappiness of her condition, which she compared to that of a slave's working in the mines, who enriches his master with the gold he digs out of the earth with incredible labour and hardship, and instead of being the better treated for it, is commonly rewarded only with drubs and bastinadoes. She continually preached to her that beauty was a blessing of a short duration, and that her looking-glass, which showed her nothing now but what was amiable, and never spoke but to her advantage, would in a short time present her with a sight that would by no means please her, and tell her most dismal news.

"Madam," says she to her, "a woman that has seen thirty, loses every sixth month one of her charms, and sees some new blemish or wrinkle rise up every day in judgment against her face and body. That wicked thing called Time makes young women old, and old women wrinkled. If a woman that has enriched herself at the expense of her chastity and reputation, is for all that despised by the world, notwithstanding her wealth and fortune, think how wretched and miserable she must needs be that joins poverty to infamy ; and what reason has she to flatter herself that any one will relieve her in her misery ? If with the money you have acquired by certain means not approved by all the world, you should free an honest fellow out of jail and marry him, you would do an act pleasing both to God and man, and the end of your life would make some sort of atonement for the beginning of it. But you on the contrary throw away yourself and all you have upon a rascal, who is as villainous as he is cowardly, and who makes it his sole ambition to fleece poor women, whom he only gains by his menaces, and keeps under by his tyranny ; now, under the rose be it spoken, this is to squander away one's wealth, on purpose to make one's self the greatest wretch alive, and to take pains to further one's ruin."

By these and such like discourses the judicious Mendez, who knew much better how to talk than act, endeavoured to remove the heroic Montafar from the good affections of the virtuous Helen, who had no other reason almost for loving him, but that she had been so long used to his company. Besides she was a woman of too good sense not to approve those reasons in her own thoughts, which the old matron had laid before her. In short, they were not urged to no purpose. Helen received them in good part, and so much the more readily, in that Mendez's interest alone was not concerned in them ; and because at that time Montafar was coming up to them, that they might enter Gaudar-rama in a body, the place where they intended to dine. They adjourned, to a more convenient opportunity, their thinking of ways and means how to give him the slip, and get rid of him. He seemed much disgusted all dinner time, and going to rise from table was seized with a great shivering, and afterwards a violent fever, which held him the rest of the day and all night, and which increasing upon him next morning, gave Helen and Mendez some hopes that this lucky distemper might assist their designs. Montafar finding himself so weak that he was hardly able to crawl, gave our ladies to understand that they must not stir out of Gaudarrama, but must send for a doctor whatever it cost, and take all imaginable care of him. He spoke this with as much haughtiness and authority as if he had talked to his slaves, and was master of their lives as well as their money. In the meantime the fever found a way to his pericranium, and brought him so low, that if he had not called now and then for drink, one would have sworn he had been as dead as a door-nail. The people of the inn wondered why they delayed so long to send for a confessor to him, when Helen and Mendez, who did not doubt but this fever would give him a lift into the other world, sitting on both sides the bed, Helen began the following discourse:

" If thou canst remember, my dear Montafar," said she, " after what manner thou hast always lived with me, to whom thou hast had all the obligations imaginable, and likewise with Mendez venerable for her age and virtue, thou mayest easily imagine we shall not much importune heaven to restore thee to thy health, but although I should desire it as heartily as I have just reason to wish thy death, yet the will of heaven must be done, and I ought to offer up with the utmost resignation what I once loved most. To deal frankly by thee," quoth she, " for this is not a time to dissemble, both of us began some time since to be so weary of thy tyranny, that our parting was unavoidable, and if Providence had not kindly visited thee with this sickness, which will soon, we doubt not, do thy business, for know to thy consolation that thou art riding full gallop to another world, we would have endeavoured at least to have settled in some place in Spain, where we should have had no more thought of thee than if thou hadst never had a being. In short, whatever foolish inclination thou mayest have to live,

since heaven, for reasons unknown to men, affords thee a
more honourable end than thou dost deserve, permitting a
fever to do that for thee which either the hangman generally
does for such villains, or fear for such mean-spirited rascals
as thou art. But, my dear Montafar," proceeded she, "before
we part for good and all, tell me sincerely once in thy life,
didst thou ever think I was such an arrant fool as to stay
here to watch thee a nights, give thee thy juleps, potions,
cordials, and administer thy clysters to thee ? Don't suffer
such vanities as these to come into thy noddle when thou
art so near death ; for though it concerned not only thy
health, but that of thy whole family, I would not stay here
a quarter of an hour longer. Cause thyself therefore to be
immediately carried to some hospital, and since thou hast
always followed my advice, don't despise this I now give
thee, and which is the last thou art like to have from me. I
mean, my poor Montafar, don't send for a physician, for he
will most assuredly forbid thee wine, and that alone,
without the help of a fever, were enough to kill thee in four-
and-twenty hours."

While Helen talked thus, the charitable Mendez every now
and then felt Montafar's pulse, put her hand on his forehead,
and finding her mistress had done speaking, she re-assumed
the discourse.

"In truth, Signor Montafar, your head is as hot as a glass-
house, and I am mightily afraid this distemper will carry
you off without so much as giving you leave to reflect on
your past life. Take therefore this chaplet," added she,
"and run over your beads devoutly till your confessor comes.
This will do full as well for the discharge of your conscience. But if we may believe the annalists of the hangman of Madrid, that have so often employed their pens to
describe your gallant exploits, your excellency's exemplary
life will not require much repentance ; besides, heaven will
reckon to you without doubt the dolorous perambulation

you made in the principal streets of Seville in the sight of so many people, and guarded by so many officers on horseback, that one would have taken you for the sheriff, but that he always marches at the head, and you were content at the time to march in the rear. And what may yet farther help to wipe off your scores, is your notable life at sea, where for six years together, you did abundance of things pleasing to your maker, working much, eating little, and always in action ; and what is more considerable, you were scarce twenty years old, when to the great edification of the neighbourhood you began that holy pilgrimage. Nor is this all," says our ancient matron, " for it is not to be supposed, but that you will be amply rewarded in the other world for the care you have taken in this, that the women that lived with you should not be lazy and inactive, making them maintain themselves, not only by the labour of their hands, but the sweat of their whole bodies. After all, if you die in your bed, it must be an inexpressible consolation to you, in that you will thereby put a pleasant cheat upon the judge of Murcia, who swore a great oath he would make you die in your shoes, who expects to have the satisfaction to see you cut capers in the air, and, in a word, who will be ready to hang himself when he comes to hear you were so malicious as to die in your bed, without the help of a third man. But I lose time in talking to thee, not considering 'tis high time to begin our journey, which we so earnestly desire. And therefore, old friend of mine," continued she, " receive this embrace with as good a heart as I give it, for I am of opinion we shall see one another no more."

As soon as she had concluded this comfortable speech Mendez threw her arms about his neck, Helen did the like, and so they went out of the chamber, and soon after out of the inn. Montafar, who had been accustomed to their raillery, and could upon occasion return them a Rowland for their Oliver, thought they had said all this merely to divert him, and had not the least suspicion when he saw them quit the room, fancying to himself they were but gone down to make him some water-gruel or posset-drink. After this he fell into a slumber, and though he could not be properly said to be fast asleep, yet it held him so long, that our damsels were got a league of their way before he awaked. He asked the woman of the inn where they were, she told him they were gone, and had given her orders not to disturb him, because he had not slept a wink the night before. Montafar then began to believe the lasses had left him in good earnest. He cursed the inn-keeper and inn to the pit of hell, threatened even the ground they walked upon, and the sun that gave them light. He must needs rise to put on his clothes, but was so feeble, he had like to have broke his neck. The good-natured hostess endeavoured to excuse the two damsels, and backed what she said with such impertinent reasons, as set our sick man a raving like one distracted, when he called her all the vile names he could think of. He was so vexed, that he would not eat a morsel for four-and-twenty hours ; and this no-diet, joined with plenty of choler, had that good effect, that after he had recruited himself with a little water-gruel, he found himself lusty enough to pursue his fugitive slaves. They were got two days' journey before him ; but two hackney mules that were sending back to Burgos farthered his design, as much as they ruined that of our two pretended pilgrims. He overtook them within six or seven leagues of Burgos, they changed countenance as soon as they saw him, and excused themselves as well as they were able. Montafar did not seem to be in the least angry with them, so great was his joy to have them again in his clutches. He laughed as heartily as they did at this merry frolic of theirs, and acted his part so well, that they believed him in their thoughts to be a downright passive blockhead. He persuaded them they had lost their way to Burgos, therefore leading them among some rocks, where he very well knew nobody would

come to interrupt him, he put his hand to a bayonet, to
which they had always paid a world of respect, and told
them, like a merciless devil as he was, that they must
immediately deliver all their gold, silver, and jewels. At
first they believed their tears would have accommodated
the business. Helen threw her arms about his neck, and
wept most plentifully; but our cavalier was so haughty,
now he had them in his power, that he was deaf to all
their prayers and entreaties, and signified to them his last
will and pleasure, that they must surrender all in a quarter
of an hour, otherwise they knew what they must expect.
Thus our poor damsels were forced to sacrifice their purses
for their safety, and it was with the last regret they parted
with their money, which they loved so dearly. But
Montafar's revenge did not stop here, for he produced
certain things called cords, which he had purposely
provided; and binding each of them to a tree, just over
against one another, told them with a treacherous smile
that, knowing how remiss and negligent they had been in
doing penance for their sins, he was resolved to give them
holy discipline with his own hands, that they might
remember him in their prayers.

He executed his pious design with some broom-branches,
and after he had satisfied himself at the expense of their
backs, he sat himself down between these two meek-hearted
sufferers, and turning towards Helen, spoke to her as
follows: "My dear Helen," said he, "take not in ill part
what I have done, but consider my good intention, and
know that every one is bound in conscience to follow his
vocation. It is thine to be malicious; for alas, the world
is composed of bad as well as good, and it is mine to
punish the malicious. Whether I have acquitted myself
as I ought, thou knowest better than any one; and if I
have heartily chastised thee, be satisfied I as heartily love
thee. If my duty did not render me deaf to all pity, I
would not leave so virtuous and honourable a damsel

naked, tied to a tree, and exposed to the mercy of the next passenger. Thy illustrious birth, with which thou didst lately acquaint me, deserves another destiny ; but I know thou wilt at the same time own, that thou wouldst do the same that I have done, if thou wert in my place. What falls out most unlucky is, that being so public as thou art, thou wilt be soon known ; and then it is to be feared that our magistrates, out of a maxim of policy, will order this wicked tree, with which thou art as it were incorporated, to be burnt, together with the wicked fruit it produces ; but know, to thy great comfort, that if thy wicked actions put thee now in bodily fear, the time will come when it will be a pleasure to thee to relate them, and when among thy other laudable qualities, thou wilt possess that of being able to pass a long winter's night, and set folks asleep with the recital of thy famous exploits. But I should give the good Mendez just occasion to complain of my unkindness should I address my discourse any longer to thee, without taking notice of her—nay, I should be wanting in my duty to my neighbour, if I should not in charity give her some advice that may be useful to her in the present posture of her affairs. They are," continues he, and turning himself towards Mendez, "in a worse condition than you imagine, let me persuade you, therefore, to recommend yourself seriously to your Maker, once in your life at least, since your old foundered carcass will scarce be able to support the fatigue of this day ; and oh ! that my prayers could as easily procure you a confessor, as it is certain you want one. Not but that your exemplary life may leave your conscience in repose ; you have been so public-spirited and charitable all your days, that instead of censuring and magnifying the faults of others, you have repaired those of a thousand young maidens ; and since you have taken such pains to study the darkest and most concealed sciences, ought you not to be commended for it ? It is true, the inquisition has no

great kindness for you upon this score, nay, and has given
you some public marks of its displeasure ; but you know
that's composed of wicked men, and that it is natural for
people of the same profession to hate one another. This
is not all, for those gentlemen have a very ill opinion of
your salvation ; but although what they say should be true,
yet a little time will reconcile one to the worst of places,
that is, even to hell itself, where you may take it for
granted you will soon receive all imaginable marks of
civility from the inhabitants, having conversed and dealt
with them from your infancy. I have one word more to
say to you, and then I have done. I might have chastised
you, madam, after another manner, but I considered that
old people, according to the proverb, turn children again,
and your ladyship is old enough to be in your first state
of innocence, and therefore whipping was more proper for
the little trick of youth you played me, than any other
chastisement. And thus, ladies, I take my leave of
you, earnestly desiring you to have a care of your dear
persons."

Having rallied them after this fashion, justly or not, as
the reader pleases, away he went, and left them rather
dead than alive, not so much for grief of their having been
whipped, as because all their money was gone, and they
were left in a lonely place tied to trees, where they might
expect every minute to be devoured by wolves. With
these melancholy contemplations in their pates, as they
were looking sorrowfully upon one another, without saying
a word, a hare crossed the road before them, and some
time after a greyhound thundering after poor puss, and a
cavalier well mounted thundering after the greyhound.
Who should this now be but Don Sancho de Villafagnan,
who had made a journey to Burgos to see his sick brother,
and kept him company at a country house not far from
thence, whither he had retired to take the fresh air. He
was extremely surprised to behold two women thus bound

to their good behaviour, but much more, when he found
one of them to resemble the beautiful stranger whom he
had seen at Toledo, whom he sought after at Madrid, and
whom he had ever since perpetually in his mind. Being
firmly persuaded she was a woman of quality and married,
he doubted whether this was she, for he could not imagine
what should bring her into that part of the world in so
wretched an equipage. But Helen's face having lost
nothing of its former lustre, though somewhat disordered
by her fright, made him to conclude that he at last had
accidentally met with that treasure which had cost him so
many desires and inquietudes in the pursuit of. So he
raised himself in his stirrups to see whether the coast was
clear, and was fool enough to suspect that this was nothing
but a diabolical illusion, which Heaven had permitted to
punish him for his sensuality. Helen on her part was
taken up with a thought full as mortifying, for she fancied
her ill stars had chosen this unlucky day to show her to
all that had anything to say to her. Don Sancho looked
upon her with great amazement, and she on him with no
less disorder; each expected when the other should speak,
and Don Sancho at last was going to begin, when a servant
came full speed to tell him that some of his relations were
going to kill one another. Upon this he spurred his beast,
attended by the servant; and when he came to the place
where he left his company, he found some four or five
drunken fellows, calling one another rogue and rascal, with
their tilters in their hands, and flourishing them notably in
the air, to the prejudice of some neighbouring trees, that
lost some of their best branches by the bargain. Don
Sancho, though enraged to be deprived of the charming
vision he had so lately seen, did nevertheless all he could
to reconcile these furious, terrible gentlemen; but all his
arguments, entreaties, and menaces had signified nothing,
had not the wine that over-loaded their brains, and downright lassitude tripped up their heels, and left them snoring

on the ground, as peaceably as if they had never fallen
out. Don Sancho seeing this, spurred his horse back
towards the happy tree, which kept the idol of his heart,
and was at his wits' ends when he saw the women were
gone. He turned his eyes round him, to see which way
they could be escaped, but saw nothing but a lonely,
melancholy place; he spurred his horse afresh, and
examined every corner, and at last came back to his
beloved oak, which like a good natured tree as it was, still
kept its old station. But as Don Sancho was a poet, and,
what is more, a tender-hearted whining poet, he had not
the same indifference for this insensible tree as other men
have. He alighted from his horse, and harangued it after
the following manner, or at least should have done so, if
he were really so great a coxcomb as I have been told
he was:

"O thrice happy trunk! since thou hast had the
honour to be embraced by that divine creature, whom I
love without knowing her, and whom I know only because
I love her, may thy leaves ever shine among the stars: let
the sacrilegious axe never presume to wound thy tender
bark; may the thunder reverence thy boughs, and the
worms of the earth not dare to approach thy root; let the
winter spare, and the spring adorn thee; let the proudest
pines envy thy condition; and lastly, may Heaven protect
thee in every part." While our worthy gentleman was
spending himself in these vain contemplations, or, if you
please, these poetical follies, which, by the by, are of
greater importance than others are, and ought not to be
used every day in the week, his servants, who knew not
what was become of him, after they had looked for him a
pretty while, at last found him and brought him home.
He returned to his brother's house very much concerned at
his late adventure; and unless I am mightily mistaken, I
have heard some people say, he went supperless to bed.
Some critics now will perhaps tell me I have left my

reader too long in suspense, who without question is impatient to know by what strange enchantment Helen and Mendez came to disappear to the amorous Don Sancho. But let him have patience, and I will soon inform him.

Montafar was at first pleased with that piece of justice he had done upon the two fugitives ; yet no sooner did the heat of his revenge begin to cool, but love inflamed him, and represented Helen to his thoughts infinitely more charming than he had ever fancied her before. He considered within himself that the prize he had taken from her would be soon spent, whereas her beauty was a certain revenue to him, so long as he kept in with her, whose absence was already become insupportable to him. So he came back the same way he went, and with those individual barbarous hands, that had so rigorously bound the two dames to the trees, and afterwards so unmercifully lashed them, broke their chains, that is to say, either cut or untied their cords, for historians differ, and by that means set them at liberty, at the same time that Don Sancho was employed not far off to reconcile his drunken companions, who were in a very fair way to cut one another's throats. Montafar, Helen, and Mendez shook hands upon this reconcilement, and after they had mutually promised to forget all was past, embraced with as much tenderness as if nothing had happened ; doing just as your great people do, who neither hate nor love, but accommodate these two contrary passions to their interest, and the present state of their affairs. They deliberated which road to take ; and it was agreed *nemine contradicente*, that it was by no means advisable for them to go to Burgos, where they would be in danger of having their quarters beaten up by the Toledo cavalier. Therefore they pitched upon Seville for the place of their retreat, and fortune seemed to favour their designs ; for coming into the Madrid road, they met a muleteer with three empty mules, who agreed to carry them to Seville at the very first proposal Montafar made him. He took care to regale our damsels on the road, to make them forget the ill treatment they had received from his hands. At first they could hardly bring themselves to trust him, and had resolved to be revenged on him the first opportunity that presented ; but at last, rather for reasons of state than any principle of charity, they became better friends than ever. They considered that discord had ruined the greatest empires, and believed they were in all probability born for one another. They did not think fit to give any specimen of their profession upon the road to Seville, for as their design by shifting their country was only to get at a distance from those that might pursue them, so they were afraid of bringing themselves into new trouble, which might hinder their getting to Seville where they had great designs to put in execution. They alighted within a league of the city, and having satisfied the muleteer, got thither about the dusk of the evening, and took up their lodgings at the first inn they found. Montafar hired a house, furnished it with very ordinary furniture, and dressed himself all in black, with a cassock, and a long cloak of the same colour. Helen took upon her the habit of a religious sister, that had devoted herself to works of piety ; and Mendez went dressed like a saint, valuing herself upon her hoary locks, and a huge monstrous chaplet, each bead of which was big enough to load a demi-culverin.

The very next day after their arrival Montafar showed himself in the streets, apparelled as I have already described him, marching with his arms across, and looking on the ground whenever he met any women. He cried out with a shrill voice, that was enough to have rent a rock, " Blessed be the holy Sacrament of the altar, and the thrice happy conception of the immaculate Virgin ! " and uttered many more devout exclamations, with the same everlasting lungs of leather. He made the children whom he met in the streets repeat the same words after him ; and moreover assembled them sometimes together, to teach them to sing hymns and songs of devotion, and to instruct them in their catechism. He repaired to the gaols, and preached to the prisoners, comforting some and relieving others, begging victuals and other provisions for them, and frequently walking thither with a heavy basket upon his back.

O detestable villain! thou wantedst nothing but to set up for a hypocrite to be the most profligate accomplished rascal in the universe. These actions of virtue, in a fellow that was the least virtuous of all mankind, procured him in a little time the reputation of a saint. Helen and Mendez likewise did all that in them lay to deserve canonization. The one called herself the mother, the other the sister of the thrice blessed friar Martin. They went every day to the hospitals, where they assisted the sick, made their beds, washed their linen, and did all this at their own expense. By these means the most vicious people in Spain obtained the universal admiration of all Seville. About this time a gentleman of Madrid happened to come thither about some private affairs. He had formerly been one of Helen's lovers, for women of her character have commonly more than one string to their bow. He knew Mendez to be a notorious cheat and Montafar to be no better. One day as they came out of the church, encompassed by a great number of persons, who kissed their very garments, and conjured them to remember them in their prayers, they were known by the aforesaid gentleman, who, burning with a Christian zeal, and not able to suffer three such notorious impostors to abuse the credulity of a whole city, broke through the crowd, and giving a hearty box o' th' ear to Montafar,

"You wicked cheats," cried he, "do you neither fear God nor man?" He would have said more, but his good intention, which in truth was somewhat of the rashest, had not the success it deserved. All the people fell on him, whom they believed to have committed sacrilege in offering this violence to their saint. He was beaten to the ground, and had certainly been torn to pieces by the mob, had not Montafar by a wonderful presence of mind undertaken his protection, by covering him with his body, keeping off those that were most enraged against him, and exposing himself even to their blows.

"My brethren," cried he to them as loud as he could bawl, " let the poor wretch alone for the love of God ; be quiet for the love of the Blessed Virgin." These few words having appeased this horrible tempest, the people made room for Brother Martin to pass, who went up to the unfortunate gentleman, well pleased in his heart to see him so used, though showing outwardly a mighty concern for him. He raised him up from the ground, embraced and kissed him all covered as he was with blood and dirt, and reprimanded the people for their rude behaviour.

" I am a wicked man," said he to the standers by, " I am a sinner, I am one that never did anything pleasing in the eyes of God. Do you believe," continued he, " because you see me dressed in this religious garb, that I have not been a robber all my lifetime, the scandal of others, and the destruction of myself? Alas! you are mistaken, my brethren. Make me the mark of your contumelies, pelt me with stones, nay, draw your swords upon me !" Having spoken these words with a counterfeit sorrow, he threw himself with a zeal yet more counterfeit at the feet of his enemy, and kissing them, not only begged his pardon, but likewise gathered up his sword, cloak, and hat, which he had lost in the scuffle. He helped him on with them again, and leading him by the hand to the end of the street, took his leave of him, after he had bestowed abundance of embraces, and as many benedictions on him. The poor man was as it were out of his wits at what he had seen, and with what had been done him, and was so full of confusion, that he durst hardly show his head in the streets all the while his affairs detained him at Seville. Montafar had won the hearts of all the city by this pretended act of devotion. The people gazed at him with admiration, and the children cried after him, " A saint, a saint," as they cried out, " A fox, a fox," when they saw his enemy in the street. From this moment he lived the happiest life in the world. Some nobleman, cavalier, magistrate, or prelate perpetually invited him to dinner, and strove who should have most of his company. If he were asked his name, he would answer, he was a beast of burthen, a sink of filth, vessel of all iniquity, and such like noble attributes, which his counterfeit devotion dictated to him. When he visited any of the ladies, he complained to them incessantly of the nothingness of his dispensation, and the deadness of the inward man : adding, he wanted concentration of heart, and recollection of spirit ; in short, he always talked to them in this magnificent cant and holy gibberish. No alms were given in Seville but what passed through his hands, or those of Helen and Mendez, who were not wanting likewise to act their parts to admiration, and stood as fair for a red-lettered preferment in the almanack, I mean to be sainted, as Montafar himself. A lady of quality, who was a widow, and devout even to superstition, sent them every day two dishes of meat for dinner, and as many for supper, and you must know these dishes were dressed by the very best cook in all Seville. Their house was too little to receive the numerous presents were daily sent them. A woman that had a mind to be with child put her petition into their hands, to the end, by their mediation it might be presented to the tribunal of heaven. Another that had a son in the Indies did the same, as likewise a third that had a brother prisoner in Algiers. Nay, the poor widow who had to contest with a powerful adversary before an ignorant or a covetous judge, did not doubt the success of her cause when she had once made a present to them according to her ability. Some gave them sweetmeats and conserves, others pictures and ornaments for their closet. Several charitable persons trusted them with great quantities of linen and woollen cloth, to dispose among the needy that were ashamed to beg, and with considerable sums of money to distribute as they saw convenient. No one came to visit them empty-handed, and their future canonization was as firmly believed as an article of faith. At last the credulity of the people ran so high, that they came to consult them about their doubtful affairs, and things to come.

Helen, who was as subtle as a devil, managed all the answers, delivering her oracles in few words, and those capable of receiving different interpretations. Their beds were mean and homely, covered in ·the daytime with coarse blankets, but at night with all the fine furniture a man could desire, that loves to sleep deliciously; their house being plentifully furnished with good feather-beds, fine coverlids, and, in short, with all sorts of movables that contribute to the convenience and pleasure of life : and all this they pretended was to be given to some poor widow, whose goods had been seized in execution, or to furnish some young woman's house who had married without any fortune. Their doors were shut up in winter at five, and in summer at seven o'clock, as punctually as in a well-regulated convent ; and then the jack was wound up, the spits turned merrily round, the capons put down to the fire, the table handsomely spread, when our hypocritical triumvirate ate heartily, and drank plentifully to their own, and the healths of those people they had cheated. Montafar and Helen lay together for fear of spirits, and their footman and maid, that were of the same complexion, copied so pious an example. As for the good Mendez, she always lay alone, being more taken up with contemplation than action, ever since she had addicted herself to the black art. This was their constant practice. instead of employing their time in mental prayer, or in doing penance. 'Tis no wonder if, living so jolly a life, they looked plump and fat. All the city blessed heaven for it, and were mightily surprised that persons of so much austerity and self-denial should look better than those that lived in luxury and ease.

For the space of three years they deceived the eyes of all the inhabitants of Seville, and by receiving presents from every one, and appropriating to their own use the alms that passed through their hands, they had heaped together an incredible number of pistoles. All good success was ascribed to the efficacy of their prayers ; they stood god-fathers to all children, made matches for all the city, and were the common arbitrators of differences. At last heaven was weary of conniving longer at their impious lives. Montafar, who was choleric in his temper, used frequently to beat his valet, who could not bear it, and had quitted his service a hundred times if Helen, who was more discreet than her gallant, had not prevented it by appeasing him with fair words and presents. One day having drubbed him immoderately for little or no reason, the boy got to the door, and, blinded by his passion, ran directly to the magistrates, to inform against these three hypocrites whom the world took for saints. Helen's diabolical spirit foretold what would happen, therefore advised Montafar to rub off with all the gold they had in the house, and retire to some place of security, till this tempest, which threatened them, had spent itself. It was no sooner said than put in execution. They carried off the most valuable things, and walking down the street as unconcerned as if they had dreaded nothing, went out at one gate, and came in at another, on purpose to baulk the scent of their pursuers. Montafar had insinuated himself into the good graces of a widow, as vicious and rank a hypocrite as himself. He had communicated this secret to Helen, who was no more jealous of this matron than Montafar would have been of a gallant

that would have promoted the good of their little common-
wealth. Here they absconded in safety, and lived luxuri-
ously, the widow loving Montafar for his own sake, and
Helen for Montafar's. In the meantime the justice was
conducted by the vindictive valet to the famed mansion
of our pretended saints. When he came there he found the
birds flown, and the maid not able to inform him whither
they were gone. However, he sealed up all their trunks,
and took an exact inventory of all that was in the house.
The serjeants found more provision in their kitchen than
would have served to regale them one day, and you may be
sure they took care to lose nothing that they could privately
sink to their own use.

In the midst of this bustle the venerable Mendez entered
the house, little imagining what had happened. The
serjeants apprehended her, and carried her to prison with
a vast concourse of people at her heels. The servant and
maids were likewise sent thither to bear her company, and
having talked too much, as well as the old matron, were
condemned, as well as she, to receive two hundred lashes.
Mendez died three days after this chastisement, it being
somewhat of the severest for a person of her age, and the
servant and maid were banished Seville for their lives.
Thus the foreseeing Helen preserved her dearly beloved
Montafar and herself from the hands of the magistrates,
who searched after them in vain, both within and without
the city. The people were all ashamed to be so notoriously
cheated ; and the ballad singers, who had sung their praises
the week before, now employed their hackney sonneteers
to expose these pretended saints in lamentable doggerel.
These insects of Parnassus exhausted all their little stock of
scandal upon this subject, and the wretched rhymes they
composed against these godly cheats, who, not long before
were the idols of the people, are still sung in Seville.

Montafar and Helen took the road to Madrid as soon as
they could do so with safety, and arrived there rich, and in

the circumstances of husband and wife. The first thing they did was to enquire after Don Sancho de Villafagnan, and finding he was not in Madrid, appeared in public ; he dressed as fine as a lord, and she in the equipage of a woman of quality, and as beautiful as an angel. She was married to Montafar, as has been said before ; but it was upon this condition, that like a husband of good sense and great patience, he should not take ill the visits her beauty occasioned her ; and she on the other hand obliged herself to receive none but such as would turn to their common advantage.

Your goers between, otherwise styled promoters of good intelligence between the two sexes, vulgarly called bawds, or, to speak more honourably of them, women of intrigue, soon came acquainted with Helen, and directed her how to manage herself. One day they made her show herself at the play, next day in the park, and sometimes in the high street of Madrid in her coach, where, bestowing a glance upon one, a smile upon another, and giving hopes to all, she soon furnished herself with a set of lovers enough to man a galley. Her dear husband religiously observed every article of the original contract ; he encouraged his wife's bashful gallants by his obliging behaviour, and led them as it were by the hand to her apartment, where he was so courteous and discreet, that he always pretended some extraordinary business or other called him out, in order to leave them by themselves. He scorned the acquaintance of any that were not rich and would not spend their money freely, and never knocked at the door till he was assured by a certain signal that always hung out of his window when his virtuous spouse was taken up in private business, that his presence would spoil no sport ; and if the aforesaid signal forbid his coming in, he trooped off merry and well satisfied, as knowing business went on in his absence, and passed away an hour or so at some gaming academy, where every one caressed him for his wits' sake.

Among the rest that paid tribute to Helen, a certain

gentleman of Granada surpassed all his competitors in his excess of love and expenses. He was descended of so good a family, that the titles of his nobility were to be found in the archives of the capital city of Judea, and those that were particularly acquainted with his pedigree have affirmed, that his ancestors were the hangmen of Jerusalem, both before and after Caiaphas. His great affection for Helen made him release a great number of pistoles out of an obscure dungeon, where he had imprisoned them for many years. In a short time Helen's house became the best furnished of any in Madrid. A coach and four that cost her nothing the keeping, came punctually every morning to receive her orders, and waited on her whither she pleased to command them till night. This prodigal lover took one of the side boxes at the play-house for her for a whole twelvemonth, and scarce a day passed over his head, but he provided some magnificent collation or other for her and her friends, at one of the summer houses near Madrid. Montafar, who loved his belly like to any churchman, never failed to make one of the number. He went as fine as a prince, had as much money in his pocket as a clerk of the treasury, ate like a Frenchman, and drank like a German. He paid a wonderful deference to our Granada gentleman who was so very liberal of his money, and indeed he had naturally an esteem for persons of that character. But at last the wind veered about, and raised a terrible storm. Helen now and then used to receive visits from a young swaggering spark, one of those furious heroes that never made a campaign in their lives, yet talk of nothing but slashing and killing, that live upon some wretched harlot, whom they insult at discretion, that go every day to the play-house to pick pockets, or create quarrels, and who at night draw their swords and hack against some passive wall, swearing next morning they had been engaged in a dangerous encounter the night before with at least half a dozen bullies. The sage Montafar often told Helen he was not at all pleased to see such a visitant in his house, from whom they could expect nothing. But for all he could say to her, she was not in the mind to part with her gallant. Montafar was angry with her, and to make himself some amends out of her carcass, treated her with the same chastisement which Mendez of happy memory and she had formerly undergone in the mountains of Burgos. Helen pretended to be easily reconciled, however meditated secret revenge in her heart. The better to accomplish her end, she caressed him so lovingly for eight days together, that he persuaded himself she was one of those tractable ladies that adore their tyrants, and use their humble servants scurvily.

One day that our Granada gallant had promised to sup with them, but by reason of some unexpected business could not come to the noble entertainment he had provided for them, Montafar and Helen drank hand to fist several bumpers to their benefactor, to whom they were obliged for all this good cheer. Montafar got fuddled according to his laudable custom, and towards the end of the repast must needs taste a bottle of perfumed hippocrass, which the gentleman had sent them as an extraordinary present. It is not certainly known whether Helen, who opened the bottle before supper, put any poisonous drugs in it or not : but this is agreed on all hands, that soon after Montafar had emptied it, he felt a strange heat in his bowels, and intolerable pains after that. He suspected he was poisoned, and ran towards his sword, at the same time that Helen did the like towards the door, to avoid his fury. Montafar went into his chamber, thinking she had hid herself there, lifting up the tapestry, but discovered Helen's young gallant, who without any more ceremony whipped him through the guts. Montafar, though he had received his death's wound, yet held him fast by the throat. The servants made such a hellish noise with crying out murder, that the justice coming that way ran into the house, just as the young bravo, who had done Montafar's business, was making his escape. In the meantime Helen, who had got into the street, and knew not which way to take, ran into the first house she found open. She saw a light in a lower room, and a cavalier walking up and down in it. Without asking him any questions, she threw herself at his feet to implore his assistance and protection, and was strangely surprised to find it was Don Sancho de Villa-fagnan, who on his part was no less astonished to see the idol of his heart thus prostrate, this being the fourth time of his meeting her by accident. Don Sancho had lately fallen out with his wife, who had procured herself to be divorced from him, upon the score of his ill usage of her, and his disorderly life. He had obtained a commission to go and settle a new colony in the Indies, and was to embark at Seville in a short time. Helen told him a thousand lies ; and he was ravished to find she was ready to follow him into America : the justice apprehended the assassin of Montafar, and made a strict search after Helen in Madrid, and seized all they could find in her house. Don Sancho and Helen arrived happily in the Indies, where several adventures befell them that cannot be contained in so short a volume as this is, and which I promise to oblige the public with, under the name of the *Perfect Courtezan, or the Modern Lais,* if I find the world inclined to receive it.

THE INNOCENT ADULTERY.

THE Spanish court at Valladolid was very much bedaggled and bemired, where they are as much bedaggled as they are at Paris, according to the observation of a famous Spanish poet, when in one of the coldest raw nights of a very cold raw winter, and about the time when most of our convents ring to matins, a young gentleman, Don Garcias by name, came out of a house where he had spent the evening in conversation, or else play. He was now got into the street where he lodged, and although the night was exceeding dark, by reason the sky was overcast, yet had he no light with him, whether it was because his footman had lost his link, or because he was a gentleman that did not stand upon these punctilios, I cannot tell; when a door opening all on the sudden, he saw somebody thrown out of it with that violence as to fall on the other side the way. If he was surprised at so odd an adventure, he was much more so when, going to lend his hand to this person that had been so rudely treated, he perceived she was in her smock, and heard her sigh and lament, without making the least effort to rise. He concluded she might be hurt with the fall, therefore by the help of his footman having set her on her legs again, he desired to know wherein he might serve her.

" 'Tis in your power to save both my life and honour,"
answered this unknown person in a voice interrupted with
frequent sobs, and which discovered she was a woman.
" I conjure you," added she, " by the same generosity that
inclined you to pity my misfortunes, to carry me to some
place of security, provided none but yourself, or such whose
fidelity you can trust, may know where I am."

Don Garcias covered her with his cloak, and commanding his footman to bear her up on one side, as he did on
the other, soon arrived at his lodging, where everybody was
gone to bed but the maid, who opened the door, and cursed
them heartily for making her sit up so late. All the
answer the footman made her was blowing out the candle,
which while she went to light, calling him a hundred rogues
for his pains, Don Garcias conducted, or rather carried the
afflicted lady, who could scarce make a shift to stand, to
his room, which was up one pair of stairs. His man soon
brought a light, and then Don Garcias beheld one of the
most beautiful women in Spain, who at the same time in-
spired him with both love and compassion. Her hair was
as bright and black as jet, her complexion a mixture of
lilies and roses, her eyes two suns, her breasts above all
comparison, her arms admirable, her hands much more so,
and her shape like that of a queen, of one's own creating :
but this black hair was in disorder, this charming complexion was eclipsed, these piercing eyes were top full of
tears, these incomparable breasts were bloody, these arms
and hands were in no better condition, in short, this fine
body so delicately shaped was covered all over with black
and blue marks, as if it had undergone the discipline of a
dog-whip a cat-of-nine-tails, or something as bad.

If Don Garcias was ravished to behold so beautiful a
creature, this beautiful creature was as much concerned
to see herself in her present circumstances, in the power of
an unknown gentleman, who seemed not to be above
twenty-five years of age. He was sensible of it, and did

all that in him lay to persuade her she had no reason to fear any ill usage from a man who should think himself happy to die in her service. In the meantime his footman made a little coal-fire, for in Spain they use scarce any other firing, which by the by is none of the best in the world. He laid a pair of clean sheets, or at least he ought to have laid them, on his master's bed, who wishing the lady a good night, left her in possession of his chamber, which he double locked, and went to lie, upon what pretence I cannot imagine, because our history is silent in the matter, with a gentleman, an acquaintance of his, that lodged in the same house. He slept in all probability much better than his guest, who wept all night long. The day appeared, Don Garcias arose, and dressed himself as spruce as a courtier for a ball. He listened at his chamber door, and hearing the poor lady still bemoaning herself, made no difficulty to come in. As soon as she saw him, her grief attacked her with new violence.

" You see," says she to him, " a woman who was yesterday the most esteemed in Valladolid, now infamous to the last degree, and that deserves more to be pitied than ever she did to be envied ; but let my misfortunes be never so great, the charitable protection you have so seasonably afforded me may still alleviate them in some measure, if at night you will see me conducted in a chair or coach to a certain convent I shall name to you. But," continued she, " after so many obligations ought I to beg the favour of you to step to my house, and inform yourself what is said and done there ; and, in short, to know after what manner the court and city talks of an unfortunate woman, whom you have so generously protected ? "

Don Garcias offered to go wherever she would please to command him, with all the eagerness of a man who begins to be in love. She gave him all the instructions that were necessary upon this occasion : he took his leave of her, promising to return immediately, when she, poor lady, fell a weeping and lamenting as violently as if she had begun but that very moment. Don Garcias did not stay a full hour before he came back, and finding his beautiful guest as much afflicted as if she already knew that he had ill news to impart to her,

"Madam," says he to her, "if you are Eugenia, the wife of Don Sancho, I have something to tell you which nearly concerns you. Eugenia is not to be found, Don Sancho is in the hands of the magistrate, accused of the murder of his brother Don Lewis."

"Sancho is innocent," cries she; "I am the unfortunate Eugenia, and Don Lewis was the most wicked of all men." Her tears which trickled down apace, and her sighs which redoubled their violence, would not give her leave to say any more; and in all probability Don Garcias was not a little perplexed to put on a sorrowful air to keep her company in her grief. At last, as violent things are never of long continuance, Eugenia's affliction began to abate, she wiped off her tears, her sighs were gentler than before, when she reassumed her discourse in the following manner:

"'Tis not enough that you know the name and quality of the unhappy woman you have so highly obliged, she is likewise willing to acquaint you with the particulars of her life, and to testify in some manner her gratitude to you by reposing this confidence in you. I am," continued she, "descended from one of the best families in Valladolid. I was born rich, and with beauty enough to give me some pretence to be proud of it. The charms of my person brought me more lovers than those of my fortune, and the reputation of both together provided me adorers in the remotest parts of Spain. Among the rest who believed they should be happy in possessing me, Don Sancho, and Don Lewis, two brothers, equally befriended by fortune and nature, signalized themselves by the excess of their passion, and the mutual emulation there was between them, who should render me the most important services. My rela-

tions declared themselves in favour of Don Sancho, who
was the eldest, and my inclination following their choice,
I gave up myself entirely to a man of above forty years old,
who, by the sweetness of his temper, and the extraordinary
care he took to please me, had made as great a progress in
my affections, as was possible for any person whose age
had been no better suited to mine. The two brothers, notwithstanding they were rivals, had all along lived very amic-
ably together, and Don Sancho when he had married me
did not lose the friendship of his brother Don Lewis by so
doing. Their houses were contiguous, or, properly speaking,
were but one house ; for the wall that divided them had a
door, which by common consent was always left open.
Don Lewis did not forbear to pay the same *dévoirs* to me
before his brother as he had done while he was his rival,
and Don Sancho, whose love increased after possession, and
who loved me better than his life, was not in the least
offended at his gallantry. He himself was used to call me
his brother's mistress, who on his side made a real love
to pass for a feigned one, with so much address, that I was
not the only person he deceived by it. In short, after he
had accustomed me to hear him talk of his passion before
company, he made love to me in private with so much importunity, and so little respect, that I no longer doubted
his intentions were criminal. As young as I was, I had
discretion enough to make him still think I took his love to
be only meant in raillery. I made a jest of what he spoke in
earnest, and though I was never more enraged than at that
time, yet I laboured as well as I could not to lose my
ordinary temper. He was provoked at it, instead of making
right use of it, and looking upon me with eyes, which his
wicked designs had made wild and staring : ' No, no,
madam,' says he, ' I feign much less since I have lost you,
than I did when I had some hopes to possess you ; and
though your rigour be sufficient to deliver you soon from
the importunities of your lover, yet have you so long accus-

tomed me to suffer, that you will do much better to———'
'Never to be alone with you if I can help it,'said I interrupting him.

"One of my women that came into my room at that
time, hindered him from carrying his insolence farther, and
me from showing him my resentment as he deserved, and I
was about to do. I was afterwards very glad I did not do
it, as well for my husband's sake, as because I was in
hopes this wicked brother of his would at last love me less,
and come to esteem me more ; but still he continued to make
feigned love before company, and to solicit me in private. I
combated his transports with all the severity I could sum-
mon to my aid ; nay, so far as to threaten him to acquaint
his brother with it. I used all my arts to cure him of this
folly. I prayed, I wept, I promised to love him as much
as any brother ought, but he forsooth would be loved as a
lover. In short, sometimes a sufferer, sometimes ill-treated,
but always as much in love as he was hated, he had made
me the most unhappy woman in Spain, if my conscience,
that can reproach me with nothing, had not preserved
tranquillity to my soul. But at last my virtue, which had
all along so well defended itself against so dangerous an
enemy, abandoned me, because I abandoned it first, and
helped to betray myself. The court came to Valladolid,
and brought all its gallantry along with it. As all new
things are apt to please, our ladies fancied they saw more
in the courtiers than they could find in the city gallants,
and the courtiers endeavoured to please our ladies, whom
perhaps they looked upon as assured conquests. Among
the other cavaliers that attended the court, in hopes of
being recompensed for their services, a Portuguese, whose
name was Andrada, had rendered himself one of the most
considerable by his wit and good mien, but much more by
his expensive way of living, the most efficacious charm to
gain women of no experience, who judge of the beauty of
the soul by that of the equipage or habits. He had no

great fortune of his own, but play had made him master of
that of other people, and his gains this way were so considerable, that he made as great a figure as the richest and
most magnificent nobleman at court. I was unfortunate
enough to please him, and when my own vanity, backed
by his continual addresses, had persuaded me I was not
disagreeable to him, I reckoned myself the happiest woman
upon earth. I can hardly express how well he knew how
to make himself beloved, or to what excess I loved him.
My husband, so good, so dear, and so respected, became to
me in a little time as contemptible as odious, Don Lewis
appeared more hateful to me than ever. In short, nothing
pleased me but Andrada. I loved none but him, and in
all places where I did not see him, I surprised all the company with my distractions and restless behaviour. Andrada
on his part loved me full as passionately. His predominant
passion for gaming gave way to his love; his presents
gained my women; his letters and verses charmed me, and
his serenades set all the husbands in our street a thinking
for whom they were designed. In short, he attacked me
so well, or I defended myself so ill, that I at last surrendered. I promised him all that lay in my power to give
him, so that now we had no other difficulty to surmount,
but that of a convenient time and place.

" My husband had engaged in a hunting-match, which
would keep him several days in the country. I sent to
acquaint my dear Portuguese with this news, and we agreed
to execute our amorous designs that very night, after my
husband was gone. I was at a certain hour to leave the
back door of our garden open, and under pretence of
passing part of the night there, by reason of the excessive
heats, was to set up a field-bed in a little summer-house,
that was open on all sides, and encompassed with orange
trees and jessamines. At last my husband quitted Valladolid, and that day seemed to me the longest I ever
knew. The night came, and my women having set me up

a bed in the garden, I pretended to be very sleepy, and as soon as my maids had undressed me, commanded them all to go to bed except one chamber-maid, who knew the secret of our amour : I had scarce laid me down, and the maid, whose name was Marina, had hardly shut the garden-door that faced the house, and opened the back-door, when my women came to tell me my husband was returned. I had but just time to shut the garden-door, which I had ordered to be left open for Andrada. My husband caressed me as he used to do, and you may imagine how I received him. He told me he was forced to come back, because the gentleman who had invited him to the sport had unluckily fallen off his horse, and broke his leg. After this he commended my judgment for choosing so cool and refreshing a place, and concluded he would likewise take up his quarters there. He got himself undressed at the same time, and came to bed to me. I did all I could to conceal my vexation at his return, and to show him by my feigned embraces that his were not ungrateful to me. In the meantime Andrada came at the hour of assignation, and finding the door shut, which he thought to have found open, by the help of his valet leapt over the garden-wall, where he had hoped to pass the night with me. He has confessed to me since, his jealousy put him upon so hardy and dangerous a design ; and that he did not doubt but some happy and better beloved rival enjoyed that happiness which I had promised him. These suspicions of his, that perhaps I diverted myself at his expense with another gallant, so inflamed his anger, that he was resolved to use me ill, in case he found what he suspected to be true, and to revenge himself upon his rival to the last extremity. He crept up to the summer-house, whereby we lay together, as softly as he could. The moon shone very bright, I saw him, and knew him as soon as he came in ; he saw I was very much affrighted, and I made a sign to him to be gone. At first he could not discern whether the person that was in bed

with me was my husband or some one else; but observing
in my countenance less fear than confusion and shame, and
seeing upon the table the clothes and plume of feathers he
had seen my husband wear that very day, and which were
as singular as they were remarkable, he was satisfied it was
Don Sancho whom he saw a bed with me, and found him
to be faster asleep than a gallant in all probability would
have been. However, he drew near that part of the bed
where I lay, and stole a kiss, which I could not well hinder,
considering the fear I was in lest my husband should awake.
He had no mind to keep me longer in this fright, and therefore went his way, lifting up his eyes to heaven, shrugging
his shoulders, and showing all the marks of a man that was
deeply afflicted at this disappointment, and so leapt back
again over the garden wall with the same facility as before.

"Early in the morning I received the most passionate
letter from him that ever was read, accompanied with a
pretty copy of verses upon the tyranny of husbands. He
spent the remainder of the night, after he had parted with
me, in writing them, and next day when I received them, I
could hardly do anything else but read them over and over,
as oft as I could do it in private. Neither of us sufficiently
reflected upon the hazard we had run to make it a warning
to us not to expose ourselves so any more. But although I
had not been inclined of myself to grant him all he asked
of me, or had loved Andrada less than I did, or had not
yielded to the insinuating flattery of his letters, yet I could
not have resisted the persuasion of my chamber-maid, who
talked to me incessantly in his favour. She reproached me
with want of resolution, which had made me to think no
more of Andrada, and talked of the passion he had for me
with the same vehemence as she would have told a sweetheart of her own what a kindness she had for him. By this
I found she was not to learn her trade now, and likewise saw
of what importance it is to be careful in the choice of persons
that are placed so near women of my age and condition.

But I was resolved to ruin myself, so that if she had been more virtuous than she was, she had enjoyed a less share in my confidence. At last she over-persuaded me to receive Andrada in a dressing-room near my chamber, where she lay by herself; and we agreed that so soon as my husband was fast asleep she should lie by him in my place, while I passed the night with my gallant. Thus we got him concealed into my dressing-room; my husband fell asleep, and I prepared to meet my lover with all the emotions of one whose desires are violent, yet who had a great deal to fear, when a terrible noise of confused voices that cried out 'Fire, fire,' alarmed my ears, and waked my husband. At the same time my chamber was all in a smoke, and I could perceive the flames through my windows. A negro maid, that served in the kitchen, had set it on fire, being drunk, and it was not perceived till it had taken hold of some dry wood, and the neighbouring stables, and now had seized my apartment. My husband was very well beloved. In an instant the house was full of neighbours that came to help us to quench the fire. My brother-in-law Don Lewis, whom the common danger had made more active and diligent than the rest, was one of the first that helped us with his servants, and who, pushed on by his passion, soon made his way into my chamber through the flames, that had already seized the staircase. He was in his shirt, and had nothing over it but his night-gown, in which he wrapped me up, when taking me between his arms, who might more properly be said to be dead than living, and that on account of the danger to which Andrada was exposed, rather than my own; he carried me to his own room, through the communication his house had with ours, and setting me down upon his bed, left me there, accompanied by some of my women.

"In the meantime my husband, and all that had concerned themselves in this accident that had befallen us, bestirred themselves so notably, that the fire was happily

put out, yet after it had done a great deal of damage.
Andrada made his escape without difficulty among the
crowd and press of people that came to help us ; and you
may imagine how joyful I was when Marina told me the
agreeable news. He writ to me a hundred foolish things
the next day, which I answered with more transport than
he had shown ; and thus we made shift by writing to each
other to soften and relieve that pain which absence occasioned us. After we had repaired all the mischief the fire
had done us, and I had left Don Lewis's room to return to
my own, Andrada easily persuaded me to let him try the
same way once more, which had not failed the last time but
for so unfortunate and unexpected an accident. That very
night we had pitched upon to make ourselves full amends
for the time the fire had made us to lose ; a cavalier of my
husband's acquaintance, who was in some trouble about a
duel, and had fled to an ambassador's house, where he did
not think himself safe enough from the civil magistrate,
was obliged to abscond somewhere else. My husband
carried him privately to his own house, and took the key of
the street door, which he caused to be locked before his
face, lest any servant through treachery or indiscretion
might discover the place of his retirement. This order, at
which I was equally surprised and troubled, was unluckily
put in execution just as Andrada made the signal in the
street, which he had told Marina of before. The poor
maid was in a strange quandary what to do, and made him
a sign from a low lattice window to stay a moment. We deliberated upon the matter a little, and afterwards she went
and told him in a low voice what new obstacle our ill-
natured destiny had trumped up to oppose our design ; so
she proposed to him to stay till all our people were gone
to bed, and then he should try to get in through one of the
kitchen windows, which she would open to him.

" Nothing seemed difficult or dangerous to Andrada, provided he could but satisfy his love. My husband saw his

friend to bed, and went to bed himself in good time, after
the example I had set him ; all our servants did the like ;
and Marina, when she thought the whole family was fast
asleep, opened the little window to Andrada, who with all
the ease in the world got half way through, but so indis-
creetly or unfortunately, that after several efforts, which
rather did him a mischief than helped him, he stuck fast by
the waist between the iron bars, without being able to stir
backwards or forwards. His valet could not help him from
the street, no more could Marina from the place where she
was, without some one else to assist her. So she went to
call up one of the maids, in whom she could repose confidence, and told her that she had been over-persuaded that
night by her sweetheart, whom she loved entirely, and was
to marry in a little time, to try to let him in at the kitchen
window, but that he stuck so fast between the iron bars,
that there was no getting him out without filing, or
wrenching them out of their places ; she desired her therefore to assist her in this extremity, to which the other
readily consented ; but for want of a hammer, or some such
like iron utensil, Andrada had not been a farthing the
better for the help of these two wenches if he had not bethought himself of his poignard, which did the business so
effectually, that after a great deal of struggling and sweat-
ing, the iron bars were by main strength wrested from the
wall, and my gentleman delivered from the terrible fear of
being found so scandalously wedged, in a place where he
could be taken for nothing but a house-breaker. However
this could not be done with so little noise but that some of
the servants heard it, who looked into the street, at the
same time when Andrada, carrying with him the iron hoop,
which enclosed him about the waist, ran off as hard as he
could drive, attended by his footman. The neighbours and
our servants cried out 'Stop thief' after them, and made
no question but that some villains had attempted to rob
Don Sancho's house, especially when they saw the iron bar,

gone. In the meantime Andrada got safe to his lodgings, and was forced to file off the iron bar, which gripped him as close as a belt, for notwithstanding all the tricks his man and he played, there was no getting it off otherwise.

" This third accident put him in a very ill humour, as I came to be informed afterwards. As for me, I took it quite otherwise ; and while Marina, not yet recovered of her fright, told me the story, I thought I should have killed myself with laughing. However, I was no less concerned than he at this series of disappointments, which rather inflamed than cooled our desires, and would not let us defer the happy minute of enjoyment any longer, than the very next day after this pleasant but unlucky adventure. My husband was in the city, endeavouring to make up his friend's business for him, which in all probability would keep him there the remaining part of the day. I sent trusty Marina to Andrada's lodgings, that were not far from my house, she found him a bed still discomposed with the fatigues of the last night, and so dejected by these unlucky crosses in his amours, that Marina was partly scandalized to see with what coldness he received the advances I made him, and to find him so backward to give me the meeting, although she often assured him this was an opportunity that was not to be lost. To make short of my story, at last·he came,"and I received him with all the transports of joy which a woman wholly abandoned to her passion can feel. I was so blinded by it, that I did not perceive, as well as Marina did, with what indifference he made his approaches to me, although it was but too visible. However my embraces at last drew on his. Hitherto our mutual joy could not be otherwise expressed than by our silence, and the thoughts of what each of us desired with so much ardour put me into so great a confusion, that I could not look Andrada in the face, and by this means gave him an opportunity to attempt what he pleased ; when Marina, who like a discreet chamber-maid had gone out of the room to be upon the watch, came in all affrighted and told me my husband was come home. She carried Andrada into my dressing-room, rather dead than alive, and seeming to be much more concerned than myself, although I had more reason to be so. My husband gave some orders to his people below, before he came up into my chamber. In this interval I had just time enough to compose myself, and Marina to empty a great coffer full of lumber, into which she put the despairing Andrada. She had scarce stowed my lover in this little sanctuary, when my husband came into the room, and only kissing me as he passed by, without any farther stay, went directly into my dressing-room, where he found a book of plays and unhappily opened it. He lighted upon a place that pleased him, and had engaged him to read longer, if Marina had not advised me to go to him, and try to bring him into my chamber. My misfortunes did not stop here, for Don Sancho, finding me strangely discomposed and thoughtful, as I had but too much reason to be, endeavoured by his own good humour to put me into a better. Never in his life did he take so much pains to divert and please me as now, and yet never did he vex and importune me more. I begged him to quit my chamber, pretending to be so sleepy that I could not hold open my eyes; but by an unseasonable fit of pleasantry, which was not usual with him neither, he kept me company in spite of all I could say to him; and though he was the most complaisant man alive, yet showed he so little of it at this time, that I was forced to turn him out. As soon as ever I had locked my chamber door, I ran into my dressing-room to deliver Andrada from his prison. Marina opened in all haste the coffer wherein she had put him; but both of us had like to have died of fear and grief, when we found him without either pulse or motion like a dead man, and so in effect he was according to all appearance.

" Imagine to yourself what terrible agonies this sight occasioned me, and what measures it was possible for me to
take in so cruel an extremity. I wept, tore my hair, grew
desperate, and I believe had had resolution enough to have
stabbed myself with Andrada's poniard, if my excessive
grief had not so enfeebled me, that I was forced to throw
myself upon Marina's bed. This maid, although she was
concerned to the last degree, yet preserved her judgment
better than I in this our common calamity, and bethought
herself how to remedy it ; which for my part I wanted
strength to execute, although my reason had not been disordered after the manner it was. She told me that perhaps
Andrada was only in a swoon, and that a chirurgeon either
by bleeding, or some other speedy relief, might restore him
that life which he seemed to have lost. I looked on her
without returning any answer, my grief having in a manner
made me stupid. Marina lost no time in asking more
questions, but went immediately to put in execution what
she had proposed ; but no sooner had she opened the door
with this intention, than my brother-in-law Don Lewis
popped in upon us, and this second disaster was yet more
terrible than the first. Although the body of Andrada had
not been exposed to his view as it was, yet the confusion
and surprise he might read in our faces would have told
him that we had been engaged in some mysterious affair,
which he would not have failed to examine to the
bottom, being so much interested in me, both as a brother-
in-law and a lover. I was therefore obliged to throw myself
at the feet of a man whom I had often beheld at mine, and,
relying upon the love he had for me, and upon his generosity, the essential quality of every gentleman, resigned the
dearest thing I had in the world entirely to his will. He
did what he could to raise me, but being resolved to continue on my knees, I frankly told him, as well as my tears
and sighs would give me leave, what a sad accident had
befallen me, at which I don't at all question but he was

pleased in his heart. 'Don Lewis,' said I to him, 'I don't implore thy generosity now to prolong my life ; my misfortunes already have made it so odious to me, that I would even take it away myself, were I not afraid that my despair could not effect it, but at the expense of my honour, from which that of Don Sancho, and even his life, are perhaps inseparable. Thou mayst believe the disdain I have all along shown thee was rather the effect of my aversion than virtue ; thou mayst rejoice at my disgrace, nay, and glut thy revenge with it ; but darest thou reproach me with a crime which thou hast so often tempted me to commit, and canst thou want indulgence for her who has so often shown it to thee ?' Don Lewis would not let me go on, but, 'Madam,' says he, 'you see heaven has justly punished you for bestowing your affections upon one whom you ought to have hated : but I have no time to lose, that I may convince you by drawing you out of this premunire, that you have not a better friend in the world than Don Lewis.'

"Having said this, he left me, and returned a moment after with two porters, whom he had ordered to be sent for. Marina and I had, in the meantime, put Andrada's body again into the great coffer. Don Lewis lent a helping hand to put it on the fellows' shoulders and bid them carry it to a certain friend's house of his, to whom he had discovered this adventure, as he had before entrusted him with the secret of his amour. Here, after he had taken the body out of the coffer, he ordered it to be laid at full length on a table, and while they were taking off his clothes he felt his pulse, and put his hand on that part of his breast where the palpitation of the heart is best to be discovered, whereby he found there were still some sparks of life remaining in him. He sent for a chirurgeon in all haste, while in the meantime they put him to bed and employed all the remedies proper to bring him to life again. In short, he came to himself, being blooded. A servant was left to attend him, and the company quitted the room to afford time to nature and rest to complete that cure which their remedies had so successfully begun. You may imagine how great Andrada's surprise was when, after so long a *deliquium*, he found himself in bed, and could only remember what a fright he had been in when they put him into the coffer ; he knew not where he was, nor what he had to hope or fear. He was taken up with these mortifying thoughts, when he heard the chamber-door open, and when the curtains were drawn saw by the light of some tapers that were brought into the room, Don Lewis, whom he very well knew to be my brother-in-law, and who, having taken a chair, spoke to him as follows : ' Am I a stranger to you, Signor Andrada, and don't you know I am brother to Don Sancho ? ' 'Yes,' replied Andrada, ' I know you well enough.' ' And do you remember,' cries Don Lewis, ' what happened to you to-day at his house ? Take my word for it,' continues he, ' if you pretend any more to carry on your intrigues with my sister-in-law, or if I ever see you more in our street, you shall sorely repent it ; and further know, that thou hadst been a dead man if I had not taken compassion on a foolish and unfortunate woman, who has been pleased to put her life and honour into my hands ; and if I were not fully assured that thy criminal designs against my brother's honour have not been put in execution. Change your habitation therefore,' continues he, ' and think not to escape my resentments if you break the promise I expect you should make me.' Andrada promised him more than he asked, he made him the meanest and most abject submissions he could think of, and protested that he owed him a life for saving his. He was weak enough in all conscience to keep his bed, but his excessive fear gave him strength to get up. From that very moment he conceived as great an aversion for me as his affection before had been violent, nay, he had my very name in horror. In the meantime I was uneasy to know what was become of him, but had not assurance to ask Don Lewis, nay, not so much as to look him in the face. I sent Marina to Andrada's lodgings, where she arrived just at the same time as he came in himself, and had ordered his trunks to be got ready, to remove to another quarter of the town. As soon as he saw her, he forbade her to come to him any more from me ; and recounting in few words all that had passed between Don Lewis and himself, added that I was the most ungrateful and most perfidious woman in the world ; that he would only consider me for the future as one that designed to ruin him, and desired I would no more think of him than if I had never seen him. Having said this, he turned Marina out of his chamber, who was extremely surprised at his treatment. However her astonishment was not so great but that she had presence of mind enough to dog him at a distance, and observing the house where his trunks were carried, by that means came to know his new lodgings.

"The vexation I felt to be accused of a crime whereof I was innocent, and to be hated by the man whom I loved so tenderly, for whom I had hazarded both my life and reputation, hindered me from taking so much satisfaction in his safety as otherwise I should have done. I fell into a fit of melancholy, which threw me into a sickness, and my distemper, which the physicians could not tell what to make of, was no little affliction to my husband. To complete my misfortune, Don Lewis began to value himself upon the important service he had done me ; he incessantly importuned me to grant him that happiness which I had intended for Andrada : reproaching me that I was in love with the latter, all the time I preached to him what I owed to my husband, and what he owed to a brother. Thus, being hated by the man I loved, loved by him I hated, seeing Andrada no more, seeing Don Lewis too often, and perpetually accusing myself for having been so ungrateful to the best husband in the world, who left nothing undone to please me, and who was distracted at my

illness, when he had the justest provocations to take away
my life; being thus troubled with remorse of conscience,
of love and hatred, two passions so contrary, I kept my
bed for two months, expecting every moment my death
with joy; but heaven, it seems, reserved me for greater
misfortunes. My youth, in spite of myself, assisted me
against this inconsolable grief. In short, I recovered, and
Don Lewis persecuted me much more than ever he had
done. I had given orders to my women, and particularly
to Marina, never to leave me alone with him. Enraged at
this usage, and the resistance I continually made him, he
resolved to obtain by the blackest piece of treachery that
ever was known that which I refused him with so much
steadfastness. I have already told you there was a way
from his house to ours, through a door that was seldom
shut. On the night he pitched upon for the execution of
his damnable design, and at the hour when he thought
every one was asleep, both at his house and ours, he got in
by this door, opened the gate towards the street, and
turned all our horses out of the stable. They immediately
ran into the court, and thence into the street. The noise
they made soon awakened the servants that looked after
them, and they my husband.

"He being very fond of his horses, as soon as ever he
knew they were got into the street, immediately ran after
them in his morning gown, swearing heartily at his
grooms, and the porter, who had forgot to shut the great
gate. Don Lewis, who had hid himself in my ante-
chamber, and seen my husband go down stairs, followed
him into the court, and having shut the street door, and
tarried a little to give the greater probability to what he
had a mind to effect, came to bed to me, personating my
husband so well, that 'tis no wonder if I was mistaken.
He was excessive cold with standing so long in his shirt.
'Good God, sir,' said I to him, 'how cold you are.' ''Tis very
true,' answered he, counterfeiting his voice, 'I had like to

have been starved in the street.' 'And are your horses,' said I to him, 'retaken?' 'My servants are gone after them,' cries he ; and then drawing nearer me, as to warm himself, embracing me very lovingly, proceeded to betray me, and dishonour his brother. As heaven permitted this crime, perhaps it reserved the punishment of it to me, that so my honour might be retrieved by my own hands, and my innocence known. Having satisfied his wicked desire, he pretended to be in pain for his horses, so up he got, and having opened the street gate, retired to his own lodging, well pleased perhaps with his crime, and rejoicing in that which would be the cause of his destruction. My husband came in soon after, and getting into bed crept close to me, half frozen and starved as he was, and obliged me by his caresses, which I thought extraordinary, to desire him to let me sleep. He thought it strange ; for my part I was surprised, and did not doubt but that some treacherous trick had been played me. I could not sleep a wink till it was day, I got up much earlier than I used to do, went to mass, and there I saw Don Lewis in his finest clothes, and with his countenance gay, as mine was sad and melancholy. He presented me with the holy water, which I received very coldly from him ; then looking on me with a malicious sneer, 'Good God, madam,' says he, 'how cold you are !' At these words, that were the same I spoke to him the night before, and which made me no longer doubt my misfortune, I turned pale and then reddened. He might easily find by my eyes, and the disorder he had occasioned me, how heinously I resented his insolence. I parted from him, without so much as looking at him, and passed all the time at mass very uneasily, as you may well imagine. I made my husband uneasy too, when at dinner, and all the rest of the day, I looked like a distracted woman, sighing incessantly, and showing that I was troubled in mind, notwithstanding all the care I took to conceal it. I retired to my chamber sooner than I used to do, pretending a slight indisposition. I thought of a hundred different designs to revenge myself.

"At last my indignation put me upon that which I resolved to put in execution. The night came, I went to bed when my husband did. I pretended to sleep, to oblige him to do the same ; and when I saw him fast, and supposed all our servants were so too, I got up, took his poniard, and, wholly blinded and transported by my passion, made a shift however by the same door, and the same way through which my cruel enemy had got to my bed, to find the way to his. My fury made me not to do things at random. I groped out where his heart lay with my hand that was free, and discovered it by its palpitation. My fear of missing my blow did not make the other tremble wherein I held the poniard. I sheathed it twice in the heart of the detestable Don Lewis, and punished him by a gentler death than he deserved. In the heat of my rage I gave him five or six hearty stabs more, and returned to my chamber in that tranquillity and peace of mind that convinced me I had done nothing but what was just. I put up my husband's poniard, bloody as it was, into the scabbard. I dressed myself in as much haste, and with as little noise as I could ; I took with me all my jewels and money, and as much transported by my love as I had been lately hurried by my revenge, ran away from my husband, who loved me better than his life, to throw myself into the arms of a young man who had not long ago taken care to let me know I was become odious to him. The natural cowardice of my sex was so well fortified by the impetuous passions that reigned in my soul, that though it was midnight, and I all alone, yet I walked from my own house to Andrada's lodging, with as much assurance as if I had being going to do a good action in the daytime. I knocked at Andrada's door, who was not at home, being engaged, it seems, at play at a friend's house. His footmen, who knew me well enough, and were

not a little surprised to see me there, received me with a
great deal of respect, and lighted a fire for me in their
master's chamber.　He came home soon after, and I
suppose little imagined to find me in his room.　He no
sooner saw me, but looking wildly upon me, cried, 'What
has brought you hither, Madam Eugenia, and what have
you to say to me, of all men living, whom you designed to
sacrifice to the revenge of your brother-in-law and gallant?'
'How! Andrada,' said I to him, 'do you put so ill a con-
struction upon an unavoidable accident, which forced me
to have recourse to the only man in the world whom I was
most afraid to be obliged by? and could you pass so
disadvantageous a judgment on a person who had given
you so many proofs of her affection? I expected something more than reproaches from you, which you would
not have been in a condition now to make, had I not
done that very thing for which you condemn me, and
charge me with as a crime.　Alas! if I had been guilty
of any, it is not against you, but against my husband, to
whom I ought to have been faithful, to whom I have
been ungrateful, because I would not be so to you, and
whom I have left to cast myself upon a cruel man that
uses me ill.　When your death, which I looked upon to be
real, had flung me into that despair, which how could a
woman avoid, that expected every moment to be surprised
by her husband? and when Don Lewis found me in this
deplorable condition, what could I otherwise do than rely
upon his generosity, and the love he had for me?　He has
most treacherously betrayed me at the expense of his own
honour, but it has been also at the expense of his own life,
which I have just now taken from him; and 'tis this, my
dear Andrada, that has brought me hither.　It is necessary
I should conceal myself from justice, till I find a proper
time to inform the world what Don Lewis's crime was, as
well as my own misfortune.　I have money and jewels
enough to maintain you with splendour in any part of

Spain, whither you will think fit to accompany a miserable woman. I shall convince the whole world in a little time that I rather deserve to be pitied than blamed, and my future conduct shall justify my past actions.' 'Yes, yes,' cried he, interrupting me, ' I will go and take Don Lewis's place, now thou art cloyed with him, and have my throat cut like him, when thou art so with me.' Ha! thou lascivious woman,' continues he, ' how well does this last wicked action of thine confirm me in my belief that thou designedest to sacrifice me to thy gallant? but think not to come off with reproaches only, I will rather be the punisher of thy crime than the accomplice of it.' He had no sooner spoke these words, but he stripped me by main force, in so barbarous a manner, that even his servants were ashamed of it ; he gave me a hundred blows, naked as I was, and after he had satisfied his rage till he was quite weary, threw me into the street, where, if I had not happily met with you, I had died ere this, or fallen into the hands of those who perhaps are now searching for me."

When she had ended her discourse, she showed Don Garcias the black and blue marks on her arms, and those parts of her body which modesty would allow her to show, and then resumed as follows :

" You have heard, generous Don Garcias, my deplorable history: tell me, therefore, I conjure you, what measures an unhappy woman ought to take, who has caused so many calamitous misfortunes."

" Ah, madam," cries Don Garcias interrupting her, " that I could as easily advise you what to do, as punish Andrada, if you would but give me leave ! Don't rob me of the honour of revenging your quarrel, and don't refuse to employ, in whatever you think fit to command, a man who is no less concerned for your misfortune, than the outrage which has been offered you."

Don Garcias pronounced these words with a heat which convinced Eugenia he no less loved than pitied her. She

thanked him in the most obliging terms her civility and
gratitude could suggest, and begged him to give himself the
trouble to go once more to her husband's house, to inform
himself more particularly what people said of her flight, and
of the death of Don Lewis. He happened to come there
just at the time they were carrying Don Sancho to prison,
together with his domestics, and those of Don Lewis, who
had deposed their master was in love with Eugenia. The
common door between the two houses which had been found
open, and the poniard of Don Sancho yet reeking with
blood, were circumstantial proofs that he had murdered his
brother, of which nevertheless he was as innocent as he was
afflicted at it. The running away of his wife, his jewels
and money that were missing, so strangely surprised him,
that he could not tell what to make on't, and this troubled
him infinitely more than his imprisonment and the proceedings of the magistrate. Don Garcias was impatient
to carry this news to Eugenia, but could not do it so soon
as he desired. One of his friends, who had business with
him, stopped him a long while in the street where his lodging
was, that happened to be over against Andrada's, from
whence he saw a servant come out booted, carrying a portmanteau. He followed him at a distance, accompanied by
his friend, and saw him stop at the post-house. He came in
after him, and found he had hired three horses, that were
to be got ready in half an hour. Don Garcias let him go,
and ordered the same number of horses to be ready at the
same time. His friend asked him what was the meaning
of this, he promised to tell him, provided he would make
one of the number ; to which the other readily consented,
without troubling himself what the matter was. Don
Garcias desired him to put on his boots, and stay for him
at his lodgings, while he made a short trip to his own.
Thus they parted ; and Don Garcias went immediately to
wait upon Eugenia to inform her what he knew of her
affair. At the same time he gave orders to his landlady

who was a woman he could trust, to furnish Eugenia with
clothes and other necessaries, and to carry her that very
night to a convent, the abbess whereof was her relation and
friend. After this he privately ordered his man to carry
his riding coat and boots to the gentleman's lodgings whom
he last parted with, and having once more conjured the
woman of the house to take care of Eugenia, and conceal
her from all the world, he went to call upon his friend, and
walked with him to the post-house, where they had not been
a minute but Andrada came thither. Don Garcias asked
him whither he was going. He told him to Seville.

"Why, then," replied Don Garcias, "we shall need but
one postilion." Andrada liked the notion, and perhaps
thought Don Garcias and his friend were a brace of cullies,
whom he might easily bubble of their money at play. They
rode out of Valladolid together and galloped a pretty
while, without doing anything else ; for I think 'tis agreed
on all hands, that when men ride post, they are none of the
best conversation. Don Garcias, finding they were now in
a fine open plain, fit for business, and remote enough from
any house, rode a little way before the company, then came
back and bid Andrada stop. Andrada asked him what he
would have. "I must fight you," answered Don Garcias,
"to revenge, if I can, Eugenia's quarrel, whom you have
mortally injured by the most cowardly and villainous action
that ever was known."

"I don't repent of what I have done," replied Andrada
to him fiercely, without seeming to be surprised, "but
perhaps you may have occasion to repent of this insolence."
He was a man of courage, and alighted from his horse at
the same time that Don Garcias alighted from his, who
would not vouchsafe him an answer. They were now
coming up to one another with their swords drawn, when
Don Garcias's friend told them they must not offer to tilt
without him, and offered to fight Andrada's footman, who
was a well-shaped young fellow, and of a promising

countenance. Andrada protested, that although he had
the best swordsman in all Spain for his second, he would
only fight one against one. His footman, not contenting
himself with his master's protestation, protested likewise,
for his part, that he would fight no man whatever, for
what cause whatever, or at any weapon whatever. So
Don Garcias's friend was forced to be an humble spectator,
or, if you please, godfather to the two combatants, which is
no new thing in Spain. The duel did not last long,
heaven so much favoured the righteous cause of Don
Garcias, that his enemy, pressing upon him with more fury
than skill, ran upon his sword's point, and fell down dead
at his feet, losing his blood and life together. Andrada's
footman and the post-boy, neither of whom were made for
heroes, threw themselves at the feet of Don Garcias, who
meant them no mischief. He commanded Andrada's
footman to open his master's portmanteau, and give him
all he had taken from Eugenia. He obeyed him immediately, and put into his hand a rich manteau, gown, and
petticoat, and a little box, which by its weight would
have made a blind man swear it was not empty. The
footman found the key of it in his master's pocket, and
gave it likewise to Don Garcias, who bid him do what he
pleased with his master's body, threatening to cut his
throat if he ever saw him in Valladolid. He commanded
the post-boy not to come back till the dusk of the
evening, and promised he should find the two horses he
had hired at the post-house. I suppose he was punctually
obeyed by these two worthy gentlemen, who were ready
to die with fear, and thought they were exceedingly
obliged to him, for not killing them as he had done
Andrada. History leaves us in the dark as to what his
footman did with his body; and as for his movables, it is
very probable he kept them for his own use. Our
memoirs likewise are wanting to inform us how the post-
boy managed himself in this affair. Don Garcias and his

friend galloped it all the way to Valladolid, and alighted
at the imperial ambassador's house, where they had friends,
and stayed till it was night. Don Garcias sent for his
footman, who told him Eugenia was in pain to see him.
The horses were sent back to the post-house by an
unknown person, who cunningly ran off after he had
delivered them to one of the ostlers. As for Andrada's
death, the people of Valladolid either talked nothing at all
of it, because they never heard a word of it ; or if they
talked anything of it, they said no more but that a cavalier
had been killed by some unknown enemy, or by thieves.

Don Garcias returned to his lodgings, where he found
Eugenia dressed in the clothes which his landlady had
taken care to provide for her. I am apt to believe she
took them up at a broker's ; for in Spain it is a common
thing for persons of quality, both men and women, to rig
themselves in such places. He restored Eugenia her
things again, particularly her jewels, and informed her
after what manner he had revenged her quarrel upon
Andrada. Being of a sweet and tender disposition, she
was extremely concerned at the unfortunate end of a
person whom she had once so dearly loved, and the
thoughts that she was the cause of so many tragical
disasters, afflicting her as much as her own misfortunes,
caused her to shed abundance of tears. That day public
notice had been given at Valladolid that no one should
entertain or conceal Eugenia, and two hundred crowns
were offered by way of reward to any that could bring any
news of her. This made her resolve to get into a convent
as soon as she could. However she passed that night in
the lodging where she was, and slept as little as she did
the night before. Don Garcias rose by break of day to
go visit the abbess of the convent, who was related to
Eugenia, and promised to receive, and keep her private, as
long as she was able. From thence he went to hire a
coach, and ordered it to stop at a by-street adjoining to

his, whither Eugenia came, accompanied by the gentlewoman of the house, both of them covered with their veils.
The coach carried them to a certain place, where they
ordered the coachman to set them down, and there
alighted that no one should find out the convent whither
Eugenia had retired. She was courteously entertained
there ; Don Garcias's landlady took leave of her, and went
to inform herself how matters were like to go with Don
Sancho. She was told things looked with an ill aspect,
and that the least they talked of doing to him was putting
him to the question. Don Garcias communicated this
news to Eugenia, who was so much concerned to see her
husband in danger of being punished for a crime he was no
ways guilty of, that she was resolved to surrender herself
into the hands of justice. Don Garcias dissuaded her from
so doing, and advised her rather to write to the judge-
criminal to let him know that only she could inform him
who it was that killed Don Lewis. Upon this the judge,
who by good luck was related to her, went attended with
several other officers of justice to discourse her. She
freely confessed to them that she had killed Don Lewis,
acquainted them with the just provocation he had given
her to serve him so, and recounted to them the particulars
of all that had passed between Don Lewis and herself,
except what related to Andrada. Her confession was
taken down in writing, and a report of it made to his
catholic majesty, who, considering the blackness of Don
Lewis's crime, the just resentment of Eugenia, her courage
and resolution, the innocence of Don Sancho and his
domestics, ordered them all to be set at liberty, and
granted his royal pardon to Eugenia, at the instance of all
the court, who appeared in her behalf. Her husband was
not much displeased with her for the death of his brother,
nay, if one knew the truth, perhaps loved her the better for
it. He made her a visit as soon as he was enlarged, and
would fain have taken her home with him, but she would

not consent to it, notwithstanding all his importunities and entreaties. She did not question but that he took Don Lewis's death as he ought to take it, yet knew very well he had heard something of what had passed between her and the Portuguese cavalier ; and that the least blemish in a woman's honour may raise her husband's jealousy, and sooner or later untie the conjugal knot, let it be never so well knit. Poor Don Sancho visited her often, and endeavoured by all the tenderest instances of kindness he could show her, to oblige her to return home, and be absolute mistress of his estate and him. She continued inflexible in her resolution, reserving for herself a pension suitable to her quality and fortune.

But though Don Sancho could not prevail on her to go home with him, yet she behaved herself so obligingly to this good husband, that he had all the reason in the world to speak well of her. But all that she did in the convent to please him only increased his concern that he was not able to get her out of it. This threw him at last into so deep a melancholy, that he fell sick, and his sickness brought him to death's door. He conjured Eugenia to afford him the satisfaction of seeing her, before he parted with her for ever. She could not refuse this sorrowful delight to a husband who had been so dear to her, who had loved her so tenderly, and who still loved her so well. She went to see him die, and had like to have died herself with grief, to observe him show so much joy at the sight of her, as if she had restored that life to him which he was going to lose. This goodness of Eugenia did not go unrewarded. He left her all he had, by which means she became one of the richest and beautifullest widows in all Spain, after she had found herself upon the very brink of being one of the most unhappy women in the world, Her affliction for the death of her husband was sincere as it was great. She gave all necessary orders for his funeral, took possession of his estate, and returned to her convent, resolving to pass the remainder of her days there. Her relations proposed to her the best matches in Spain, but she was resolved not to sacrifice her repose to her ambition ; and finding herself everlastingly persecuted by crowds of pretenders, whom her beauty and wealth drew after her to the parlour of the convent where she was, she would at last be seen by nobody but Don Garcias. This young gentleman had served her so opportunely upon so important an occasion, and with so much zeal, that she could not see him without saying to herself that she owed him something more than bare civilities and compliments. She discovered by his livery and equipage that he was not over rich, and she was generous enough to offer him some assistances, which a person in ordinary circumstances may receive without shame from one that is richer than himself. In the little time she had been at his lodgings, and in the conversation he had often had with her, he made her sensible he had a lofty soul, elevated above the common pitch, entirely disengaged from all sordid interests, and wholly devoted to honour. She was therefore afraid she should affront him if she made him any present, which to be sure would have been answerable to her generous temper ; and on the other hand she feared he would have but a sorry opinion of her gratitude, if she did not give him some proofs of it by her liberality. But if Don Garcias gave her some pain upon the aforesaid occasion, she gave him no less on her part, and so was even with him. In short, he was in love with her, but though the respect he bore her could not have hindered him from acquainting her with it, yet how durst he mention love to a woman, whom that word had so lately exposed to such terrible misfortunes, and that at a time, too, when the sorrowful air of her face, and the tears which trickled down her cheeks incessantly, were evident demonstrations that her soul was yet too full of grief to be capable of admitting any other passion.

Among the rest that made their visits to Eugenia, in

quality of her thrice humble slaves, in hopes I suppose to become one day her thrice imperious masters ; among the rest, I say, who had offered themselves to her, and whom she had refused, there was one Don Diego, who having nothing else to distinguish him, was resolved to signalize himself by his constant persecutions. He was foolish as it is possible for a young fellow to be, as unmannerly as he was foolish, as troublesome as he was unmannerly, and hated by all the world for being thus troublesome, un-mannerly, and foolish. His body was of a piece with his soul, ugly and ill-fashioned ; he was as poor in respect of the blessings of this transitory world, as he was covetous to obtain them. But being descended from one of the best families in Spain, and nearly related to one of the principal ministers of state, which only helped to make him the more insolent, people showed him some little respect for the sake of his quality, although it was not recommended by the least merit. This Don Diego, who was for all the world such a spark as I have described him, thought Eugenia had every-thing a man could desire in a woman, and hoped to obtain her with ease by the credit of his friends at court, who had promised to make up the match for him. But Eugenia was not to be so easily persuaded as they imagined into an affair of that importance, and to favour a private man the court would not commit a violence that must needs have disgusted all the world. Eugenia's retiring into a convent, her resolution never to leave it, her positive orders to receive no more visits, the coldness of those that at first encouraged Don Diego in his pretensions, made him to despair of ever obtaining her without difficulty. For this reason he was resolved to carry her by main force out of her convent, an attempt the most criminal that can be undertaken in Spain, and which none but a fool like himself would ever have dreamt of. He found for his money fellows that were as great fools as himself, and gave orders to have fresh horses left upon the road down to the sea-side, where a vessel lay ready for him ; in short, he forced the convent, carried off Eugenia, and that unfortunate lady had become the prey of the most dishonourable wretch alive, if Heaven had not raised up an unexpected champion for her relief, even then when she thought herself most abandoned by it. One single gentleman, whom Eugenia's cries drew after her ravishers, opposed their whole body, and hindered them from passing farther, with so much valour, that he immediately wounded Don Diego and several of his accomplices, and gave time to the townsmen, who had taken the alarm, and to the civil magistrate to come down upon them with such numbers that quickly forced Don Diego and his companions to surrender, or else to run the hazard of losing their lives on the spot.

Thus Eugenia was delivered, but before she would suffer herself to be carried to her convent, she desired to know what was become of that valiant gentleman who had so gallantly exposed his life for her sake. They found him wounded in several parts of his body, and he had almost lost all his blood as well as his senses. Eugenia had a mind to see him, and no sooner cast her eyes upon him, but she knew him to be Don Garcias. If her surprise was great, her compassion was no less, and she gave such tender proofs of it, that the standers by might have interpreted it to her disadvantage, if she had not had a just occasion besides to afflict herself. She prevailed with them, through her entreaties and prayers, not to carry her generous defender to prison, whom Don Diego, who was upon the point of expiring, and his accomplices confessed not to belong to their company, but to be the man that had attacked them. So he was carried to the next house, which happened to be that where Don Sancho lived formerly, and now belonged to Eugenia, who had left all her furniture, and a few servants in it. He was put into the hands of the chirurgeons belonging to the court and city. Eugenia retired to her convent, but was forced the

next day to leave it, and return to her own house, because
a new order was issued out, which prohibited all convents
of nuns to receive any seculars among them. Next morning Don Diego died, and his relations had interest enough
to hinder his process being made after his death ; but his
accomplices escaped not so, for they were all punished
according to their deserts. In the meantime Eugenia was
almost distracted to see Don Garcias out of hopes of a cure.
She implored the assistance of Heaven, and offered to give
the chirurgeons whatever they could demand ; but their
art was exhausted, and they had no hopes but in Heaven,
and the youth of the sick party. Eugenia would not stir
from his bedside, and attended him night and day so carefully, that she was in danger of bringing herself into the
same condition ; I mean, of wanting another to do the same
offices for herself. She heard him often pronounce her
name in the delirious fits of his fever, and among a thousand
incoherent things, which his disturbed imagination made
him to say, she heard him often talk of love, and discourse
like a man that is a fighting or quarrelling.

At last, nature, assisted by so many remedies, surmounted
the obstinacy of his illness ; his fever abated, his wounds
began to close up, and the chirurgeons assured Eugenia
there was now no danger, provided no unexpected accidents
befell him. She gave them handsome presents for their
pains, and ordered prayers to be put up in all the churches
of Valladolid for her champion's recovery. It was at this
time Don Garcias was informed by Eugenia that she was
the woman whom he had saved, and that she came to be
informed by him how he happened to come so seasonably
to her relief as he was returning home from a friend's house.
She could not forbear to let him know how many obligations she had to him, and he on his part could not conceal
his excessive joy for having served her so opportunely, but
yet durst not presume to acquaint her with a thing of
greater importance. One day as she was all alone with

him, and had conjured him not to let her be any longer
ungrateful to him, but to make use of her upon some important occasion, he thought it a proper time for him to
discover the real sentiments of his soul. He sighed at the
very thought of what he was going to do, he looked pale,
and the disorder of his mind was so visible in his countenance, that Eugenia was afraid something extraordinary
ailed him. She asked him how his wounds fared ?

" Alas, madam," answered he, " my wounds are far from
being my greatest misfortune."

" And what is the matter ? " said she to him, very much
affrighted.

" It is a misfortune," replied he, " that is without remedy."

" It is true," answered Eugenia, " you were unfortunate
to be so dangerously wounded for an unknown person,
who was not worth your exposing your life for her ! But
still, it is a misfortune that can't last always, for your
chirurgeons don't doubt but that you'll be well in a little
time."

" And this it is that I complain of," cries Don Garcias :
" if I had lost my life in serving you," continues he, " I had
died gloriously, whereas I must drag on a wretched life
against my will, and live to be the most unhappy man in
the world."

" With all the good qualities you possess, I cannot believe
you to be so unhappy as you talk," replies Eugenia.

" How, madam," says he to her, " don't you think that
man very unhappy who knows your value, who esteems
you more than any one living, who loves you better than
his life, and with all this who cannot pretend to merit you,
though Fortune had been as favourable as she has hitherto
been averse to him ? "

" You mightily surprise me," said she to him, blushing,
" but the great obligations I have to you give you a privilege
over me which under my present circumstances I should
allow in none but yourself. Only think of getting well,"

continued she, " and rest assured your misfortunes shall not trouble you long, when it is in Eugenia's power to put an end to them."

She would not stay for his answer, and by that means saved him a world of compliments ; which fell out luckily for him, because he must have strained hard to make good ones, and that perhaps might have done him harm in this present weakness. She called to some of her servants to look after him, and went out of the room just as the chirurgeons came in. Satisfaction of mind is a sovereign remedy to a sick body. Don Garcias gathered such hopes of the happy success of his amour from Eugenia's words, that from the deep melancholy wherein he had been plunged before, like a despairing lover, he now gave up himself to joy, and this joy contributed more to his cure than all the remedies the chirurgeons could use. In a little time he was perfectly cured, and out of mere good manners quitted Eugenia's house, but not his pretensions to her heart. She had promised to love him, provided he did not make any public discovery of it ; and after all perhaps she loved him as much as he could love her ; but having lately lost her husband, and been engaged in some adventures which rendered her the common subject of conversation in court and city, she thought it not advisable to expose herself afresh to the malicious censures of the world, by a marriage so unseasonable, and against the rules of decency.

At last, Don Garcias overcame all these difficulties by his merit and constancy. He was so well made in his person as to make any rival whatever despair. He was a younger brother of one of the best families of Arragon, and although he had not actually signalized himself in the wars, yet the long services his father had done the crown of Spain might very well make him hope to find a reward of as great profit as honour at court. Eugenia could not defend herself against so many noble qualities, nor was she willing to be any longer in his debt after she had received so many obligations from him. In short, she married him. Both court and city approved her choice ; and that she might not have any reason to repent it, not long after the King of Spain bestowed a commandery of St. Jago upon Don Garcias. And before that happened, it so happened that our bridegroom convinced Eugenia the first night of his bedding her, that he was another sort of a man than Don Sancho, and she found in him what she had not found in the Portuguese Andrada. They had abundance of children, because they took abundance of pains to get them ; and the people of Spain to this day tell their history, which I have given you here, for a true one, as it was given me.

THE GENEROUS LOVER;

OR,

THE MAN OF DEEDS, AND NOT OF WORDS.

UNDER a King of Naples, whose name I cannot tell, however suppose it might be Alphonso, Leonard de St. Severin, Prince of Tarento, was one of the greatest lords of his kingdom, and one of the celebrated generals of his time. He died, and left the principality of Tarento to his daughter Matilda, a young princess about seventeen years old, as beautiful as an angel, and as good-tempered as she was beautiful. She was so extremely good conditioned, that those that did not know she had an infinite deal of wit would not have been apt to have called her having any in question. Her father, long before his death, had promised her in marriage to Prosper, Prince of Salerno. He was a person of a haughty, disagreeable temper, and the sweet and gentle Matilda, by virtue of her being long accustomed to bear with him, was so well prepared to love and fear him, that never did slave depend more upon the imperious will of his master, than this young princess did upon that of old Prosper. I think a man of the age of forty-five may very well be called old, especially where he is mentioned with one so young as Matilda. Her affection to this superannuated lover may be said to have proceeded rather from custom than inclination, and was as sincere as his was interested. Not but that he was as fond of her, too, as it was possible for him to be, and this was no more than what any man would have been, as well as he, for indeed she was all over amiable ; but it was not in the nature of the beast (I beg his pardon for this expression, but it is out) to love very much, and he rather esteemed a mistress for her dirty acres and unrighteous mammon, than for her merit and beauty. The truth is, he made love but awkwardly ; Matilda however was so happy, or, to express myself more properly, she was so easy to be pleased, that although he did not pay her half the respect and complaisance which one might expect from a generous lover, yet for all that he was absolute master of her heart, and had brought her to such a pass as to submit to all his ill conditions. He found fault with all her actions, and plagued her incessantly with those musty advices that old men in their great wisdom so often inculcate to the young and which they so little care for. In short, he would have been a greater thorn in her side, than a peevish, malicious governess, if he could but have found any faults in her conduct. It is true, when he was in good humour, he would tell her stories of the old court, play on his guitar, and dance a sarraband before her. I have already told you his age, but to go on with his character. He was spruce in his person and clothes ; curious in his periwigs, an infallible sign that his hair was none of the best ; took mighty care of his teeth, though time began to play tricks with them ; valued himself upon his lily-white hands, and suffered the nail of his left little finger to grow to a prodigious length, by the same token he thought it one of the prettiest sights in the world. He was nice to admiration in his feathers and ribbons, punctually twisted up his moustachios every night, was always perfumed, and ever carried some tit-bit in his pocket to eat, and some verses to read. As for himself, he was an execrable versifier, a walking magazine of all the new songs, played upon most instruments, performed his exercises with a grace, but his chief talent was dancing. He loved the wits that asked him nothing, had performed some actions in his time that were brave, and some that were otherwise, and, as one might say, had two buzzards for one hawk, or if you please two blanks to one benefit. In short, I may properly apply to him a burlesque song of my own making, the latter part of which is almost worn into a proverb.

SONG.

" Here lies a fine wight,
That could sing you at sight,
And dance like a sprite,
Could verses indite,
And bravely recite.
What's more, he could fight
(I swear by this light)
Like fury, or knight.

" He knew what was what,
Could gallop or trot,
And toss off his pot,
And swear at the shot.
Yet with all he had got,
It was the hard lot,
Of this boaster, God wot,
To be a damned sot."

With all these fine qualities, one of the loveliest princesses in the world was desperately in love with him. It is true, indeed, she was but seventeen years old ; but our noble Prince of Salerno did not stand much upon that. There is no doubt but the Princess Matilda, being so rich and beautiful as she was, would have had a hundred gallants more, if it had not been universally believed in Naples that her marriage with Prosper was as good as concluded in her father's time, or if that prince's quality had not discouraged other pretenders, who (though they wanted his title) were men of fortune and birth good enough to be his rivals. Thus the greatest part of these lovers, either governed by a principle of fear or discretion, were content to sigh for her in private, without daring to speak. Hippolito was the only man that had the courage to own himself in public the rival of Prosper, and the respective lover of Matilda. He was descended from one of the best families in Spain, and came in a direct line from the great Ruis Lopez d'Avolos, Constable of Castile, who was so remarkable an instance of the inconstancy of fortune, since, from the richest and most powerful grandee of his own country, he was turned out of it poor and miserable, forced to borrow of his friends, and fly to the King of Arragon, who took him into his protection, and gave him a fortune sufficient at Naples to support him suitable to his quality. This Hippolito was one of the most accomplished cavaliers of his time ; his valour had gained him reputation in several parts of Europe, and all the world owned him to be a man of the nicest honour.

As I have already told you, he was a humble admirer of Matilda, and though he could never hope to succeed so long as she loved Prosper, yet he resolved to love her on to the end of the chapter. He was liberal even to prodigality, whereas his rival was thrifty even to avarice. He omitted not the least opportunity to show his magnificence to Matilda, and although he carried it as far as his fortune would give him leave, yet she seldom saw it ; for her tyrant Prosper hindered her from giving any countenance to these gallantries of love, let them come from what quarter of the world they would. Our obstinate lover frequently ran at the ring before his mistress's window, often gave her serenades, and diverted her with tilts and tournaments. The cipher and colours of Matilda were to be seen in all his liveries. The praises of Matilda rang through all Italy, in the verses he composed, and in the airs and songs he caused to be made ; but she was no more moved with all this than if she had known nothing of the matter. Nay, by the express order of the Prince of Salerno, she must go out of Naples, whenever there was to be any running at the ring, dancing, or any gallantries of the like nature, which the amorous Hippolito provided for her. To make short of my story, she affected to disoblige him upon all occasions, with a cruelty that seemed to be a violence upon her nature, and made all the world to exclaim against her. This did not in the least discourage Hippolito, and the ill-treatment of Matilda increased his love instead of lessening it. He did more than this : he showed that respect to Prosper which he did not owe him ; and to please Matilda, paid him the same deference which is usually shown to persons of superior quality, although there was no other difference between the Prince of Salerno and him than in their estates. In short, he respected his mistress in his rival, and perhaps forbore to hate him because he was beloved by Matilda. But Prosper was not so complaisant. He hated Hippolito mortally, made a hundred scurvy jests upon him, nay—would never have scrupled to tell lies of him, if he had thought any one would have believed them. But Hippolito was the delight of Naples, and his reputation was so well established there, that, although he had actually deviated from his character, he could hardly have destroyed it.

Thus Prosper was the happy man, and stood possessed of Matilda's affection, though he did nothing to deserve it. That beautiful princess did not think she saw him often enough, though she saw him every day, when fortune all on the sudden threw her from the height of happiness into the extremity of misery. She had a cousin german by her father's side, who might have passed for a man of merit, had he been a person of less ambition and avarice ; he had been bred up with the king, was of the same age, and had insinuated himself so far into his good graces, that he was the sole manager of all his pleasures and sports, and the dispenser of all his favours. This Roger de St. Severin for so he was called, was possessed with a fancy that the principality of Tarento belonged to him, and that a daughter could not legally inherit it to the prejudice of the male line. He spoke to the king about it, who encouraged him to claim his right, and promised to support him by his authority. The affair was kept secret; Roger made himself master of Tarento, and had placed a good garrison there, before Matilda had the least mistrust of it. Our poor princess, who had never been in any trouble before, was as it were thunderstruck with this news. No one but Hippolito declared in her favour, who scorned to truckle to the king's favourite; and Prosper, who was more obliged to her than any man living, did even less for her in this case than any man, whereas Hippolito not only discharged his duty, but was carried by his zeal beyond it. He waited on her to offer her his service, but she durst not accept it, for fear of disobliging her Prince of Salerno, who since her misfortune did not visit her so often as he had used to do when she was peaceable mistress of Tarento. In the meantime Hippolito talked boldly of the injustice was done her, and sent a challenge to Roger; for which he had guards placed upon him, and was commanded to desist; but as he was generally beloved by all people, he might have easily raised a party in Naples strong enough to have made the favourite doubt the success of his ill designs. He made several attempts upon Tarento, all which miscarried by reason of the great care Roger had taken to prevent all accidents of that nature.

At last the breach between the two pretenders growing wider every day, and most of the Italian princes interesting themselves one way or the other, the Pope employed his mediation to procure a peace, made them lay down their arms, and prevailed with the King of Naples to refer the decision of the dispute between his favourite and Matilda to judges of known integrity. The reader may easily guess what an extraordinary expense Hippolito had been at, being head of the party, and so liberal in his temper ; he may likewise easily imagine that Matilda, as much a princess as she was, was in a short time reduced to very pressing necessities. Roger had possessed himself of her lands. He had persuaded the king she kept private intelligence with his enemies ; her rents were no longer paid, and no one durst lend money to the woman whom the favourite had a mind to ruin. Prosper abandoned her at last, but she still loved him so violently, that she less resented his ingratitude, than forgetfulness.

Hippolito would not offer her money, because he knew she would refuse it, but went a more generous way to work. He sent her some by one of his friends, who took the honour of it upon himself, and without telling her it came from Hippolito, obliged that princess by oath never to speak of it, lest his kindness might draw upon him the indignation of the favourite.

In the meantime the process came on, and sentence was given in favour of Matilda. The king was displeased at it, Roger was enraged, the court was astonished, every one was vexed or rejoiced according to his own inclination or interest, but yet the generality of people admired and praised the probity of the judges. Matilda, who to her glory had obtained so important a process, sent a gentleman to Prosper, in a transport that can hardly be imagined, to acquaint him with the happy success of her affair. Prosper rejoiced exceedingly at the news, and to testify his satisfaction to this gentleman, hugged and embraced him after a strange rate, and moreover promised to serve him whenever an opportunity should offer. Hippolito knew nothing of the matter till after his rival, yet he bestowed a diamond ring of great value upon the person that brought him the news. He feasted all the court, prepared lists before Matilda's window, and for eight days together ran at the ring against all opposers. Gallantries of this nature generally make a great deal of noise. Several princes of

Italy, and most of Matilda's relations and friends were there present, and signalized themselves. Nay, the king himself, who passionately admired this sort of exercise, was pleased to honour it with his royal presence. Roger had interest enough with his master to have hindered him, but by a cunning fetch of politics he had reconciled himself to Matilda, and declared to all the world, that unless he had really thought Tarento had belonged to him, he would never have attempted to make himself master of it. The king was mightily pleased with his so readily submitting to the sentence of the judges, and that he might recompense him for the loss of his trial, and his pretensions upon Tarento, gave him one of the most important governments of the kingdom, besides the places he had before. Hippolito performed wonders at running at the ring, and carried away the sole honour of it. Prosper had a mind to dispute it with him, so all be-plumed and be-feathered that any one would have taken him for an American prince. But he was thrown the very first course, either through his own fault or that of his horse, and was sufficiently bruised to boot, or at least pretended to be so. He was carried to Matilda's house, who out of vexation quitted her balcony, and cursed the amorous Hippolito a hundred times for his pains. He came to hear of it, and was so concerned that he broke up the assembly, and retired in the greatest despair to a fine house he had within a league of Naples. In the meantime Prosper was so enraged at his fall, that he treated Matilda after a most terrible manner, telling her she was the cause of his disgrace, and reproached her with being in love with Hippolito. Matilda, always gentle, always humble, and always blindly fond of her haughty tyrant, begged his pardon, and, in short, was as chicken-hearted as he was brutal. Hippolito had a sister that was bred up with the Queen of Spain, and was lately returned to Naples, for reasons I do not know, but which would signify nothing to our history if I did. Besides she

was beautiful to a miracle, and was a lady of so extraordinary merit, that rendered her deserving of the vows of
the best men in the kingdom. At her return from Spain,
she found her brother's affairs in so low a condition, that
when he set up the running at the ring, she would not
appear at court, because she wanted an equipage suitable
for a person of her quality, yet always kept at her brother's
house, which was all was left him of his estate, for he had
already parted with his lands. She came *incognito* to see
the running at the ring, and observing her brother to break
up the assembly, and leave Naples so abruptly, followed
him home, and found him in the most lamentable condition
that could be. He had broke his lances, tore his feathers
and hair, mangled his clothes and face ; and, in short,
was in such a distraction, that she would have despaired
of ever seeing him come to his senses again, had she not
known very well that a smile, nay, an indifferent look
from Matilda, would have made him to forget a thousand
ill-treatments. She did all that lay in her power to bring
him to good humour, gave way to his passion instead of
combating it, railed at Matilda when he stormed against
her and said all the good things she could think of her
when after all his transports the scene changed, and she
found him the most amorous lover that ever was.

But the surly Prosper had not the same complaisance
for Matilda ; his fall still broiled in his stomach, and he
daily laid it to her charge, though she was by no means
accessary to it. One day, when after having thanked her
judges, she went to wait upon the king to thank him likewise, although he had been against her—but at court it is
a point of indiscretion to speak one's real thoughts, or receive a denial otherwise than with fawning and cringing—
one day, therefore, when she was in the king's ante-chamber,
she saw the obsequious Prosper come in. Ever since his
fall he had never made her a visit but to scold and quarrel
with her for suffering Hippolito to run at the ring under

her window. Nothing could be more unjust than Prosper's complaints. It was not in Matilda's power to hinder a public diversion, even though it had not been designed for her sake, since her palace took up one side of the great square. And although it had been in her power, yet ought she not to have done it, unless she had resolved to be thought a woman of neither manners nor gratitude. Prosper was the only man who by his false way of reasoning fancied she had done him an irreparable injury, and his anger soured him to that degree that he went no more to visit her, as if he had broke with her for good and all. The poor princess was ready to run distracted about it, and no sooner saw this tyrant of hearts, who was just going into the king's chamber, but she threw herself in his way and stopped him. He endeavoured to avoid her, and pressed forward. She caught him by the arm, and casting a look at him that was enough to have charmed any one but this haughty brute, asked him what she had done, that he should shun her thus.

" What have you not done?" replied this prince arrogantly ; " and how can you ever retrieve the reputation you have lost by suffering the gallantries of Hippolito ? "

" I cannot hinder them, nor prevent his loving me," answers Matilda, " but it is in my power not to approve either his love or gallantry ; and I think," continues she, " I sufficiently testified my dislike of them, when I went from my balcony before the show was over."

" You should not have appeared there at all," replies Prosper ; " and the reason why you went away at last was only because you saw all the company pointed at you for being there. But your love for Hippolito has made you to lose all your reason, and his gallantries have quite effaced the services I am capable of doing you."

Matilda was vexed to the heart to hear this, and was going to answer, but he would not give her leave   Besides the anger that appeared in his countenance made the princess so afraid of him that she was perfectly speechless. "When you were no more mistress of Tarento," said he to her, "and the king ordered you to be apprehended, I had a mind to see how far your indiscretion and mean spirit would carry you, and whether adversity could cure your faults. For this reason I made no feasts like your gallant, nay I pretended to be no longer in your interests. In the meantime Hippolito made a mighty bustle, and did you little service, and your affairs for a long time seemed to be in a desperate condition. Then you could condescend to make some advances towards me, in order to bring me back to you again, but this was only a copy of your countenance, since you still preserved your Hippolito. Your politics, I confess, were not amiss. You drained this poor despicable gallant while he had a drop to part with, flattering yourself, that after you had exhausted him to all intents and purposes, you should do me an extraordinary favour to take me in his room ; and you made account, that although you should lose Tarento at your trial, yet your beauty would make you princess of Salerno, whenever you pleased. But no sooner did a favourable decree revive your hopes, than you changed your maxim of state for your maxim of love. You thought a young ruined prodigal would better fit your turn than me, and considered, that if you married the prince of Salerno, you must expect to live with a master, authorized by custom, and the laws, whereas you would find in Hippolito a supple slave that would make it all his business to please you. Imprudent princess !" continued he, "durst such a poor needy wretch as Hippolito pretend to make love to a woman of your quality unless you gave him encouragement, and can any one believe, that for bare hopes only, he would have put himself to such an expense, that he is utterly beggared by it, and so foolishly too, that he enriched, with one single present, the man that came from you, to bring him the news that you had gained your cause ? Yet after all these testimonies I have of your indiscretion and infidelity, you are vain enough to believe I love you never the worse for them. Be happy if you can with your Hippolito, but delude yourself no longer that I will be unhappy with Matilda."

He would have left her after he had spoke these words, but the princess still kept her hold, and once in her life had the courage to contradict him.

"Ungrateful prince!" said she to him, 'one of the greatest proofs I can give thee that I yet love thee, is not to hate thee, after thou hast said so many disobliging things to me. They rather make against thee than me, and I cannot employ them better to thy confusion and my own advantage, than by confessing they are true. Yes," continued she, "Hippolito has loved me; Hippolito to serve me, neither feared the hatred of a favourite, nor the indignation of a king; he respects me, he does everything to please me. He would have protected me when I was abandoned by all the world, nay, he has done more, for he has ruined himself for my sake. What didst thou ever do like this? Thou wilt tell me perhaps thou lovest me; how! Love me, and not show common civility to me; thou who oughtest to have shown it to my sex, although it were not due to my quality. And yet what ill-conditioned master ever treated slave more unworthily than thou hast done me, and who would have thus trampled on a person that loves thee so well as I do? No, no, prince, thou hast no reason to complain, and art obliged to me that I don't. But I will go farther than this: I will own, if thou wilt have me, crimes I never committed. I will never see Hippolito more, nay will be ungrateful to him, that thou mayest not be so to me. In fine, to regain thy heart, there is nothing so difficult but I will put it in execution."

"And there is nothing impossible to those bright eyes," says the prince to her, adjusting his periwig. "They have already disarmed me of my anger, and provided they always keep their favourable glances, the too happy Prosper will never adore any other than the beautiful Matilda."

The amorous princess thought herself over-paid with these few compliments of her old gallant. In a less public place perhaps she would have thrown herself at his feet, to thank him for this mighty condescension, but neither time nor place would give her leave to answer here. The king came out of his chamber. She begged Prosper to stand by while she spoke to him, but he shrinking away told her, it was not convenient for them to be seen together, for some reasons he could tell her. She perceived well enough, he was afraid of making his court ill, but she was so near the king, that she had not time to reproach Prosper with being a better courtier than a lover.

She presented herself to the king, paid her respects to him, and made her compliment of thanks. The king received her very coldly, and his answer was so ambiguous, that it might as well be interpreted to her disadvantage as otherwise. But the sweet things Prosper had said to her, gave her such satisfaction, that his last ingratitude, in refusing to introduce her to the king, made no impression upon her, no more than the ill reception his majesty had given her, so much transported was she to be reconciled to her imperious lover. That day she was visited by all the ladies of quality in Naples, who agreed to go a-hunting next morning a-horseback, in a campaign dress, and caps set off with feathers. The greatest gallants at court were there, so we may easily imagine, the Prince of Salerno, who was gallantry itself, made one of the company. This was not all ; he resolved to make the princess a present, which he had never done before. He sent her a most passionate letter, accompanied with a fine cap ; but to tell truth, he himself had sorted and ordered the feathers, by the same token there was not one new amongst them. As I take it, I have already observed, he had an admirable fancy in feathers. This was the only vanity on which he would lay out his money, though to do him justice, he husbanded his plumes to a miracle, for he would often diversify, and trans-

plant them from one cap to another, and let them be never
so old, knew how to make them appear fresh; and gay upon
occasion, as well as if he had served seven years apprentice-
ship to the trade. I am willing to believe he sat up the
best part of the night to put this cap in order, that nothing
might be wanting to so magnificent a present. The princess
received it as if it had been sent her from heaven, gave him
a hundred more thanks than it deserved, and promised in a
letter she sent in answer to his, that she would honour herself with this miraculous cap as long as she lived. I will
not tell you what sport they had in the chase, because the
particulars never came to my knowledge. But we may
reasonably suppose some of their horses foundered, that
the cavaliers were so well-bred as to wait upon the ladies,
that Prosper displayed all his gallantry, and that he
engrossed the whole discourse to himself, being the
greatest talker of his age.

Our ladies were so well pleased with the sport, that they
resolved to take their pleasure the next day; and in order
to change their diversion, designed to go by sea to Pozzuolo,
where the princess Matilda promised to give them a
collation and music. They no less spruced themselves up
for this voyage, than they had done the day before for
hunting. The boats they went in were finely adorned,
covered with rich tapestry, whether of Turkey or China, I
won't be positive, and the meanest cushions were of silk or
velvet. Prosper would needs go thither by land, and had
none but his dear self to accompany him, either to save
money, or because he was melancholy, for some folks are
so out of pride. He was mounted upon his finest horse,
had dressed himself in his richest campaign suit, and
loaded his head with the spoils of many an ostrich.

Hippolito's house lay on the road to Pozzuolo, near the
sea, and the prince of Salerno must of necessity ride just
by it. He no sooner saw it, but a noble thought came
into his head. He knew Hippolito was at home, and

therefore alighted from his horse to have a little conversation with him. Hippolito received him with all the respect and civility due to his quality, although the other had not the manners to return it. Prosper made him a very rude compliment upon his presuming to be in love with a princess, who was to be his wife. Hippolito bore his impertinence for a long while, and answered him with all the sweetness imaginable, that he ought not to be offended at his gallantry, which a love without hopes put him upon. But at last Prosper's insolence forced him to change his language, and he had already called for his horse to go out and fight him when word was brought, that the sea was very tempestuous, and that the boats wherein the ladies were, which they could behold from the shore, were in danger of being dashed against the rocks. Hippolito did not doubt but that these ladies were Matilda and her company ; he persuaded Prosper to run to the relief of their common mistress, but who excused himself upon his not being able to swim, and that he was not yet recovered of the bruise he had received when he ran at the ring. The generous Hippolito, detesting in his soul the ingratitude of his rival, ran or rather flew to the sea-shore. His servants followed, threw themselves into the sea after his example and by the assistance of some fishermen, who happened by good luck to be at that time upon the coast, they made a shift to save Matilda's life, and the ladies in her company. Their boats were overturned within a hundred yards of the shore ; and Naples had bewailed the loss of all its beauties at once, had it not been for this seasonable relief.

Hippolito was so happy, that Matilda owed her life to him. His love made him soon to distinguish her from the other ladies, whom the waves were going to dash against the rocks that bounded the shore. While the fishermen and his servants helped the first persons they found, he caught hold of the princess just as she rose above water and holding her with one hand, while he swam with the

other towards the shore, he happily gained it without any
one to help him.   Matilda found herself much more ill
upon her shipwreck, than the rest of the ladies that were
saved with her.   After they had vomited their salt-water,
changed their clothes and recovered from their fright, they
were well enough that very day to take coach for Naples.
As for the princess of Tarento, it was a long while before
they could bring her to herself.   Even then they much
doubted her life, and Hippolito and his sister Irene took all
the care of her that was possible.   He sent to Naples for
the ablest physicians, besides him that belonged to the
princess, and quitted his house entirely to her and some of
her domestics that came to wait on her.   He and his
servants made shift to lodge at a little farm not far from
his own house, whence he sent every moment to inquire
how the princess did, when he could not go thither himself.
As for Prosper, who was very well pleased with the rough
compliment he had passed upon Hippolito, he left Matilda
and the rest of the ladies to shift for themselves as well as
they could, without troubling his head what became of
them ; thinking, perhaps, that since he was none of the
fittest to help them, he ought not to pollute his eyes with
so sad a spectacle, and so jogged on gently towards Naples,
expecting the doubtful event of the shipwreck to rejoice at,
or otherwise, according as it would have made him happy
or unhappy.   In the meantime Matilda, assisted by her
youth, and the remedies that were given her, recovered both
her health and beauty at once, and was extremely satisfied
with the great care of Hippolito and his sister, who dexterously insinuated to her with what indifference Prosper
had beheld the peril she was in.   Matilda did not discover
the least token of resentment in her face or discourse ;
whether it were because her love had mastered it, or
because she dissembled her ill-usage, I cannot tell.

The night before she designed to leave Hippolito's house
to return to Naples she could not sleep, and therefore

called for a book and a candle to divert her. Her women were gone out of her chamber to sleep or do something else, when she saw Prosper come into the room. We may easily guess what a surprise she was in, to see him at so unseasonable an hour, and how much she looked upon herself affronted by so disrespectful a visit. She spoke to him of it with some warmth. Prosper was warmer than she, and as if this princess had thrown herself into this danger of losing her life on purpose to give Hippolito the glory of saving it, reproached her with her shipwreck, as a blemish on her honour, and taxed her with infidelity, by reason she was in the house of one that was in love with her, lodged in his chamber, and lay in his bed. Matilda would not condescend to show him how unjust his reproaches were but retorted on him for not having endeavoured to save her, and in a cutting way of raillery, complained of his not being able to swim, as also for not being fully recovered of his late dangerous fall. Prosper reddened with anger and confusion, treated her with opprobrious language, and told her he would never see her more, since Roger, the king's favourite, offered him his sister, and with her all the advantages he might expect from the alliance of a person in his post. Matilda could not hold out against so terrible a menace ; her blood curdled within her, and her love soon conquered her indignation. She had begun to exert herself a little, but all on the sudden became a suppliant. He relented too on his side, when he saw her humbled as much as he thought convenient, and according to his custom cajoled her, and said the same soft things he ought to have done, if in all the love quarrels he had had with her, he had never trespassed against the respect and tenderness he owed her. He made new protestations of love to her, and straining hard to surprise her by some topping compliments, made very impertinent ones ; for he wished her all sorts of adversities, to the end he might have an opportunity forsooth of convincing her how much he was her humble servant.

"For God's sake, madam," said he to her in a passionate tone, "why are you not out of favour at court? Oh that you were still persecuted by Roger! Oh that you were yet out of your principality of Tarento! that you might see with what zeal and ardour I would solicit the king for you! with what vigour I would espouse your cause against your enemies, and whether I should be afraid to venture my person, and all I were worth in the world, to reinstate you in what was usurped upon you."

"Come, come," says the princess, "there's no necessity I should be more unfortunate than I am, to give you the opportunity of showing your generosity; and I would not willingly put your love to so dangerous a trial." They were engaged in this discourse when a noise of confused and dreadful voices, that cried out fire, made them to run to the windows, where they saw all the lower part of the house vomiting fire and smoke, and that at the same the flames beginning to enter the chamber by the stair-case, took from them all hopes of saving themselves that way, as Prosper was preparing to do. The princess, all in a fright, conjured him not to abandon her in so great a danger, and proposed to make use of the sheets and hangings to get out of the window. The prince, as much affrighted as she, told her they could not have time to do it; and measuring with his eye the height of the windows, and considering which would be the best way to leap into the court, told Matilda very plainly that upon these occasions every one ought to shift for himself.

"But thou shalt not go without me," said she to him very resolutely, "and I will run no danger here which the most ungrateful and ungenerous man alive shall not partake with me." She had no sooner said these words, but she caught hold of Prosper, and her indignation at his baseness gave her so much strength, that in spite of all his striving and and struggling, he could not disengage himself from her. He swore, called her names, was brute enough to threaten

to drub or kill her, I don't know whether, and had certainly
been as good as his word, if at the time he was struggiing
with her, as rudely and fiercely as if he had been to deal
with an enemy, the generous Hippolito had not come into
the room.   The princess seeing him, left Prosper, and came
up to Hippolito, who without giving her time to speak,
covered her with a wet sheet, which he had brought on
purpose, and taking her up in his arms, threw himself like
a lion with his prey through the flames, which now had
filled all the stair-case.   He had no sooner set her down in
a place of safety, but he was so generous as to do the like
service for his rival.   It is true, he burnt his clothes, and
singed his hair and eye-brows ; but I would fain know what
signifies the burning one's clothes, or singing one's hair, to
a man whose heart had been already burnt to a coal by
love ?

While Matilda recovered her spirits, and Prosper
got back to Naples, without so much as thanking his
deliverer, Hippolito beheld his house burnt down to the
ground, together with his furniture, horses, and in short, all
that his former profuseness had left him.   Matilda was
afflicted at it, I will not say more than he was, for alas he
scarce thought of it at all, but as much as if she had seen all
that was dear to her in the world destroyed.   She looked
upon herself to be the occasion of this misfortune to him,
and indeed was not mistaken.   Her cousin Roger, who had
reconciled himself to her with no other intent than to accomplish her ruin more easily, had bribed some of Hippolito's
servants, that were villains enough to take his money, to lay
a great deal of combustible stuff in the vaults and cellars
which they were to set on fire in the dead of the night, when
all the family were asleep.   This unjust favourite made no
conscience to ruin a poor gentleman, nay, procure his death
too, provided he could but do the same to a relation,
whose estate he hoped by this means to inherit ; and as if
her death would not satisfy him, which had most infallibly

happened, in case his design had succeeded, he likewise endeavoured to make her memory odious. At the time when Hippolito's house was on fire, Roger had managed his cards so dexterously, that messengers were ordered to search Matilda's palace, who opening her closet found some forged letters there, which seemed to be written to the Duke of Anjou, and which plainly convicted her of keeping a private intelligence with that dangerous enemy of the government.

Our unfortunate princess received this unlucky news just as she was going to send to Naples for her coaches to bring her home. She was extremely troubled at it, and without staying any longer, ran to Naples with all her servants a-foot in the most lamentable condition that can be imagined. Hippolito offered to accompany her, but she positively forbade him, fearing, I suppose, to disoblige her musty spark Prosper ; and thus our unhappy lover saw her depart, and was infinitely more concerned at this last misfortune which had befallen the princess, and at her commanding him to leave her, than at the burning of his house. Matilda no sooner came to Naples, but she was taken into custody. She demanded to have audience of the king, but it was refused her. She sent to speak with Prosper, but the old gentleman pretended to be wondrous sick, and thus Matilda beheld herself all at once abandoned by her friends, as if she had been infected with the plague. The very same day she received an order from the king to leave Naples. Her own domestics basely and scandalously deserted her ; her creditors, without any respect to her quality, persecuted her most unmercifully : In short she was reduced to so wretched a condition, that she could not procure either coach or horse, to carry her to a certain prince of Italy, who was the nearest relation she had in the world next to Roger, and who had always espoused her quarrel against that haughty favourite.

Being thus forsaken by all her friends, destitute even of

the necessaries of life, and incapable of obeying so rigorous an order, she took sanctuary in a convent, where they would not receive her without his majesty's permission, who granted it, on condition that she should leave it that very night. She went out of it in disguise, and so secretly, that with all the search and inquiry Hippolito could make, he could not meet the least information which way she was gone. However, he resolved to follow her just as chance directed, rather than sit still at home, and make no inquiry after her. While he was in quest of her, or at least fancied he was, she thought no more of him, and Prosper no more of her. He represented her as a state criminal, made his court very regularly to the king and his favourite. And as the generality of mankind use to alter their measures with the time, he made love to Camilla, Roger's sister, and begged of the king to help on the marriage. The king, who looked upon this as an advantageous match for his confidant's sister, whom he loved the best of any subject in his dominions, spoke about it to this favourite, who always liked that which his master liked.

This sister of Roger's was one of the most beautiful ladies of Naples, and though she shared in her brother's good fortune, yet had she no hand in his wicked designs. As she was looked upon at court to be the best match in the kingdom, she in like manner looked upon Hippolito to be the completest gentleman of his time, and perhaps loved him, or at least would have loved him, if she had not observed him so passionately in love with another. She took Matilda's misfortune so to heart, and was so generous in her temper, that if she had in the least suspected it was all owing to her brother, she would most undoubtedly have reproached him for so black an action, and been one of the first that should have exclaimed against it. She was so afflicted at Hippolito's late loss, that not valuing what the world might say of her, she went to find him at his habitation that was burnt down, to offer him money, or whatever else he wanted that lay in her power to bestow on him. She met with his sister there, who little expected such a visit, much less to be invited to take up her quarters at Camilla's house. This beautiful lady could not refuse so obliging an offer, and accordingly went with her to Naples. What better course could a young person of her sex and condition take, who found herself without a farthing to relieve her, without a house to cover her, without hopes of mending her fortune, in a country too where she scarce knew any one but her brother, who was nevertheless as good as lost to her, since as soon as ever he had been informed that Matilda had left Naples, he ran in quest of her like a madman, without knowing whither she was gone.

The day on which Camilla went to find Irene at her brother's house, with design to carry her home with her, the king was pleased to honour her with a visit, and presented other our gallant prince of Salerno with all his gallantry. Camilla, who had Hippolito always in her thoughts, received Prosper's compliments with as great indifference as she expressed thankfulness to the king for condescending to visit her. The sorrowful Irene bore her company, and under all her affliction appeared so charming to the young king, that he fell in love with her. His love was violent even in its infancy. He approached her with as much respect and awe as if she had been in his condition, and he in hers. He said a thousand fine things to her upon her beauty, and this lovely young lady, who demeaned herself neither with too much haughtiness nor submission, discovered at once so much wit, prudence and modesty, that he considered her from that very moment as the only happiness that was wanting to his fortune. He stayed at Camilla's house as long as he possibly could, and the pleasure he took in conversing with Irene, was so much the more taken notice of, as the young king had always seemed insensible to love, and behaved himself with great coldness towards all the most celebrated beauties of Naples. Irene was so charming that it was impossible for a man, though never so little inclined to love, and never so incapable to judge of her merit, to avoid falling in love with her. Camilla before she knew her, intended to serve her for her brother's sake only, but no sooner came she acquainted with her, than she loved her for her own. She easily believed the king was in love with her because she desired it ; and being far from envying her good fortune, as any other handsome lady but herself would have done, she rejoiced at it exceedingly. She congratulated Irene upon so important a conquest, and had without question flattered the vanity and hopes of any lady less presuming than her. But this modest damsel could not be persuaded but that the king was more a gallant than a lover ; that he had no other design than only to divert himself, and that he would think no more of her, when he was out of her sight. But she was mistaken : for it was not long before the king came again, to acquaint her with his passion, which was so impetuous that it would not suffer him to be longer without seeing her than that very evening after he fell in love with her. He told the Prince of Salerno he was re-solved to go *incognito* after the Spanish mode to make love to Irene under Camilla's balcony. Prosper was mightily pleased to be made the confidant of his master's pleasures, and to accompany him in an amorous adventure. In all probability Roger had been chosen for this affair, or at least had bore his share in it, had not he that very day taken his leave of the king to go to Tarento, whither some important business had called him.

The night came, and the king, accompanied by Prosper armed like himself after the Italian manner, that is to say, with more offensive arms than a single man can be supposed to want, came under Camilla's balcony, who had been beforehand acquainted with his coming by Prosper. She knew the method and good breeding of the court too well, not to leave the king at liberty to entertain himself with his mistress in private. For this reason she retired to another balcony, notwithstanding all entreaties Irene could use to get her to stay with her. The king reproached this young lady for her uneasiness to be alone with him, and told her, she owed at least some complaisance to a king, who had for her something above it.

"I should owe all to your majesty," replied Irene, "if I did not likewise owe something to myself, which I cannot owe to any one else."

"And what do you owe to yourself?" says the king, "which you do not owe to my love?"

"Why not to believe you have any for me," answers Irene.

"Alas!" cries the king, sighing, "there is nothing so sure, and nothing I would not willingly do to hinder you from doubting it."

"If I could believe what you tell me," says she, "I should have more reason to complain of your majesty, than to thank you."

"How! cruel damsel," answered the king, "and can a passion so sincere as mine offend you?"

"It would be an honour to some great queen," replies Irene; "but it would very much call in question the judgment of any one else."

"It is true indeed," says the king, "you are no queen; but she that deserves to be one, is in a possibility of being one."

"I am not so conceited of my own merit," answers Irene, "as to expect any such alteration in my fortune, and your majesty I hope has more goodness than to divert yourself any longer at the expense of an unhappy creature."

"Beautiful Irene," says our amorous prince, "I love you as much as it is possible for the most passionate and faithful lover in the universe to love, and if my tongue has informed you what my looks and sighs could not have acquainted you with in so short a time, don't think I have any design to dispense on account of my quality with any of the pains of a long servitude, or the services and cares which the most charming woman upon earth may expect from the most respectful lover. But so violent a pain as mine wants a speedy remedy, and you ought to rest satisfied in my opinion, however scrupulous and rigid you may be towards a king, who is afraid to displease you with this declaration of his love."

He said to her abundance of things more passionate than this, which the person who overheard them might unluckily forget, as I can assure you he did. So I leave the discreet reader to imagine them; for to make a king of Naples express himself so tenderly as ours did, and at the same time not to maim his thoughts, a man must be as much in love as he was, which I humbly presume is none of my business to be at present. Irene always answered him with her usual modesty, and without showing herself either too hard, or too easy to be persuaded, she disengaged herself so handsomely from so nice a conversation, that it increased the king's esteem for her, who parted from her infinitely more in love than he had been before. From that time there passed not a day in which he did not visit Camilla and Irene, nor a night but he came to that lady's balcony, where he employed all his amorous eloquence to persuade her of the sincerity of his passion.

One night when he had given orders to his guards not to attend him, he walked in disguise through the streets of Naples, accompanied only by the Prince of Salerno. He took so much diversion in this ramble, that the greatest part of the night was spent when he came to Camilla's balcony. He found his post already taken up by two men, or at least they stood so near it, that they must needs overhear whatever he should say to Irene. One of these parted from the other and went into Camilla's house, while his companion tarried in the street. The king stayed a while to see whether he would not go away of himself, and leave him the street free ; but finding he stirred no more than a statue, he grew impatient, and commanded Prosper to go and see what the fellow meant by staying there, and to oblige him to retire. The prince of Salerno walked toward him, with as much apprehension as if he had been sent upon some dangerous enterprise. The other seeing him come up, retired. Prosper was resolved to see who he was, the other mended his pace, and seeing Prosper did the like, very fairly betook himself to his heels, when the prince of Salerno ran after him, and coursed him into another street. In the meantime the king did not stir from his post, expecting every moment when Prosper would come back, that he might send him to Camilla and Irene, to let them know he expected them under the balcony, and in all probability was wholly taken up with his amour, for a lover does nothing else when he is alone ; when the man who had parted from him whom Prosper pursued, came out of Camilla's house, and mistaking the king for his comrade :

"Look Calixtus," said he to him, " here is your dispatch. The governor of Cajetta will order you a vessel to carry you to Marseilles."

The king, without returning any answer, received the packet of letters which he presented to him. "Calixtus," adds this unknown person, " the rest depends upon thy diligence. And thou hast in thy hands the fortune of the Duke of Anjou, thy master and mine."

"Ha ! ungrateful villain and traitor ! What wicked designs art thou carrying on against me ?" cries the king, laying his hand upon his sword.

Roger, for it proved to be him, distracted at his making so fatal a mistake, and hurried on by his despair to be more wicked than he was, thought of nothing now but losing his life, or taking away that of the king, who had loved him so tenderly. The reproaches he so justly expected for his unparalleled ingratitude and villainy affrighted him as much as the severest torments that could be inflicted on him. He put his hand to his sword almost at the same time the king did, who charged him with so much vigour and fury, that Roger, troubled with a remorse of conscience for his crime, was for a long time forced to defend himself.

At last, his rage filling him with new strength and courage, he pushed furiously at the king, whom he looked upon now to be no otherwise than his enemy ; and by the desperate thrusts he made at his sacred person, obliged him likewise to defend himself. But kings, who may be valiant as well as other men, are usually assisted by a more powerful genius than that of ordinary mortals. Roger, as brave, furious and desperate as he was, could not have maintained his ground long against his incensed prince, although the clashing of swords had now brought several persons upon the spot, who could hardly be kept from hacking to pieces an execrable villain, who durst attack the life of his sovereign. His own domestics, and those of Camilla, were the first that came with lights into the street, and were strangely surprised to see their master engaged with the king.

The unfortunate Roger no sooner saw the light which exposed him to the terrible looks of his prince, but he was utterly confounded. His rage and valour abandoned him both at once, and his sword dropped out of his hand. The king, who had the pleasure to see him wounded, after he had had occasion for all his valour to hinder himself from being wounded by him, seized him with his own hands, and gave him to the captain of his guards, who came luckily by with a party of soldiers, and had received order to watch all night the avenues leading to Camilla's house.

In the meantime Prosper ran after his man, who, flying from him as fast as his legs could carry him, unluckily fell into the hands of the watch, who were walking their rounds that night, as their custom was, to prevent all disorders in the streets. He seemed so astonished, and faltered so strangely in his answers, that they had certainly stopped him, although Prosper, who pursued with sword in hand, and had made himself known to them, had not commanded them in the king's name to secure him, and to be responsible for his forthcoming. He immediately sent back to acquaint the king with what he had done ; and if he was surprised to see such a number of flambeaux in the street, and the king surrounded by such crowds of people, he was much more so to find what had passed between the king and Roger ; and to see that favourite, whom all the court so lately adored, cursed by all the company, and in the hands of the guards, who were carrying him to prison. That night the king did not see Irene, because he would avoid the sight of Camilla, whom he ordered Prosper to wait upon, and assure her from his mouth that he distinguished her from her brother, whose crime should not in the least lessen his esteem for her. Irene writ to him in favour of Roger ; and to oblige Camilla, did that which the repeated instances of an amorous prince could not obtain from her. Next day Roger was examined, and found guilty of high treason, for maintaining a private correspondence with the Duke of Anjou, who had a great party still in the kingdom of Naples. He had been informed by some of them of the insatiable ambition of Roger, and having offered him in marriage a princess of his own blood, with certain advantages, which he could not hope from his present master, this ungrateful favourite, violating his faith and honour, had engaged to receive the French into Cajetta and Castellamara, whereof he was governor. The same judges who convicted him of treason against his prince, discovered his villainous plot against the Princess of Tarento ; and now that mirror of constancy the Prince of Salerno, who had abandoned her when he saw her in disgrace, to offer his services to Camilla, whom he saw in favour, no sooner found the king to repent of the ill treatment he had given her, and resolved not only to re-instate her in her former honour and fortune, which had been unjustly taken from her, but likewise to confer new ones upon her, than this generous lord, who had so lately importuned the king to marry him to Camilla, now humbly entreated him to dispense with his promise, and give him leave to carry on his pretensions to Matilda ; and at the same time desired his majesty, who designed to make inquiry after her, to leave the care of that to him, and give him a commission to go and find her wherever he could hear any news of her, in order to bring her again to court. The king's affection was too deeply settled on the beautiful Irene not to think of her brother Hippolito, and be concerned that nobody could tell where he was. He dispatched couriers into all parts of Italy, who had orders to inquire after him as they searched for Matilda, and in case they found him, to bring him again to Naples. He hoped by this means to convince Irene how cordially he espoused the interests of her family, and how much it afflicted him that she knew not what was become of her brother, whom she loved so dearly.

This amorous cavalier, after he had searched a long time for his princess with the utmost care and diligence without being able to find her, resigned himself to that blind guide chance and rambled wherever his horse carried him, making no longer stay in any place than his horse and that of his servants, who we may suppose were not so solicitous as he in the search of Matilda, had time to rest themselves. As for his own part, he enjoyed no more repose than a condemned criminal, and after he had passed whole days in sighing on horseback, spent whole nights in complaining to the trees and rocks of the cruelty and absence of Matilda, and in quarrelling with the innocent stars, that generally lighted him to bed by reason he lay in the open fields and under the canopy of heaven. One day, when he was so taken up with these melancholy thoughts that he did not consider that his servant and horses could not, like himself, feed upon so slender a diet as love, he found himself towards sun-setting near a solitary inn, which rather looked like a retreat for cut-throats and banditti, than a place to lodge travellers.　Hippolito had rode beyond it, for your true lover is an indefatigable animal, when his valet informed him his horses were not able to stir a step farther, out of mere lassitude and hunger, not to speak of himself, who wanted to eat and repose as well as they ; upon this our despairing lover condescended to alight, but the inn-keeper, who stood before his gate, together with his wife, and an ill-looked fellow, who seemed to be a soldier, told him rudely, he had no place to entertain him in, and that his rooms as well as stables were all taken up.　Hippolito was not much concerned he could not get a lodging here, and his servant had despaired of getting one, when the soldier that stood by the inn-keeper, after he had whispered a few words in his ear, told Hippolito in Calabreze, that if he pleased he might come in, and that he should be very proud to lend his room to so fine a gentleman ; and while Hippolito made scruple to accept so courteous an offer, the man of the house, that had spoke so rudely to him a little before, came and held his stirrup, while he alighted, with a smiling cut-throat look, which showed he designed to make a penny of him.　Thus Hippolito was persuaded to come into the inn.　He would not eat a bit, and having only drank a glass of water, for philosophers have observed that love and sorrow are very dry, he walked out to take a turn or two in a place very proper for his melancholy contemplations, which he had observed not far from the inn.　In the meantime his valet sat down to supper with the landlord and his wife, and the civil Calabrian, who had so obligingly parted with his chamber to Hippolito.　He fell like a man that was half starved, and did not guzzle down so much wine as he could have done, because he was

forced to call upon his master to put him in mind of going
to bed, which was a thing he frequently forgot.   He went
to look for him among the rocks, where he found him feeding his melancholy by reflecting on the ill condition of his
affairs and his love, and brought him back to the inn,
where they showed a vile room, with a bed yet more vile,
and which having no curtains, lay exposed to the sun and
wind on all sides.

Hippolito would not undress, but threw himself in his
clothes upon the bed, as his man did upon another, where he
slept so heartily that it would have made any man but his
master to have envied him, who for his part could not sleep
a wink : but a true lover would think he had committed an
unpardonable sin should he sleep like other mortals.   In a
short time all the people in the inn were got to bed, and
everything was hushed, when some persons on horseback
disturbed their repose, and thundered at the gate like to
persons that were impatient to be let in.   The man of the
house, that got up to see what the matter was, knew them
and opened the gate to them.   Soon after Hippolito heard
the next chamber to his open ; several persons went into it
and some of them went out again immediately, while the
rest that stayed talked to one another.   He was too much
taken up with his own private affairs to have any great
curiosity for those of other people, and had not listened to
their discourse, if one of them had not talked so loud, that
he fancied he was not unacquainted with the voice.   This
made him desirous to know what they talked of, and at
last he heard them speak the following words distinctly :
" Yes, my dear Julia, I must once more say it, few persons of
my condition have been treated worse by fortune than
myself ; she has plunged me in miseries that are not to be
paralleled ; but as great and vexatious as they are, yet they
don't so much disturb me as the ingratitude wherewith the
basest of men requites my affection for him ; and this
ingratitude does not sit so heavy on me, as mine to the

man whom I ought to love. I blame myself incessantly for it, and my inquietude on this score is infinitely more afflicting than all the losses I have sustained, and all the calamities that oppress me."

The other person that took up the discourse talked so low, that Hippolito could hear nothing but a few incoherent words, that were frequently interrupted by sighs. He got up and crept to the wainscot which divided the two rooms, but the noise he made was heard by the persons whom he had a mind to listen to, so their conversation ceased, but not the sighs of the afflicted party, whose voice he imagined to resemble that of Matilda. The reader may easily guess how impatient he was to know whether he was mistaken, and to satisfy himself in so important a doubt, was preparing to go out of his chamber, when all on the sudden the door opened, and by the light of a dark lanthorn he saw four men come into his room with their swords in their hands, among whom he observed the Calabrian soldier and the master of the house. If he was surprised at so unseasonable a visit from these men, who did not seem to come with any good design, they were no less so to find him up and awake, who they hoped was in a sound sleep. Hippolito, clapping his hand to his sword, asked them what they wanted in his chamber at such an hour, and in such an equipage ; and he no sooner saw them put themselves in a posture to attack him, but he fell upon the foremost with such bravery and skill, that he soon made the room too hot for them. In the meantime his footman awaked, followed the noise, and seeing his master set upon by so many enemies, seconded him very valiantly, when, having wounded all that had attacked him, he laid the most dangerous of them at his feet. These men defended themselves like fellows that did not value their lives ; but though they had been more in number than really they were, yet could they not have resisted the valiant Hippolito, seconded by so courageous a servant. He killed another of his enemies, and the two that were left very fairly betook themselves to their heels. He was so vexed at a slight wound he had received in his arm, that he was resolved to pursue them, and in all probability had cleared the world of them, as well as he had done of the other sparks, had not these villains been so wise in their fear, as to make one leap of it down the staircase and to shut the door after them. Hippolito was a long while before he could open it, which gave the two murderers time enough to make their escapes, so that he and his man returned to the inn without them. He ran directly to the chamber where he thought he had heard Matilda's voice, but found it open and no one in it, no more than in the rest of the rooms in the house, which he searched with as much care as inquietude.

"Fulvio," said he to his man, "I heard Matilda talk, I knew her voice, and no one but such an unhappy wretch as I could have missed her when she was so near me." He afterwards repeated to Fulvio the words he heard Matilda speak, interpreted them to his advantage, as he had some reason to do, but instead of giving him consolation they only increased his affliction; for he thought this was a trick of fortune, to let him hear Matilda's voice, for no other end than to make him more concerned for not being able to see her, or know what was become of her. He looked after this princess in all the places thereabout, and was so besotted as to come back to the inn to search for her there, but not a soul was to be seen, except only in the stable, from whence Fulvio took four horses besides his own and his master's.

Hippolito quitted this inn in the most pensive condition that can be imagined. Fulvio proposed to carry off the thieves' horses as lawful prize, and represented to him that perhaps they might find Matilda, and then they should want a steed to mount her upon. Hippolito did not hear what he said, or else would not vouchsafe to make him an answer, so strangely was he taken up with his melancholy thoughts. Fulvio took his master's silence for consent, and tying the horses by the tail, drove them before him designing, I suppose, to make ready money of them the first chapman he could find. They rode part of the day together, without Hippolito's answering so much as one of the many questions Fulvio put to him, in order to divert him. They lost their way, and at last were got among a parcel of barren rocks by the sea-side, and which ended in a sandy plain.

Among these rocks, in a creek where the sea ran into the land, as they came from a narrow lane, they fell in among a company of peasants, armed with all sorts of clubs and other weapons, who at first were surprised to see two men on horseback, followed by so many horses without anybody to ride them ; but at last taking heart of grace to see so few, and themselves so many, for there were at least a hundred of them, they encompassed our adventurers in a tumultuous manner ; and holding the butt ends of their muskets up at them, some cried, "Who goes there ?" Others, "Who are you for ?" Others, "Knock them down," and lastly, some more conscientious than the rest, "Who are ye ?" Hippolito could not answer so many questions at once, and if he could these ill-bred clowns made such a confounded noise that there was no hearing of him. At last an old man of a tolerable good aspect, who afterwards discovered himself to be the commander of these formidable heroes, for then every man set up for himself, partly by speaking aloud to them, which set him a coughing like an alderman at church, and partly by the rhetoric of a good oaken cudgel, made shift to compose the mutiny. He asked Hippolito peaceably and civilly who he was, and what business he had in so solitary and so remote a place from the great road. Hippolito told him he was a cavalier of Naples, and had lost his way to Ancona. He then asked the old spark what occasion had brought so many people together, who in-

formed him that some corsairs of Barbary having landed a
great number of soldiers, they had pillaged some places
near the sea, and finding none to oppose them, and being
covetous of a greater booty, were so foolhardy as to march
higher up into the country. He added that most of those
men he saw armed had been robbed, wherefore they
resolved under his conduct to wait the coming of the
enemy, and fight them as they came back with their slaves
and the plunder of a neighbouring village, which in all
probability they were gone to attack ; that 'twas impossible
for the Moors to escape, there being no other way for them
to get back to the sea but this ; and that it was not so much
the loss of their goods that had encouraged these peasants to
attempt so bold a design, as that of their wives and children.

Hippolito offered to venture his life in their quarrel, and
they took him at his word. The old man gave him the
command-in-chief, which he accepted, to the great satisfaction and joy of our boors, who now promised themselves
mighty matters from Hippolito's military phiz. Four of
the likeliest among them, of whom the old fellow was
one, were mounted upon the four horses which the provident Fulvio had brought along with him from the inn.
Hippolito divided his men into three parties. One he
posted among the rocks, where they could not be seen by
the enemy, with orders not to stir before they came up to
them. He posted the second in a narrow passage that led
towards the sea to hinder the infidels from getting back to
their ships ; and he placed himself with his men on horseback at the head of the third, encouraging them to behave
themselves bravely, and fall in with the enemy to render
their arrows ineffectual. He had scarce given these orders,
and posted his men, but the enemy appeared to the number
of a hundred and fifty. They drove several horses before
their main body laden with booty, together with the women
and children whom they had made slaves. Being old
experienced soldiers, they were not a whit discouraged to see

Hippolito and his troop marching towards them, or else perhaps they despised so small a number. I will not trouble myself to relate the particulars of this noble battle between the Moorish corsairs and our peasants, although Hippolito did abundance of gallant actions there, which deserve to be remembered. I will only tell you that his orders were well executed, that the arrows of the Moors did them little or no harm, because they fell in with them so gallantly, that he began their overthrow with the death of their captain, and concluded it by that of their stoutest men.

Our peasants when they had been once blooded put all the Moors to the sword, whether they cried quarter or not, and notwithstanding all the endeavours Hippolito used to prevent this massacre. The dead were lamented as much as the common joy would give leave, and the wounded bound up their wounds. Hippolito received a thousand commendations, and as many thanks from these poor people, who verily believed they should not have got the better if it had not been for him. They offered him the better part of the booty they had recovered from the enemy, which nevertheless he refused, as likewise to go and make merry with them after the victory.

Just then Fulvio brought two women before him in the habit of pilgrims, one of whom had no sooner taken off a great hat which hid her face, but he knew her to be Matilda. He alighted, or, I might rather say, leapt from his horse to throw himself at the feet of this princess, who embraced him with all the marks of tenderness that savoured nothing of that disobliging treatment which the tyranny of the Prince of Salerno had obliged her formerly to offer him. This faithful lover wanted expressions to let Matilda know how glad he was to see her ; never did his eloquence leave him so in the lurch, never did he so strain to declare his thoughts, which notwithstanding he murdered. In short, he did not know what he did, so great was the disorder of his mind. He was uncertain for some time whether he should in form Matilda of the pains he had been atto find her, so much did his excessive modesty keep him from valuing himself upon his services. However he gave her at last a true recital of his adventures, ever since he had left Naples for her sake ; and forgot not to acquaint her what had happened to him in the inn, where, as he fancied, he had heard her voice. Matilda gave him abundance of thanks for these last obligations she had to him, adding that she looked upon herself to owe both her life and honour to him, since the defeat of the Moors was entirely owing to his bravery and conduct. She owned that it was she who was in the next chamber to him at the inn, promised to inform him by what accident she had been carried thither, and, in short, to give him her whole history, whenever she had a convenient time and place to relate it.

The other pilgrim that accompanied Matilda was one of her chamber-maids called Julia, being the only servant that had fidelity enough to follow the fate of her mistress, and bear a part in all her afflictions. 'Tis probable that Fulvio and she were glad to see one another ; and for my part, I am apt to believe that they said abundance of fine things and displayed their subaltern eloquence to each other, if I may so express myself, very plentifully upon this occasion. Our victorious peasants that had observed with what concern Hippolito and Matilda received one another, re-doubled their courteous offers to Hippolito, who made no difficulty to accept them for the princess's sake. Among the rest the old man, who, as I have already taken notice, led the peasants on to battle before Hippolito came up to them, begged of him and Matilda that they would do him the honour to take a sorry lodging at his house, which they accepted. He sent one of his sons in all haste to get things ready at home for the better reception of these guests, and now they prepared for their journey. Matilda and Julia were mounted upon the two best horses they could find. . Among several women, whom they had freed from out of the hands of the Moors, Fulvio observed one whom he thought he had seen somewhere, who avoided as much as she could his looking at her, as if she knew him but had no mind to be known by him. At last he came up to her, and found her to be the inn-keeper's wife that had designed to murder them. He went to inform his master of it, and desired some peasants to look after her. Towards the dusk of the evening they arrived at the village. Matilda and Hippolito were received by our old man with all the marks of esteem and gratitude. The other peasants of the village went home to their several houses, to make merry after so notable a victory, and those that lived farther off marched homewards likewise. Hippolito commanded the inn-keeper's wife, whom Fulvio had apprehended, to be brought before him, and upon the very first threatening to deliver her into the hands of justice, she confessed that their inn was a meeting place of banditti and robbers, that her husband kept a correspondence with all the thieves of the country, and that the reason why he at first had refused to entertain Hippolito, was because he expected a famous highway-man that night, companion to the Calabrian whom he had seen at the inn, to confer with him about some robberies they had in hand. She likewise informed Hippolito that the Calabrian had a great mind to his horse and equipage, to rob him of which after he had whispered with her husband, and persuaded him to join in the action, he had lent him his room. History does not tell us what they did to this woman, after they had learnt from her all they desired to know. Hippolito and Matilda, the better to conceal their quality, made Fulvio and Julia, the old man and his whole family, to sup with them. After supper, I cannot tell whether it was a good or bad one, Matilda would not suffer Hippolito to languish any longer under his impatience to know her adventures, and therefore informed him by what accident she came to the inn, and afterwards into the hands of the Moors.

" After the King had commanded me," said she to him,
"to quit Naples, and through the great interest of my
enemies, I had but one night allowed me to put myself in
a condition to obey so rigorous an order. I implored the
assistance of some gentlemen at court, whom I thought I
had obliged enough to be my friends, but I found to my
disappointment, that they were only such to my fortune,
and not to me. I had reason also to complain of my
domestics, who had all abandoned me in this extremity
but Julia. She had a brother married in Naples who had
the generosity to leave his family at the entreaty of his
sister, to conduct me to the place whither I designed to
steer my course. He bestirred himself so effectually, that
the very night I was commanded to leave Naples, I had
got everything ready for my journey, before break of day.
We dressed ourselves in the habit of Loretto pilgrims, by
which means we were not discovered at the city gates. I
walked that day as many miles as could be expected from
one of my sex, who had never been used to travel before,
and we jogged on peaceably after the same manner for
several days together without any cross adventures to disturb us. Yesterday a little before night, we were met in a
narrow way by three men on horseback, that had the looks
of villains. I designed to avoid them, which I endeavoured
with so much haste, and so unluckily, that my foot slipping
against a piece of rising ground, I fell at the feet of one of
the horses that came thundering after me. The large hat
which covered my face and my head-clothes, tumbled off
with the fall, and my hair fell about my shoulders. My ill
stars would so have it, that these men saw something in me
that did not displease them. They talked awhile together,
then alighting from their horses, one of them seized Julia,
another caught hold of me, while the third attacked Julia's
brother, who had put himself in a posture to defend us, but
whom we saw soon after fall being, it seems, run through
the body. After so many misfortunes which had happened

to me, and which from a happy princess, at least so in appearance, had made me the most miserable woman in the world, I had some reason to believe that all the prudence and all the precaution imaginable would signify nothing against the power of fortune ; that we must e'en suffer her to act as she pleases, and persuade ourselves that her inconstancy, which makes us to feel her hatred, then when we thought ourselves most secure from it, will in like manner restore us to her friendship when we least expect it. Thus I resigned myself," continues Mathilda, "to my peculiar destiny, and when I found myself stopped and seized by these strangers, submitted without any struggling to be mounted on one of their horses because I knew they could otherwise have done it by force ; and although I was in their hands, yet death could deliver me from them whenever their insolence should oblige me to have recourse to that last remedy. Julia, who fell a screaming and crying out as loud as she was able, when she saw her brother drop, yet suffered herself to be carried off after my example, though she still continued afflicted. At night we arrived at the inn where you heard my voice. Your engagement with the robbers troubled us exceedingly at first, but when we saw you had driven them out of the house, and the noise was over, Julia and I quitted our room. Finding nobody in the inn, we resolved to make our escapes out at the garden door, which then stood open, and the fear of being retaken made us to redouble our speed. We travelled all night, and part of the next day, till the heat of the sun, and our weariness together, forced us to rest ourselves among the rocks, not far from this place, where we found a convenient shade, and were taken asleep by the Moors whom you defeated."

Matilda concluded the recital of her adventures with fresh protestations to Hippolito, that she would never forget what he had done for her. However she did not tell him the name of the place to which she intended to retire, and for his part he did not ask her about it. No doubt it was to some petty prince or other of Italy, in which cattle that country abounds, for any man that has money enough may there be easily made his highness, without any other qualification to merit it. I might with as little difficulty have bestowed what name I pleased upon him, since history has been silent in the matter ; but I found upon second thoughts, that his name would be no great ornament to my narration, and therefore omitted it. Hippolito offered to conduct her whither she had an inclination to go, but she would by no means suffer him ; however she was forced, at the repeated instances of our officious cavalier, to take his servant Fulvio with her, and two horses for herself and Julia. I will not mortify the reader with a recital of the melancholy parting between Hippolito and Matilda. I'll e'en let her go in quiet to Ancona, where she sold part of her jewels, and bring back the poor Hippolito to the sad ruins of his house, where he arrived without a farthing in his pocket, all the earthly goods he had in this transitory world being the horse he rode on. He had scarce set foot to ground, before he met a Neapolitan gentleman who was in quest of Matilda, as well as several others, whom the king had dispatched into all parts of Italy to find her if possible. He acquainted Hippolito with Roger's disgrace, after what manner Matilda's innocence came to be discovered, the orders the king had given to find her out, and, in short, with all that had happened at Naples ever since he had left it, except his majesty's violent love to the beautiful Irene, which was nevertheless known to all the world ; however our gentleman thought fit to conceal it from him, whether out of an excess of discretion, or for some other reason I don't know.

You may imagine that Hippolito, generous as he was, and loving Matilda better than his life, was extremely pleased to hear of so unexpected a revolution in her favour, although at the same time he came to know that his own condition was more desperate than ever; this gentleman having withal assured him that the king had promised Prosper he should marry this princess as soon as ever she returned to Naples.　This last news hindered the wretched Hippolito from going to court, it made his life odious to him, insomuch that he avoided all manner of company so carefully, that he was the only man in the kingdom who did not know what a great ascendant his sister had over the king.

In the meantime Matilda was nowhere to be heard of, although the gentleman that had accidentally met with Hippolito went to Ancona, whither he told him she was gone, yet could he hear no news of her, notwithstanding all the inquiries he made for that purpose.　A report ran of this princess's death, and some people pretended to relate the very circumstances of it, which at last coming to Hippolito's ears, it threw him into such a fit of sickness, that had like to have cost him his life.　But in short, his body at length recovered a little strength, in spite of the indisposition of his mind.　He was accustomed sometimes to ride on horseback along the sea-shore, and 'twas in one of these melancholy freaks, that after he had made several reflections upon the misfortunes of his life, he resolved to go and end his days in the wars which the Grecian princes were at that time carrying on against the Turk, who now began to extend his conquests from Asia into Europe.　At last Matilda was found, and Hippolito was so ravished with joy, that he bestowed his horse, the only movable he had left him in the world, upon the man that brought him the news.

The same day his servant Fulvio came to him, and was exceedingly astonished to find his master so melancholy, and in so bad an equipage, at a time when all Italy talked of nothing but the great power his sister Irene had over the king, by the love he bore her.　He told Hippolito the

princess's name, to whom Matilda had retired, he informed
him after what manner Prosper came to compliment her
from the king, how he conducted her to Naples, and, according to the laudable custom of servants, that always make
haste to tell their masters ill news, he exaggerated to him
the joy Matilda had conceived at the sight of Prosper, and
the marks of affection she showed him. " Her passion for
him is so increased," continues this indiscreet valet, " that
she has newly spruced up the old cap of plumes he formerly
presented her with, which he has so often upbraided her
with, and which is so well known at Naples, by the many
jests that have been made upon it at court. I can't
imagine," says he, "where the devil she had laid it up, to
find it at so critical a juncture, but to be sure she must set
a mighty value upon it."

After this rate trusty Fulvio began to rail at the Princess
of Tarento a little more than became him ; but Hippolito
bid him to hold his tongue, and perhaps had cudgelled him,
had he not given off, or altered his language. Fulvio likewise told his master that the princess desired him to come
and meet her. "How!" cries Hippolito, " and does she not
sufficiently afflict me by not loving me, but to enhance my
affliction she must make me see how well she loves
another, and will she caress Prosper before me ? It may
be so, to give him, I suppose, the pleasure of seeing me die
with grief, as if their happiness wanted nothing to complete it but my death. But," continues Hippolito, " I
must obey her, and see how far her injustice will go."

He was in a good vein to complain of his ill treatment,
and was about to have done it, as he had just provocation,
when he saw afar off a body of horse, which Fulvio assured
him came with the Princess of Tarento, who, designing to
see Hippolito, would needs pass by his house, in hopes to
find him there. Although the king had sent his coaches
for her, yet she was resolved to make her entry into Naples
on horseback. Prosper looked as big upon his prancer as

a holiday-hero, and being all over covered with feathers like to any Indian monarch, rode by her side. He entertained the princess with a world of treble refined compliments, and every other moment sung some amorous ditties to her, very methodically, and like a man of art. Hippolito, who was out of sorts, both as to his mind and body, would fain have declined seeing his rival, as well as appearing before so much company ; but Matilda, who knew. him afar off, because perhaps she saw Fulvio with him, who had parted from her so lately, rode up to him, and Prosper and the rest of the company did the like. Matilda reproached Hippolito after the most obliging manner that could be, that being her best friend, he had not done her the honour to meet her on the road, as some of the best quality of the city and court had done. Hippolito protested he had never heard of her happy return till now, and added, that although he had known of it, he had not presumed to meet her, for fear such an unhappy wretch as he might infect and disturb the public joy. Matilda assured him he had effectually disturbed hers, if she had not been so happy as to have met him. She conjured him to come and share in her good fortune, as he had done all along in her adversity : and added, that having a design to marry, because she had found by woeful experience that a young princess, without either father or mother, had occasion for a husband of power and interest to protect her, and that having cast her eyes upon the man she designed to make Prince of Tarento, she desired him to do her the honour to assist at her wedding, which she would not celebrate without him. Prosper, as having the principal interest in this affair, joined his prayers to those of his mistress, and, contrary to his custom, spoke abundance of civil things to his rival, pretending to be overjoyed to have his good company. A despairing, unhappy man interprets everything to his disadvantage, as a sick body beyond all possibility of recovery turns the best ailments to poison. Hippolito took the civilities and obliging words of Matilda as so many cruelties she was minded to persecute him with. He could not conceive how she could have so hard a heart as to make him be the spectator of her nuptial ceremonies. He could not tell what answer to make her, and therefore looked on her with astonishment. The faithful Fulvio, who was as much scandalized as his master, cursed her heartily behind his back, and, whispering him in the ear, desired him of all love not to go ; swearing that she was a fury incarnate to ask him to see her married to Prosper. In the meantime Matilda redoubled her petition with so much importunity, that Hippolito was not able to refuse complying with her. She would have him that very minute get up upon a horse she had brought for him, though perhaps it might so happen at that time that he was not master of a pair of boots. Thus we see Hippolito mounted, very much out of humour, and out of countenance, by Matilda's side, who rode between him and Prosper. The princess still continued to talk very obligingly to him. She exaggerated the obligations she had to him, and entertained the company with a recital of all the valiant actions he had performed, both against the robbers that attacked him in the night, and against the Moors, whom he attacked in the day, although they were much superior to him in number, and with but a small body of unexperienced peasants. She was interrupted by Prosper, who with an impertinence peculiar to himself, must needs acquaint her with the miracles of that famous night, in which Roger was taken, and with what swiftness he had pursued the abovementioned Calixtus, who was privy to the correspondence which that chief minister had kept with the enemies of the state. Matilda did not bestow much attention upon his discourse, but still addressed herself to Hippolito, although he seldom made her any answer. But Prosper, by telling the same story a hundred times over, made people to

Y 2

listen to him whether they would or no ; and whatever
happened to be talked of, he perpetually loaded the conversation with the important service he had done the king
and government, by his pursuit of Calixtus.

He had mortified the company much longer with this
important exploit, if the king had not appeared, attended
by all the topping persons of both sexes at court and city.
Prosper, to show what a fine figure he made, rode towards
the king, and then without knowing why or wherefore
rode back again to Matilda, with full as little reason, and
presented her to his majesty, although there was no occasion
for it. She was received by him as well as she could
desire or expect. He excused himself for all his ill-treatment of her, laying the blame thereof upon Roger, and
told her that to make her some reparation for the injuries,
which through the instigations of this treacherous favourite
he had done her, he now bestowed upon her one of the
best preferments in the kingdom. Matilda thanked his
majesty with a great deal of humility, but much more wit.
I will not here pretend to set down any of the fine compliments that her gratitude suggested to her upon this
occasion. I will only tell you that they were admired,
nay, and applauded by all the company, as I have been
credibly informed. Prosper interposing to make acknowledgments for her, only repeated what she had said before.

In the meantime Irene rode up to Hippolito, whom she
knew from behind, and seeing herself out of the king's
sight, threw her arms about the neck of her dear brother,
who had made her shed so many tears, and drew some
from her now. Hippolito, who loved Irene as much as so
amiable a sister deserved, embraced her in so tender a
manner, that the sight thereof was enough to soften a heart
of iron or marble, according as the reader pleases. The
king, who missed Irene, and could not be long without her,
looked for her in the crowd, and at length perceiving her
with her brother, his amorous impatience must needs make

him ride up to her. He did not receive Hippolito as a
bare subject when she presented him to his majesty.
Matilda, Prosper, and in short all the persons of quality
about the king, observed that he talked to him after such a
manner, as made some of the politicians in the company
then conclude, that this cavalier would make no little
figure at court. But all the king's smiles could not cure
him of that mournful air which the gaiety of his rival had
occasioned in him, who appeared as jolly and well satisfied
as if he had the whole world at his beck. All this while
the sun, who darted his rays very fiercely upon this noble
company, warmed most of their heads deliciously, but
especially those that were bald. All the flies from the
sea-shore, the gnats from the neighbouring places, those
which the horses belonging to the king's retinue had
brought along with them from Naples, and those which
Matilda's horses had brought with them from more distant
parts ; in fine, all these buzzing insects, which we may call
the parasites of the air, incommoded their faces exceedingly, tormented their horses cruelly ; and those poor tits
were the most exposed that had the least tails to whisk
about them. I must own indeed that the umbrellas protected them a little from the beams of the sun, but not
from the burning reverberation of the earth, or from the
clouds of dust, with which the *sistole* and *diastole* of the
lungs commonly called respiration, filled the throats of all
the company, his majesty not excepted. In a word, the
place was not tenable ; but to the great consolation of
those who suffered most by the sun and flies, the king, who
was never weary where Irene was, had not as yet told
Matilda all that he had a mind to tell her ; and therefore
talking loud enough to be heard by those that were about
him, he pronounced the following numerical individual
speech to her, for it was faithfully repeated to me word
for word.

" Beautiful princess, after the persecutions you have

suffered from me, and in some measure by my orders, and after all the losses you have sustained, you would have little reason to be satisfied with me, and I should have as little to be satisfied with myself, if I did not do all that lay in my power to contribute as much to your happiness, as hitherto I have done to your misfortunes. It is not enough that I have declared you innocent, that I have restored to you all that was taken from you ; nay, that I have increased your fortune by my favours, for if I don't see you married to the Prince of Salerno, I do nothing. By making you this present of the prince, I acquit myself in part of what I owe you ; and by rewarding him with so beautiful a lady, I think I have sufficiently requited him for all the great services he has done the state."

"Ah ! sir," said Mathilda, "let your majesty take care that while you intend to be just to me, you be not so to Prosper. Acknowledgment has its excess, as well as ingratitude. You will not give Prosper all he deserves in giving him only me, and in giving me the great Prince of Salerno, you will give me more than I deserve. I am as well satisfied with your majesty, as it is possible for me to be ; and these last testimonies of your goodness, which I owe to my misfortunes, render them so dear to me, that they will be the most agreeable things I can think of as long as I live. But, sir," continued she, "since your majesty is so religious as to pay what you think you owe, and since a subject ought to govern herself by the good example of her prince, will not your majesty give me leave, now you have put me in a capacity to pay my debts, to do it immediately upon the spot, and pay others in the same coin they have paid me ? Draw near therefore, brave Hippolito," said she to this cavalier, turning towards him, "come and thank my gratitude, after you have had so much reason to complain of my unkindness. I owe you a love of many years, which is not in the least lessened by my ill-treatment of you. I owe you, besides the expenses wherein this constant passion has engaged you, and besides the greatest part of your estate which you have spent to support my quarrel, and your fine house, which was burnt all along of me ; I owe you, I say, my honour and my life, that were both in danger between the robbers and the Moors ; and I owe you likewise a life which you hazarded in my deliverance. I will now take care to acquit myself, generous Hippolito, of all these obligations ; but those I have to Prosper, being of the oldest date, are consequently the more pressing, and must be first discharged." Hippolito looked as pale as death at these last words of Matilda, and immediately reddened after he had looked pale. Prosper smiled upon him, and gazed at Matilda with a very amorous look, who spoke to him as follows :

" Prince of Salerno, you would make me believe that you loved me from my infancy, and indeed you have always treated me like an infant. You made yourself to be feared by her whom you called your pretty mistress ; you have always amused her with fine compliments and songs, or treated her with reproaches and reprimands, at the time when she expected the most important services from you. In fine, the greatest token of love you ever gave me, was a present of some of your old feathers, which I promised to keep for your sake, and have been as good as my word." With this she took the cap off her head, which Prosper had given her in the days of yore, and presenting it to him, " At the same time," continued she, " that I discharge my debt, by returning you the fair words and feathers you gave me, I bestow myself upon Hippolito and make him Prince of Tarento, to acquit my obligations towards the most generous of all men, whom I have always found to be a man of deeds and not of words."

When she had said these words, she gave Prosper his fatal cap with one hand, and with the other took that of the despairing Hippolito, who from that happy moment ceased to be so, and no more dreamed of this unexpected happiness than Prosper did of being repaid with his cap. The king, as well as his courtiers, was not a little surprised at this sudden change of the scene ; but Irene's great interest with him, and the justice as well as generosity of Matilda's action, made him to approve it. Besides the commendations he bestowed upon the princess at the same time kept the Prince of Salerno in his duty, who, blushing with shame and confusion, could not tell how to behave himself, and we may suppose, had it not been for the fear he lay under of displeasing his master, he would have quarrelled with Matilda, according to his ancient custom, in case the interest of his fortune had not been too prevalent for his natural arrogance. The king took pity on him, and presenting Camilla to him after he had talked a while in private with her and Irene, told Prosper that so beautiful a lady with all her own charms, and her brother Roger's estate, might very well comfort him for the loss of Matilda. In the meantime all the court strove who should be most forward to congratulate this princess upon her just choice of Hippolito, and to assure this happy lover how overjoyed they were at his good fortune. They were most plaguily embarrassed on both sides to find out compliments to answer every one, and were forced to repeat the same thing over and over again. But the king came very luckily to deliver them out of this trouble.

"Beautiful princess," says he to Matilda, "you have taught me that we ought to discharge our debts when we are able. I therefore acquit myself of the debt I owe to Irene's beauty and wit, and this day make her queen of Naples."

This unexpected declaration of his majesty surprised, as we may imagine, the company infinitely more than that of Matilda had done. Irene throwing herself at his feet, testified to him by her respect and silence, her humility and resignation. The king raised her up, kissing her hand, and from that very moment treated her as he would have done the greatest queen in the world. All these strange adventures so took up people's thoughts, that those that were most incommoded by the heat complained no longer of it. In short, they turned back towards Naples, where all sorts of rejoicings began, till all things were prepared for the king's marriage, who caused that of Hippolito and Matilda, as likewise that of Prosper and Camilla, to be deferred, to the end that the same day might be signalized by three such illustrious weddings. The king never repented of choosing Irene for his wife. Matilda, who was of so loving a temper, that she loved Prosper more than he deserved, for no other reason than because he happened to be loved by her first, yet loved Hippolito exceedingly, who for his part loved her as much when a husband, as he had done when a gallant. Only Camilla lived unhappily with Prosper. She durst not refuse him for fear of offending the king, who had punished Roger only with banishment; and thus to save her brother's life, she rendered her own uneasy, being married to a covetous, impertinent, jealous prince, who, while he lived, was the scorn and laughter of the court of Naples.

THE END.

O